Issei Buddhism in the Americas

THE ASIAN AMERICAN EXPERIENCE

Series Editor
Roger Daniels

A list of books in the series appears at the end of this book.

Issei Buddhism in the Americas

Edited by
DUNCAN RYŪKEN WILLIAMS
AND TOMOE MORIYA

University of Illinois Press
URBANA, CHICAGO, AND SPRINGFIELD

Manufactured in the United States of America
1 2 3 4 5 C P 5 4 3 2 1
∞ This book is printed on acid-free paper.

Library of Congress Cataloging-in-Publication Data
Issei Buddhism in the Americas / edited by
Duncan Ryûken Williams and Tomoe Moriya.
p. cm. — (The Asian American experience)
Includes bibliographical references and index.
ISBN 978-0-252-03533-3 (cloth : alk. paper)
ISBN 978-0-252-07719-7 (pbk. : alk. paper)
1. Buddhism—America. 2. Japanese—America.
3. Immigrants—America. I. Williams, Duncan
Ryûken, 1969– II. Moriya, Tomoe, 1968–
BQ724.I87 2010
294.3'928086912097—dc22 2009048711

Contents

Foreword

ROGER DANIELS

Although the study of the religions of most immigrant groups to what is now the United States has been a major element in their historiography, up to now this has not been particularly important for Asian American groups. In addition, when such study has occurred, the focus is usually on the immigrants' adaptation to the various forms of Christianity they found in their new homeland or, in some instances, to the missionary-inspired religion they had acquired in Asia. Only rarely has significant attention been paid to the religions they brought with them.[1] The present volume is particularly welcome. Its authors focus on the varieties of the Japanese Buddhist immigrant religion experiences in Hawaii, the United States mainland, Canada, and Brazil. They treat both the formal religious structures and the largely religious language schools that became bones of political contention in Hawaii and North America. Until recently almost all English-language literature on Buddhism in America focused solely on the relatively few Caucasian converts while ignoring the much larger and expanding numbers of Asian American Buddhists.

Although it seems clear that the Buddhist newcomers were essentially just another variety of immigrant religion, they were not regarded as such by New World governments. From the 1920s on these governments, led by the United States, became increasing hostile to both Buddhist churches and language schools. The Japanese language schools in the United States found protection from onerous government restriction in a 1927 Supreme Court decision, *Farrington v. Tokushige* (273 *US* 284), but when war came in 1941 constitutional protections for Japanese Americans and Japanese American churches were simply disregarded. Buddhism was regarded as an enemy religion, and Buddhist priests and language teachers were well represented on the Department of Justice's lists of persons to be interned at the onset of hostilities. After 1942, when the War Relocation Authority began the phased release of incarcerated Japanese Americans for resettlement in the interior, its regulations made it more difficult for Buddhists to regain their liberty.

The editors point out that, viewed from a Japanese perspective, the trans-Pacific expansion of Buddhism into the New World was a continuation of its eastward transmission from India through Southeast and East Asia to Japan. The offshoots planted in the New World received direction and financing from various church headquarters just as Christian churches that were part of the westward plantation from Europe looked to ecclesiastical authorities in London, Amsterdam, and Rome for direction and support.

Since many, perhaps most, readers will be unfamiliar with even the basics of Japanese Buddhism, the editors have provided a double set of introductions: the initial one at the beginning of the volume, and four mini-introductions, one at the beginning of each of the four parts into which the essays are divided. It might be prudent for some readers to read them all before beginning the essays themselves.

Note

1. An earlier volume in this series, David K. Yoo and Ruth H. Chung, eds., *Religion and Spirituality in Korean America* (2008), focused on variants of Korean American Protestantism, Catholicism, and Buddhism.

Introduction

Dislocations and Relocations of Issei Buddhists in the Americas

DUNCAN RYÛKEN WILLIAMS
AND TOMOE MORIYA

> [Nishi] Hongwanji was the first Japanese [Buddhist denomination] to start an American mission, which in itself exemplifies the history of an eastward transmission of the Buddhist teachings (*Bukkyō tōzen*). This means that American Buddhists have considerable responsibility as pioneers for spreading the teachings around the world.[1]
>
> —Kōyū Uchida, Bishop of the Buddhist Mission of North America (1905–1923)

Bukkyō tōzen: The Eastward Transmission of Buddhism

Buddhists in Japan had long employed the idea of "Bukkyō tōzen," literally "the eastward transmission of Buddhism," to describe the geographic advance of their religion from its roots in India, across the Asian continent, and finally to Japan. In this formulation, Japan was conceived of as the last stage in the progression of Buddhism. In the late-nineteenth and early-twentieth centuries, however, Buddhist "missionaries" such as Bishop Uchida advocated a new eastward movement of Buddhism: this time, from Japan across the Pacific Ocean to the Americas. These pioneering Issei (or "first-generation") priests and the devout Japanese Buddhist laypeople they served established a Buddhist presence in lands further east by constructing temples, transmitting Buddhist teachings and practices, and to a lesser extent, through converting non-Buddhists in the Americas. This volume explores these pioneering efforts in the contexts of late-nineteenth- and twentieth-century Japanese diasporic communities and immigration history on the one hand and the early history of Buddhism in the Americas on the other.

The eastward reorientation across the Pacific to the Americas allows us to question certain disciplinary boundaries and categories that have traditionally located Buddhism solely in Asia or defined "America" in Anglo-Christian terms. By examining the "eastward transmission of Buddhism" in conjunction with the lives of the Issei in the Americas, we will explore how Buddhism negotiated local, translocal, and transnational boundaries as well as how a multiethnic, multilingual, and multireligious vision of America emerged from the realities of transplanted Asian religious practices in Hawaii, South America, and the West Coast of the United States and Canada. In this way, we hope to build on the emerging scholarship of historians such as Thomas Tweed who have begun to "retell" America's religious history with sustained attention to Asian religions in America.[2]

The rhetoric of the American West and its "opening" by "pioneers" suggest that America faces only Europe and is centered in a New England Anglo-Protestantism every other immigrant group and religious tradition ought to "assimilate" into. Instead of the "American West," especially for the first Japanese sojourners and settlers, the Americas should be viewed as the "Pacific East." This is a perspective that is in part inspired by an emergent scholarship on American religious history at its "frontiers" such as that of Laurie Maffly-Kipp who focuses on the American West as part of the Pacific Rim or America's "Pacific borderlands."[3]

Further, given Japan's own colonial and imperialist ambitions, Japanese Americans could be located, in the words of Eiichiro Azuma, as "between two empires": Japan and America.[4] Yet, neither the simplistic frameworks of a Japan-centered diaspora ignoring local conditions and community formations nor an America-centered assimilationist model that reduces religious change to "Americanization" are adequate for understanding the place of religion in the lives of Buddhists in the Americas. The study of Issei Buddhism, thus, opens up the possibility for retelling American religious history from the perspective of those for whom Asia, rather than Europe, constituted the homeland.

Dislocations: Religion and the Sense of "Home"

After a period of over two hundred years in which Japan had discouraged international exchange, Japan's emergence into modernity in the late-nineteenth century coincides with its government establishing diplomatic relations with the West and the subsequent approval of the emigration of its subjects. The new Meiji-period (1868–1912) government also established a system of state-sponsored Shintō, withdrew support from the Buddhist tradition, and allowed Western Christian missionaries into Japan for the first time in centuries. This was the context in which, starting with the so-called *gannen mono* (people of the first year [of Meiji]), Japanese students, businessmen, and laborers began emigrating to the Americas. Even though its treaty with the United States assured Christian missionaries the freedom to proselytize, the Japanese were so wary of Western religious and imperialist ambitions in Asia that the *gannen mono* were issued passports that explicitly prohibited them from converting to Christianity during their journeys abroad.[5]

This policy eased over time, and by the late-nineteenth century some Japanese Christian converts made their way to the Americas for further study and economic opportunities. Still, the overwhelming majority of Japanese immigrants were Buddhist, hailing primarily from certain regions of Japan such as Hiroshima, Yamaguchi, and Fukuoka prefectures. They initially went as laborers to the sugar plantations in the Kingdom (and later Territory) of Hawaii, followed by journeys further east to the North or South American mainland to work on farms, railroads, canneries, fisheries, and logging operations.

Although many were sojourners and returned to Japan at the end of their labor contracts, thousands remained in the Americas, where they formed various kinds of community organizations, families, and even Japantowns. It was amid this "dislocation" that the necessity of religion, particularly Buddhism, became clear. The hardships of labor, the lack of proper Buddhist funerals for those who had perished in the "foreign land," and the need for spiritual, moral, and social centers all propelled those in diaspora, especially those from the fervently Pure Land Buddhist regions of Hiroshima and Yamaguchi, to call for the establishment of Buddhist missions in the Americas.

Buddhist organizations in Japan had already begun to respond to similar requests from Japanese who had emigrated to other parts of Asia, reflecting both Japan's colonial ambitions and the promotion of Japanese forms of Buddhism to other Asians. For example, the Higashi Honganji (one of the large Pure Land Buddhist organizations) had been the first to send a missionary priest to China, as early as 1873.[6] By 1889, however, the voices of those in Hawaii had been answered with small-scale nonofficial propagation by Buddhist priests such as Reverend Sōryū Kagahi of the Nishi Hongwanji. The headquarter organizations in Japan shifted some personnel to look "east" across the Pacific; Kagahi's Nishi Hongwanji, for instance, formally opened its Hawaii mission in 1898. The pattern of sending missionaries to East Asia first, and then to Hawaii, was followed by other mainline Buddhist sects of the Pure Land tradition and the Nichiren, Zen, and Shingon schools: the Jōdoshū established its Hawaii mission in 1894,[7] the Nichirenshū in 1899,[8] the Sōtōshū in 1903,[9] and the Shingonshū in 1914.[10]

These denominations eventually opened temples on the North American continent, but largely due to different policies in Japan, some established their respective North American headquarters later and on a smaller scale than others. For example, Cristina Rocha's chapter describes how the Brazilian government, with its deference to the country's strong Catholic tradition, restricted official propagation by Buddhist missions to the Japanese immigrant community until the 1950s.[11] The early years of Buddhism in the Americas had thus both translocal and highly localized elements. On the one hand, the simple fact of "dislocation" meant that Japanese Buddhists, whether in Manchuria, the Philippines, or the United States, shared common concerns, and Buddhist institutions served as their spiritual link to Japan and family through funerary and memorial services. On the other hand, as a number of chapters of this volume suggest, each locality—Canada (Masako Iino), Hawaii (Keiko Wells), and Brazil (Cristina Rocha)—brought on a different set of conditions to which Buddhism had to adapt.

The challenges faced by these pioneer Buddhists came from the fact that they were located "in-between" localities, nations, and empires. On the one hand, those who left Japan would in many respects never be completely accepted as "Japanese" in Japan; and on the other hand, racially discriminatory laws in the Americas—such as naturalization laws, voting rights, and alien land laws—meant that it was nearly impossible to be considered fully "American." Here, the role of religion in national identity was evident on both sides of the Pacific. Even though both nations constitutionally protected the freedom of religion, those who had converted to Christianity in Japan and those who refused to convert to Christianity in the Americas faced serious questions about their national identities. Buddhists in America faced serious obstacles to really feeling at "home" in a nation that seemed to assert the normalcy and superiority of one particular race (Anglo white) and one particular religion (Christianity, especially Protestantism—or in the case of Brazil, Catholicism).

Hybrid forms of American Buddhist formation or "creolization," as Cristina Rocha's chapter on Brazil explores, continued in the new lands with the dynamic interaction between Buddhism and certain aspects of Christian and other religious traditions popular in the Americas. This ongoing process of identity construction through the interface of religious and cultural differences is also highlighted in Keiko Wells' analysis of Buddhist musical traditions among wartime Buddhists in Kona, Hawaii. Both Rocha's examination of life-cycle rituals and Wells's study of music emphasizes the extent to which the Buddhist religion served simultaneously as a repository of Japanese spiritual and cultural patterns and practices and served as a vehicle to enter and mold a new religious landscape emerging in Hawaii, the U.S. mainland, Canada, and Brazil.

This volume's strength lies in both its contributors' extensive use of Japanese-language sources and their commitment to explore these encounters—or more precisely, an increasingly complex network of transnational exchanges from both sides of the Pacific. For example, to counter the Japanese state's orientation toward a new form of national identification centered on the emperor, some Buddhists sought to "modernize" the tradition by employing Western scholarship for the study of Buddhism as a pan-Asian tradition.[12] The influence of these Buddhist reform movements is the subject of Lori Pierce's chapter, which explores "Buddhist modernism" and the relationships between Asian Buddhists and European and American sympathizers. She uncovers "a neglected and more complex reality" by analyzing publications such as the *Light of Dharma,* an English-language Buddhist journal published between 1901 and 1907 by the Nishi Hongwanji mission, as well as a host of other English-language Buddhist periodicals. This "universal" Buddhism—one that emphasized its trans-sectarian and multiethnic aspects—locates its "peculiar hybrid faith" in a process of transnational encounters hitherto not seen.

Meanwhile, this new international arena offered an opportunity for the Japanese Mahayana Buddhists to propagate their teachings. Tomoe Moriya's chapter on publication ventures presents the new discourses of Japanese Buddhists, including those of the young D. T. Suzuki and a number of Nishi Hongwanji ministers. In the words of Bishop Uchida, the ideal of *Bukkyō tōzen* was the driving force behind many Japanese priests' desire to spread the Mahayana teachings among Euro-American converts/sympathizers (*kaikyō,* or the opening of the dharma), even though their actual target audience seems to have been the Japanese immigrants and their children (*tsuikyō,* or the teachings following [immigrants]). These Issei Mahayana Buddhist intellectuals were responding in their own way both to Westerners' penchant for Theravada Buddhism and to the xenophobic criticisms from American society by using journals and other publications, which had been the preferred method of spreading Christianity in Asia.

Ethno-Religious Formations and Civic Space

Although many sojourners and immigrants thought of themselves first and foremost in terms of their local identities (particularly their regional or prefectural identities), their "dislocation" outside of Japan led them increasingly to identify as Japanese nationals. Although national identity formation did not completely overshadow previous local identities—as evidenced by a number of the chapters highlighting the significance of prefectural organizations (*kenjinkai*) in helping new arrivals settle, find connections, and build Buddhist temples, especially after the military success in the Russo-Japanese War of 1904–5—feelings of national pride were celebrated in Japan as well as in the diaspora. Japanese pride in national origins was clearly linked in many respects to their religious beliefs. When white officials in Hawaii refused to recognize marriages conducted and authorized in Japan (in the so-called picture bride marriage) and forced mass Christian marriage ceremonies on the piers of Honolulu Harbor, the Japanese community organized protests against what they felt was an affront to their religion's and their nation's dignity. Eventually, the Hawaiian Territorial government provided certifications allowing Japanese Buddhist and Shinto priests to conduct marriages, an implicit admission that freedom of religion meant that coming to America did not necessitate accepting Christian standards.

By this period, many Japanese in the Americas had begun to form families (the addition of women, including picture brides, meant the birth of a new second generation or Nisei) and communities (forming majority populations on some parts of the Hawaiian Islands and concentrating in ethnic enclaves such as Japantowns on the mainland). The earlier Buddhist missions, which were often all-male youth groups, increasingly developed into full-fledged temples complete with women's organizations and religious and language instruction for the Nisei youths. Masako Iino's chapter focuses on the formation of this type of ethnic-religious enclave in the Canadian Issei community and its struggles in the face of calls for "a white man's province" by politicians in British Columbia. Although some Issei were initially indifferent to religion, the more they encountered a demeaning external identification of themselves as "Orientals" and "Japanese," the more incentive many felt to educate their Nisei children with "not just religious doctrines, but manners and moral education," including loyalty to their parents, the elderly, and the emperor. Iino looks in particular to the Japanese oratorical contests of the 1930s to demonstrate just how much the "*yamato damashii*" (Japanese spirit) was emphasized even among the second generation who simultaneously understood themselves as Canadian citizens.

The nexus of ethno-religious formations came to a head most dramatically in the Japanese language school controversies in Hawai'i. Noriko Asato's exhaustive study of this controversy during the 1920s sheds new light on the "religious rivalry" between Buddhists and Christians, discussing various pieces of legislation that targeted the Japanese language schools run by Buddhists. Very much a feature of debate in civic space (both in terms of press coverage in Hawaii as well as legal consequences when the U.S. Supreme

Court ruled in favor of the language schools), at stake in this struggle were larger questions about whether Anglo-Christianity or a multicultural and religiously pluralistic society (including Japanese-speaking Buddhists) would define "America."

Buddhism in the civic sphere is also discussed by Michihiro Ama in his chapter on the establishment of Higashi Honganji Pure Land sect in North America, by Reverend Junjō Izumida. Ama analyzes several court cases from the 1920s (using both legal documents filed in Los Angeles and press reports from the period) that pertained to Izumida and the legal "ownership" of the temple that would eventually become the Higashi Honganji headquarters in North America. Groundbreaking as one of the first studies of Buddhism and American law, Ama explains that the differences between American "democratic" board governance (as accepted by the court) as opposed to Japanese "customary" practices of temple management was a key feature of this hotly disputed legal case.

As Buddhism became an increasingly visible part of the religious landscape in the Americas, it faced resistance from those who thought it undermined the notion of a Christian, English-speaking, and whites-as-racially-superior America. Between the Japanese victory against a "white" imperial power in the Russo-Japanese War and their confidence as a economic and military power in its colonialist projects in Asia, the growing number of Japanese in the Americas caused increasing concern among those who viewed this group as simultaneously too inferior to be assimilated and too powerful to treat equally. Whether it was Buddhist language schools in Hawaii challenging anti-Japanese legislation or Buddhist temples leading the charge for higher wages in the sugar plantation strikes whereas Japanese Christians supported the plantation owners, Buddhists were beginning to be viewed in the mainstream public opinion as troublemakers and "un-American."

Relocations: Wartime Loyalty and Japanese American Religions

By the mid-1930s, when the Japanese military seized political leadership in Japan and began their imperialist incursions in the name of creating "co-prosperity" in Asia, a strong anti-Japanese sentiment was growing not only among white Americans, but Filipinos, Chinese, and Koreans in America as well. As it became increasingly obvious that a clash of two empires (American and Japanese) was inevitable, U.S. and Canadian intelligence agencies began collecting information and compiling lists of persons of Japanese ancestry to arrest in case of war. Akihiro Yamakura's chapter expands this volume's focus on Buddhism to trace the process of targeting Shintō (Tenrikyo) priests alongside others considered national security threats, describing how these religious leaders were arrested almost immediately after the Japanese attack on Pearl Harbor on December 7, 1941.

Race eventually trumped religion as nearly 120,000 persons of Japanese ancestry—whether Buddhist, Shintō, or Christian, whether Japanese or American citizens, including babies who could hardly be considered a national security threat—were incarcerated in internment camps run by the Department of Justice or the U.S. Army: the so-called "ghost towns" in the Canadian interior, or "relocation centers" run by the War Relocation Authority in the months that followed Pearl Harbor. Yamakura documents Shintō religious life during this "relocation" as involving both racial prejudice continued along with religious discrimination (Shintō was banned altogether and Buddhism was discouraged by American and Canadian authorities).

Although "dislocated" once again, newly discovered letters, diaries, and sermons of Issei Buddhist and Shintō priests reveal how they provided not only a spiritual refuge for internees during these hard years, but also served the social function of maintaining family and communal cohesion through ancestral, life-cycle, and traditional Japanese rituals. Although the Japanese in Hawaii were not caught up in the mass incarceration (individual Shintō and Buddhist priests were arrested), under martial law and with the absence of priests most temples and shrines on the island had to close for the duration of the war. However, from both within the "relocation centers" and the islands of Hawaii, thousands of Nisei (the vast majority of them Buddhists) volunteered for military service either in the legendary 100th Infantry Battalion and the 442nd Regimental Combat Team in the European front, or as linguists for the MIS (Military Intelligence Service) in the Pacific, many of them having studied the Japanese language at one of the Buddhist-run schools. Many of these young men sacrificed their lives, serving in the most highly decorated unit in U.S. Army history (the 100th/442nd) or a unit that shortened the Pacific War by at least two years according to General MacArthur's intelligence chief (the MIS) and were clearly loyal Americans. The majority of them were also Buddhists. Keiko Wells's chapter offers an insightful analysis of the Buddhist folk songs written by the parents of these soldiers on the Hawaiian islands as news of their sons' deaths became nearly a daily occurrence. Although the notion of an "American Buddhist" might have seemed inconceivable just decades earlier, no one—including the army, which after the war officially added the option of a "B for Buddhism" designation for a soldier's dog tag—could deny that this seemingly anomalous combination was a part of the American religious landscape.

Inevitably, the trauma of war and "relocation" shaped Japanese American Buddhism as it reemerged in the postwar period. *Bukkyō tōzen* continued on during the "resettlement" of many Japanese in cities such as Chicago, New York, and Toronto as thousands of Buddhists sought new lives away from a hostile Pacific coast. Further research on this and subsequent periods will be crucial to re-visioning Buddhist and American religious history faithful to these experiences.

Each section of this volume begins with a brief essay by the editors to provide some contexts for the chapters. We hope with this volume to not only stimulate further research on these topics, but to reorient Buddhist studies toward the emergence of the religion in areas beyond Asia, to recall Asian American studies to the significance of religion in ethnic communities, and within American religious history to keep studying Asian immigrant religion.

Notes

1. Kōyū Uchida, "Hokubei kaikyō sanjūnen no kaiko to shōrai no tenbō," In *Sōkō bukkyōkai kaikyō sanjūnen kinenshi,* Sōkō Bukkyōkai Bunshobu, ed. (San Francisco: Kageyama Tetsujirō, 1930), p. 20.

2. See *Retelling American Religious History* (Berkeley: University of California Press, 1996) edited by Thomas Tweed and *Asian Religions in America: A Documentary History* (New York: Oxford University Press, 1998) edited by Thomas Tweed and Stephen Prothero.

3. See Laurie Maffly-Kipp, *Religion and Society in Frontier California* (New Haven, Conn.: Yale University Press, 1994) and "'Eastward Ho!' American Religious History from the Perspective of the Pacific Rim," in *Retelling American Religious History,* Thomas Tweed, ed. (University of California Press, 1996), pp. 128–47.

4. Eiichiro Azuma, *Between Two Empires: Race, History, and Transnationalism in Japanese America* (Oxford: Oxford University Press, 2005).

5. Hawaii Nihonjin Iminshi Rengō Kyōkai, ed. *Hawaii Nihonjin iminshi* (Honolulu: Hawaii Nihonjin rengō kyōkai, 1964), p. 226.

6. Yūsen Kashiwahara, ed., *Shinshū shiryō shūsei* (Kyoto: Dōbōsha, 1975); Jidong Chen, "Kindai ni okeru Nicchū bukkyō no saisekkin: Ogurusu Kōchō no Beijing nikki o chūshin to shite," *Kindai Bukkyō* 9 (2002): 52–71.

7. Sadanobu Washimi, "The Issei and the Jōdo Denomination in Hawaii during the 1920s: Research from the 'Propagation Records,'" paper presented at the Issei Buddhism Conference, University of California, Irvine, September 3–5, 2004; "Jōdoshū kaigai kaikyō no ayumi" Henshū Iinkai, ed., *Jōdoshū kaigai kaikyō no ayumi* (Tokyo: Jōdoshū henshūshitsu, 1980), p. 188.

8. Naofumi Annaka, "Nichiren-shū Mission in Early 20th Century Hawaii: Findings from Its Early Documents in the 1910s," paper presented at the Issei Buddhism Conference, University of California, Irvine, September 3–5, 2004; Naofumi Annaka, "Hawaii ni okeru Nichirenshū no kaikyō katsudō ni tsuite," *Indogaku Bukkyōgaku Kenkyū* 52/2 (2004): 572–77.

9. Senryō Asai, "Sōtōshū in Hawaii in the Early Twentieth Century," paper presented at the Issei Buddhism Conference, University of California, Irvine, September 3–5, 2004.

10. Eiki Hoshino, "Hawaii ni okeru Daishi shinkō no tenkai to Shingonshū jiin no katsudō," in *Hawaii Nikkeijin shakai to Nihon shūkyō: Hawaii Nikkeijin shūkyō chōsa hōkokusho,* Keiichi Yanagawa and Kiyomi Morioka, eds. (Tokyo: Tokyo daigaku shūkyōgaku kenkyūshitsu, 1981), pp. 137–53. In the case of Nishi Hongwanji, among the 202 Issei ministers who were assigned to the United States from 1899 to 1941, 16 were transferred from the Asia-Pacific region and 10 were assigned to the same region after resigning from the North American mission. See Buddhist Churches of America, ed., *Buddhist Churches of America: A Legacy of the First 100 Years* (San Francisco: Buddhist Churches of America, 1998), pp. 53–119.

11. See also Takashi Maeyama, *Ihō ni "Nihon" o matsuru: Buraziru Nikkeijin no shūkyō to esunishitī* (Tokyo: Ochanomizu shobō, 1997); Masako Watanabe, "Tenkanki o mukaeta esunikku chāchi: Buraziru Nikkei shakai ni okeru dentō bukkyō no mosaku," *Meiji Gakuin Daigaku Shakaigakubu Fuzoku Kenkyūjo Kiyō* 34 (2004): 169–85.

12. Yūsen Kashiwahara, "Gohō shisō to shomin kyōka," in *Kinsei Bukkyō no shisō* Yūsen Kashiwahara and Manabu Fujii, eds. (Tokyo: Iwanami shoten, 1973), pp. 533–56; Judith Snodgrass, *Presenting Japanese Buddhism to the West* (Chapel Hill, N.C.: University of North Carolina Press, 2003). For "transsectarianism," "transnationalism," and "cosmopolitanism" in Meiji Buddhist history, see James Edward Ketelaar, *Of Heretics and Martyrs in Meiji Japan: Buddhism and Its Persecution* (Princeton: Princeton University Press, 1990), pp. 174–212.

Suggestions for Further Reading

Ama, Michihiro. 2007. *Immigrants to the Pure Land: The Acculturation of Shin Buddhism in Hawaii and North America, 1898–1941.* Ph.D. diss., University of California, Irvine.

Asato, Noriko. 2005. *Teaching Mikadoism: The Attack on Japanese Language Schools in Hawaii, California, and Washington, 1919–1927.* Honolulu: University of Hawai'i Press.

Buddhist Churches of America, ed. 1974. *Buddhist Churches of America, Vol. 1: 75 Year History, 1899–1974.* Chicago: Nobart Inc.

———. 1998. *Buddhist Churches of America: A Legacy of the First 100 Years.* San Francisco: Buddhist Churches of America.

Cadge, Wendy. 2004. *Heartwood: The First Generation of Theravada Buddhism in America.* Chicago: University of Chicago Press.

Cheah, Joseph. 2004. *Negotiating Race and Religion in American Buddhism: Burmese Buddhism in California.* Ph.D. diss., Graduate Theological Union.

Douglas, Thomas James. 2004. *Crossing the Lotus: Race, Religion and Rationality among Cambodian Immigrants in Long Beach and Seattle.* Ph.D. diss., University of California, Irvine.

Fujimura, Bunyū. 1995. *Though I Be Crushed: The Wartime Experiences of a Buddhist Minister.* Los Angeles: The Nembutsu Press.

Fujita, Stephen, and Marilyn Fernandez. 2002. "Religion and Japanese Americans' Views of World War II Incarceration." *Journal of Asian American Studies* 5/2: 113–37.

Horinouchi, Isao. 1973. *Americanized Buddhism: A Sociological Analysis of a Protestantized Japanese Religion.* Ph.D. diss., University of California, Davis.
Hunter, Louise. 1971. *Buddhism in Hawaii.* Honolulu: University of Hawai'i Press.
Ichikawa, Akira. 1994. "A Test of Religious Tolerance: Canadian Government and Jodo Shinshu Buddhism During the Pacific War," *Canadian Ethnic Studies* 26/2: 46–69.
Imamura, Jane. 1998. *Kaikyo: Opening the Dharma, Memoirs of a Buddhist Priest's Wife in America.* Honolulu: Buddhist Study Center Press.
Iwamura, Jane. 2003a. "Altared States: Exploring the Legacy of Japanese American *Butsudan* Practice." *Pacific World* 5 (Third Series): 275–92.
———. (ed. with Paul Spickard). 2003b. *Revealing the Sacred in Asian and Pacific America.* London: Routledge.
Kashima, Tetsuden. 1977. *Buddhism in America: The Social Organization of an Ethnic Religious Institution.* Westport, Conn.: Greenwood Press.
Kawamura, Leslie. 1977. "Buddhism in Southern Alberta." In *Religion and Culture in Canada.* Peter Slater, ed. Waterloo, Ontario: Wilfrid Laurier University Press, 491–506.
———. 1978. "Changes in the Japanese True Pure Land Buddhism in Alberta: A Case Study, Honpa Buddhist Church." In *Religion and Ethnicity.* Harold Coward and Leslie Kawamura, eds. Waterloo, Ontario: Wilfrid Laurier University Press, 37–55.
Kikuchi, Shigeo. 1991. *Memoirs of a Buddhist Woman Missionary.* Honolulu: The Buddhist Study Center Press.
Koda, Tara. 2007. *Meiji "Buddhism" in America: A Study of the Effects of Shinbutsu Bunri on Jodo Shinshu and Its Development in Hawaii and California.* Ph.D. diss., University of California, Santa Barbara.
McLellan, Janet. 1999. *Many Petals of the Lotus: Five Asian Buddhist Communities in Toronto.* Toronto: University of Toronto Press.
Maffly-Kipp, Laurie. 1994. *Religion and Society in Frontier California.* New Haven: Yale University Press.
———. 1996. "'Eastward Ho!' American Religious History from the Perspective of the Pacific Rim," In *Retelling American Religious History.* Thomas Tweed, ed. Berkeley: University of California Press, 128–47.
Masatsugu, Michael. 2004. *Reorienting the Pure Land: Japanese Americans, the Beats, and the Making of American Buddhism, 1941–1966.* Ph.D. diss., University of California, Irvine.
Moriya, Tomoe. 2000. *Yemyo Imamura: Pioneer American Buddhist.* Honolulu: Buddhist Study Center Press.
———. 2001. *Amerika bukkyō no tanjō: Nijū seiki shotō ni okeru nikkei shūkyō no bunkateki henyō.* Tokyo: Hannan daigaku sōsho 64, Gendai shiryō shuppan.
———. 2008. "Buddhism at the Crossroads of the Pacific: Imamura Yemyo and Buddhist Social Ethics." In *Hawai'i at the Crossroads of the U.S. and Japan before the Pacific War.* Jon T. Davidann, ed. Honolulu: University of Hawai'i Press, 192–216.
Mullen, Eve. 2001. *The American Occupation of Tibetan Buddhism: Tibetans and Their American Hosts in New York City.* Münster, Germany: Waxmann Verlag.
Mullins, Mark. 1987. "The Life-Cycle of Ethnic Churches in Sociological Perspective." *Japanese Journal of Religious Studies* 14/4: 321–34.

———. 1988. "The Organizational Dilemmas of Ethnic Churches: A Case Study of Japanese Buddhism in Canada." *Sociological Analysis* 49: 217–33.

———. 1989. *Religious Minorities in Canada: A Sociological Study of the Japanese Experience.* Lewiston, N.Y.: Edwin Mellen Press.

Muneto, Tatsuo. 1997. *Dharma Treasures: Spiritual Insights from Hawaii's Shin Buddhist Pioneers.* Honolulu: Buddhist Study Center Press.

Nishimura, Arthur Jiro. 2003. *Religion, Ethnicity and Organization: An Organizational Analysis of the Buddhist Churches of America.* Ph.D. diss., University of Washington.

Numrich, Paul David. 1996. *Old Wisdom in the New World: Americanization in Two Immigrant Theravada Buddhist Temples.* Knoxville: University of Tennessee Press.

Payne, Richard K. 2005. "Hiding in Plain Sight: The Invisibility of the Shingon Mission to the United States." In *Buddhist Missionaries in the Era of Globalization.* Linda Learman, ed. Honolulu: University of Hawai'i Press, 101–22.

Pierce, Lori Anne. 2000. *Constructing American Buddhisms: Discourses of Race and Religion in Territorial Hawai'i.* Ph.D. diss., University of Hawai'i.

Prebish, Charles. (ed. with Kenneth Tanaka). 1998. *The Faces of Buddhism in America.* Berkeley: University of California Press.

———. (ed. with Martin Baumann). 2002. *Westward Dharma: Buddhism Beyond Asia.* Berkeley: University of California Press.

Rocha, Cristina Moreira. 2005. "Being a Zen Buddhist Brazilian: Juggling Multiple Religious Identities in the Land of Catholicism." In *Buddhist Missionaries in the Era of Globalization.* Linda Learman, ed. Honolulu: University of Hawai'i Press, 140–61.

———. 2006. *Zen in Brazil: The Quest for Cosmopolitan Modernity.* Honolulu: University of Hawai'i Press.

Rust, William Charles. 1951. *The Shin Sect of Buddhism in America: Its Antecedents, Beliefs, and Present Condition.* Ph.D. diss., University of Southern California.

Seager, Richard Hughes. 2000. *Buddhism in America.* New York: Columbia University Press.

Snodgrass, Judith. 2003. *Presenting Japanese Buddhism to the West: Orientalism, Occidentalism, and the Columbian Exposition.* Chapel Hill, N.C.: University of North Carolina Press.

Spencer, Robert Francis. 1946. *Japanese Buddhism in the United States, 1940–1946: A Study on Acculturation.* Ph.D. diss., University of California, Berkeley.

Suzuki, Lester E. 1979. *Ministry in the Assembly and Relocation Centers in World War II.* Berkeley, Calif.: Yardbird Publishing.

Suh, Sharon. 2004. *Being Buddhist in a Christian World: Gender and Community in a Korean American Temple.* Seattle: University of Washington Press.

Tanabe, George J., Jr. 1994. "Glorious Gathas: Americanization and Japanization in Honganji Hymns." In *Engaged Pure Land Buddhism: Challenges Facing Jōdō Shinshū in the Contemporary World.* Berkeley, Calif.: Wisdom Ocean Publications, 221–37.

———. 2005. "Grafting Identity: The Hawaiian Branches of the Bodhi Tree." In *Buddhist Missionaries in the Era of Globalization.* Linda Learman, ed. Honolulu: University of Hawai'i Press, 77–100.

Tanaka, Kenneth K. 1998. "Issues of Ethnicity in the Buddhist Churches of America," In

American Buddhism: Methods and Findings in Recent Scholarship. Duncan Williams and Christopher Queen, ed. London: Routledge Curzon Press, 3–19.

Tsunemitsu, Kōzen. 1964. *Nihon Bukkyō tōbeishi.* Tokyo: Bukkyō shuppankyoku.

———. 1971. *Hawaii bukkyō shiwa.* Tokyo: Bukkyō dendō kyōkai.

Tuck, Donald R. 1987. *Buddhist Churches of America, Jodo Shinshu.* Lewiston, N.Y.: Edwin Mellen Press.

Tweed, Thomas. 1992. *The American Encounter with Buddhism, 1844–1912: Victorian Culture and the Limits of Dissent.* Bloomington: Indiana University Press.

———. (ed). 1996. *Retelling American Religious History.* Berkeley: University of California Press.

———. (ed. with Stephen Prothero). 1998. *Asian Religions in America: A Documentary History.* New York: Oxford University Press.

Van Esterik, Penny. 1993. *Taking Refuge: Lao Buddhism in North America.* Tempe, Ariz.: Arizona State University, Program in Southeast Asian Studies.

Washimi, Teishin. 1984. "'Kaikyōku kiroku' ni mirareta Hawaii Jōdoshū." In *Shūkyō bunka no shosō.* Takenaka Shinjō Hakase Shōju Kinen Ronbunshū Kankōkai, ed. Tokyo: Sankibō busshōrin, 1265–82.

———. 1998. "Hawaii Jōdoshū to Nihongo gakkō." In *Bukkyō kyōka kenkyū.* Mizutani Kōshō Sensei Koki Kinenkai, ed. Kyoto: Shibunkaku, 481–96.

Watada, Terry. 1996. *Bukkyo Tozen: A History of Jodo Shinshu Buddhism in Canada, 1905–1995.* Toronto: HpF Press/Toronto Buddhist Church.

Wells, Keiko. 2002. "Shin Buddhist Song Lyrics Sung in the United States: Their History and Expressed Buddhist Images (1), 1898–1939; (2), 1936–2001." *Tokyo daigaku Amerika taiheiyō kenkyū* 2: 75–99; 3: 41–64.

Williams, Duncan. (ed. with Christopher Queen). 1998. *American Buddhism: Methods and Findings in Recent Scholarship.* London: Routledge Curzon.

———. 2002. "Camp Dharma: Japanese-American Buddhist Identity and the Internment Experience of World War II." In *Westward Dharma: Buddhism Beyond Asia.* Charles Prebish and Martin Baumann, eds. Berkeley: University of California Press, 191–200.

———. 2003. "Complex Loyalties: Issei Buddhist Ministers during the Wartime Incarceration." *Pacific World* 5 (Third Series): 255–74.

Yoo, David K. 1996. "Enlightened Identities: Buddhism and Japanese Americans of California, 1924–1941." *Western Historical Quarterly* 27: 281–301.

———. (ed.) 1999. *New Spiritual Homes: Religion and Asian Americans.* Honolulu: University of Hawai'i Press.

———. 2000. *Growing Up Nisei: Race, Generation, and Culture Among Japanese Americans of California, 1924–49.* Urbana: University of Illinois Press.

PART 1

Nation and Identity

American Buddhism began in the mid-to-late-nineteenth century with the transmission of ideology, artifacts, and people: Buddhism, Buddhist art, and Buddhists. These ideas and objects found their way to the Americas as part of transnational exchanges of translated texts or transported statuary made possible by the process of modernity and colonialism. For example, a Burmese Buddha statue could end up in New York via London, or a French translation of the *Lotus Sutra* might appear in New England. In this section, we attempt to track some aspects of the sociopolitical, economic, and cultural history of what scholars now call "Buddhist modernism" in an effort to understand the larger context of the early years of Buddhism in America.

In many ways, large-scale emigration of Japanese Buddhists to the Americas was part of a larger transnational process of identity-formation necessitated by increased global interaction. Virtually all Asian forms of Buddhism in the late-nineteenth and early-twentieth centuries were undergoing similar dynamic transformations. In Japan, Buddhists were being forced to develop strategies to counter the domestic anti-Buddhist ordinances of the new Meiji government that identified the Japanese nation with an emperor-centered state Shintō. At the same time, a new "Japanese" Buddhism was being constructed in relation to other forms of Buddhism in the Asian world: notably the Indo-Tibetan, Theravada, and Chinese. Buddhism itself was, in the international arena, being defined against other major religions (especially Christianity). However, the growth of nativism and nationalism that Japan experienced at the turn of the twentieth century also meant that Buddhism also served as a repository of Japanese nationalism and identity for its expatriates. Modern Japanese Buddhism thus emerged as *both* "national/Japanese" and "transnational/non-Western," notions that became central to the experience of Buddhism for Japanese in the Americas.

The origins of Japanese American Buddhism (and thus, to some extent of Buddhism in the Americas) cannot be fully understood outside of the context of the religious landscape of United States at the time. In Hawaii in particular, the influx of tens of thousands of Buddhist "heathens" prompted Christian clerics and American government officials to fret about the future of an American territory that did not have a clear Christian majority. National and religious identity-formation was also a major theme in the Americas at that time: Notions of the United States as a Protestant nation were also being contested on the East Coast in response to the influx of Catholic immigrants from Ireland and Italy. American nativism and nationalism at the turn of the century rhetorically foregrounded demands that Jews, Catholics, and Buddhists conform to a core Anglo-Protestant American identity. But while other ethnic groups might assimilate to "whiteness"—a racial, if not religious, "melting"—Japanese Buddhists faced the double bind of religious and racial differences. Despite similar motivations for immigration, Asian immigrants were distinguished from their European counterparts by unequal treaties, low wages, and hostility to "heathen religions," and ineligibility for citizenship, voting rights, and land ownership.

It was in this context that pioneer Issei Buddhists started establishing temples in the Americas: first in Hawaii, then in the mainland United States, South America, and Canada. These temples established by and for immigrants were more than just religious sites: like the Christian churches and Jewish synagogues of many European immigrants, they became centers of social and cultural life that addressed the practical needs of a growing and increasingly more settled community. This sociocultural dimension of Buddhism set the stage for a dynamic process of identity formation, both religious and national. Although here the focus is on Japanese American Buddhism, we hope to foreground the importance of these kinds of studies in coming to a more complete picture of Buddhism in the United States.

Both the transnational-translocal characteristics shared by Buddhism in the Americas and the religion's highly localized nature are the primary focal points of the following chapters by Cristina Rocha and Masako Iino, who explore the impact of Buddhism in Brazil and Canada, respectively. Rocha's study of Brazilian Zen argues that an understanding of local-translocal interactions can best be understood through the notion of "creolization," a term Rocha uses in lieu of the more commonly used "syncretism" (associated with two clear systems that become "impure" when mixed) and "hybridity" (a term originating in the biological sciences and carrying the implication that hybrids are "native to nowhere"). Although the concepts of syncretism and hybridity have held theoretical importance in the study of this kind of interaction between so-called "universal religions" and local cultures, Rocha finds that both are inadequate to describing how dynamic "indigenizing" processes generate new identities and homes for Buddhism.

Although Rocha is neither the first to propose the concept of "creolization" (it has been theorized in Caribbean studies and linguistics) nor to critique theories of cultural encounters that seek "origins" and "purity" (Vijay Prashad's notion of "polyculturalism" is a good example of the latter), she uses this creolization framework to discuss broad processes of cultural exchange and encounter in ways that are extremely relevant to the study of Buddhism in the Americas. Through an exploration of Zen Buddhist funerary rituals, ancestral practices at the temple, *butsudan* altars in the home, and Buddhist-Catholic weddings, Rocha explains how both Buddhism and Catholicism become part of a "dynamically hyphenated religious practice." She convincingly shows that creolization in the case of Brazilian Zen is "not a product but a *process* of interaction and change."

In the second essay in this section, Masako Iino focuses on early encounters between Japanese immigrants to Canada and the majority Anglican Church population there that demanded religious conformity and sought to defend British Columbia as a "white man's province" even though it had the largest concentration of Chinese and Japanese immigrants in Canada. Iino's study revolves around the question of how to become Canadian while maintaining a Buddhist and Japanese spirit (*yamato damashii*). Iino follows this discussion to the second-generation (Nisei) Buddhists who experienced a national identity distinct from their parents but who were at the same time being confronted by racial and religious barriers to full acceptance into a Canadian identity. Her analysis of publications such as *Otakebi* (1930) and *Buddha* (1935 and 1940), put out by Canadian Young Buddhist Associations, reveal how Buddhists negotiated a complex process of ethnic and national identifications and differentiations spanning several generations despite pressures to "assimilate" or "Americanize."

Some young Buddhists even went so far as to challenge Anglo-Protestant conformity, claiming in 1940 that "Assimilation in the true sense is not to assimilate with the white people who claim they are superior to us, but to stand in a status equal to that of the white, to accept, together with the white, the habits and the values of Canada, and to contribute to Canadian culture." The Canadianization experience, for these Nisei, meant organizational independence both from Japan as well as from the U.S.-based Buddhist Mission of North America. At the same time, Issei and Nisei Canadian Buddhists also thought of themselves as transnational cosmopolitans who, they hoped, would be able to contribute to a new "Pacific era civilization" that could span multiple nation states by highlighting their Buddhist and Japanese "spirit."

Both Rocha and Iino provide critical perspectives from Issei Buddhists that force us to rethink how Buddhism becomes variously identified with national and transnational identities in an era of boundary crossing through migration. Through the kind of specific, locally based case studies they present, we can see the intricate dynamics of the encounter between Buddhism and local cultures that ultimately produced distinct American, Canadian, Hawaiian, and Brazilian forms of Buddhism.

1 “Can I Put This Jizō Together with the Virgin Mary in the Altar?”

Creolizing Zen Buddhism in Brazil

CRISTINA ROCHA

In this essay, I analyze the religious practices of Japanese Brazilians who adhere to Sōtō Zen, the only Japanese Zen Buddhist tradition represented in Brazil. I argue that the multiple influences that have shaped Japanese religious practices since their arrival in Brazil in 1908, along with the recent strong interest in Buddhism in Brazilian society, have given rise to creolized religious practices. I use the concept creolization to underscore the notion that identity is not formed through a seamless synthesis of two or more worlds, but rather it emerges from a dynamic process of exchange and interaction. In this context, the concept of creolization can shed light on the various ways in which Japanese immigrants and their descendants have overlaid a Brazilian religious “vocabulary” onto their Buddhist “grammar.”

I examine several cases of how Japanese Brazilians strategically draw their religious identity from different sources at different occasions. While until the 1990s the main religious identities were derivations of Catholicism, French Spiritism, and Afro-Brazilian religions, more recently, some Japanese Brazilians are returning to Buddhism as a result of the status and prestige that it has acquired in Brazilian society in general. I show how symbolic and cultural capital—previously associated with Catholicism, and now associated with Buddhism as well—are strategically used to negotiate and construct a distinctive religious identity.

Catholic and/or Buddhist? What Is in a Ritual?

In January 2001, I was at Tenzuizenji, a temple-cum-Zen center recently established by Coen sensei, a non–Japanese Brazilian nun in São Paulo city,[1] where I participated in the one-year memorial service that Nícia Takeda, a sansei, organized for her deceased mother. Her mother's seventh-day mass had been at a Catholic church,[2] but the forty-ninth-day memorial service was officiated by Coen sensei at Busshinji, the Sōtōshū headquarters for South America situated in São Paulo city. Although Nícia and her family did not know what Buddhist tradition they belonged to, all the memorial services she remembered (those of her grandfather, grandmother, father, and mother) had been held at Busshinji because, as she put it, "my mother's sister-in-law's aunt was a nun at the temple, which made things easier." After having meditation sessions with Coen at her local martial arts and massage school, Nícia decided to follow Coen when she left Busshinji to establish Tenzuizendo. She had already studied Tibetan Buddhism for three years and visited her lineage's Rinpoche in India, but after her mother's passing, Nícia started a long search into her family's history and traditions. This is how she describes her search:

> Upon my mother's death, we realized we didn't know Buddhism. For instance, we didn't know what the meaning of the altar was. My mom was the one who took care of the *butsudan* [Buddhist altar] and without her, we didn't know how to tend to it. Hence, someone suggested we talk to a monk at Busshinji and my sister and I made an appointment. The monk explained the meaning of having a *butsudan* at home and how to organize it, the meaning of the *ihai* [mortuary tablets] and of the offerings, who the historical Buddha was and so on. We, then, set another time when we would come back to show him what we had in our *butsudan*. This time he explained every little bit of what we had: *ihai* [mortuary tablets] of brothers who had passed away as children, photos of my grandfather. He told us what had to be kept with us and what could be kept at Busshinji. So we kept my grandmother's, grandfather's, and my father's *ihai* and had a new one made for my mom.

At the one-year memorial service, Nícia revealed to me that her family and friends were not Buddhists but Catholic Japanese Brazilians.[3] Interestingly, this included her deceased mother as well. The only Buddhists at the service were Coen sensei, her non–Japanese Brazilian disciples who were assisting the service, and the new sympathizer Nícia. "What should we make of that?" I asked her. Was Nícia betraying her mother's memory by giving her a Buddhist memorial service? Were her family and friends upset? Why was Nícia so interested in Buddhism after having been a Catholic herself? Nícia's response unveiled a world and a story echoed by the other Japanese Brazilians I interviewed.

A Dynamically Hyphenated Religious Practice

Nícia's mother was Catholic, but her grandmother and grandfather, who came from Japan, were Buddhists. Arriving immediately before World War II, they were prohibited from speaking Japanese, so their children went to Brazilian schools and were baptized as Catholics.[4] Despite their ostensible conversion, Nícia's grandmother maintained several Japanese cultural practices, including keeping a *butsudan* in her bedroom. Nícia's mother, by contrast, kept a Catholic altar in her own bedroom. When Nícia's grandmother passed away, her mother brought the *butsudan* to her own home and started tending for both altars equally. According to Nícia:

> Everyday my mother would bring offerings such as water, rice, flowers, candles, incense, and an occasional treat received from a visiting friend to both altars. She kept this tradition because my father was the first-born son, so she felt the obligation to maintain the Buddhist altar. While at my grandmother's altar there was an image of the Buddha, photos and *ihai* of deceased members of the family, in her own altar she had an image of the Virgin Mary. Although my mum was Catholic, when my father passed away, she had an *ihai* made for him and put it on the forefront of the *butsudan*. My father was neither Buddhist nor Catholic, so my mother had my father's 7th day mass at the Catholic Church, but had his 49th day-mass [*sic*] and 3-year mass [*sic*] in Busshinji.

Nícia's family and friends were not upset about going to the Buddhist temple for the service. In fact, they welcomed the opportunity to get together in the temple for lunch after the service because many of them lived out of São Paulo city and had not seen each other in a long time. This would not have happened in a Catholic church because parishioners do not get together for a meal after a memorial mass. They were also happy Coen spoke Portuguese to them during and after the service. Nícia pointed out that her mother's best friend, who was eighty-two years old and also in attendance, was as active a Catholic as her mother, but also had a *butsudan* at home and did Buddhist memorial services for deceased family members.

This story mirrors those of many other Japanese Brazilian families I interviewed. They also told me that it is common practice to have a seventh-day Catholic mass for the deceased family member (because the family has usually become Catholic) and have Buddhist memorial services held at fixed intervals thereafter (forty-nine days, first anniversary, third anniversary, and sometimes extending to seventh, thirteenth, and twenty-third anniversaries) because the late family member was a Buddhist. This choice reflects the fact that in

Catholicism the seventh-day mass is a very important service, whereas the forty-ninth-day memorial service is meaningful to Buddhists, who consider it as the moment when mourning ends and the deceased's soul becomes an ancestor. On this day, the new Buddhist name given to the departed (*kaimyō*) is finally engraved on the *ihai,* which is then placed in the *butsudan.* It is noteworthy, however, that the *shonanoka,* the Buddhist seventh-day service, is also considered an important service in Japan, because it is the first in the series of memorial services. Perhaps because of the strong Catholic influence in the culture at large, the Catholic rite here trumped the Buddhist one.

On another occasion, a family member told me it was the first time the family had gone to Busshinji, as the deceased mother was the last Buddhist in the family. All her children were practicing Catholics and the grandchildren were nonpracticing Catholics. As I had lunch with them in the Busshinji basement after the memorial service, one of the grandchildren grimaced and exclaimed upon drinking green tea: "Ahh, this is yuck!" and immediately returned to his *guaraná* (a Brazilian soft drink). I gathered that going to Busshinji was not the only thing they were doing for the first time that day. Roberto Teruya, the son who organized the memorial service, told me his mother had a connection with the Higashi Honganji (a sect of the Jōdo Shinshū school) as well, so in this case, the first memorial service was held there. But, as with Nícia's mother's service, his family was happy to have a priest who spoke Portuguese and explained a little about Buddhism. When I interviewed Roberto, he asked me excitedly: "What is Zen? I don't know anything about Buddhism. I see many Brazilians interested in Buddhism. It is more a philosophy now. They read everything about it!"

Innovation and Continuity: Japanese Buddhism in Japan and Japanese Brazilians

These stories reveal the constant cultural negotiations Japanese immigrants and their descendents have been through since their arrival in Brazil. It is important to note, however, that a hyphenated religious practice does not imply that each category—Buddhist and Catholic—is stable, distinct, or homogeneous. On the contrary, these stories show how second- and third-generation Japanese Brazilians strategically draw their religious identity from different sources on different occasions at their own will.[5] Indeed, these stories show that dynamic interactions between Japanese Brazilians and Brazilian society at large enabled creolization and consequently innovation.

However, the process of innovation needs to be understood in the context of continuity. Belonging to two religions simultaneously is not strictly a

Japanese Brazilian phenomenon. In Japan, for example, it is a commonplace that practicing Buddhism does not exclude practicing Shintoism as well. As Ian Reader has noted, "praying to one does not prevent one from praying to the other."[6] Likewise, for Japanese Brazilians, being a Catholic does not exclude keeping one's previous cultural and religious traditions, which include Buddhism.

I believe that for the majority of the Japanese Brazilians who have converted to Catholicism, Buddhism and the Buddhist temple are still regarded as repositories of long-forgotten, old Japanese cultural traditions. Much like the *butsudan,* which holds memories even when as in Nícia's story, they are not fully understood by the family members anymore, I argue that Buddhism is not regarded merely as a religion, but as a niche of "forgotten" memories and traditions. In a diasporic community, cultural objects are frequently divorced from their original cultural meaning, acquiring other significant connotations. In this case, *butsudan* and Buddhism become a connection to Japan and family roots. When there is a death in the family, Japanese Brazilians often feel the need to reinforce those connections.

Continuity between Japan and Japanese Brazilians is also evident in the lack of knowledge of these families about which school of Buddhism they have historically belonged to. Connections with Buddhism have undoubtedly been severed in the past for lack of a dense Buddhist environment and because of pressure to learn Brazilian ways in order to achieve social mobility. But we see the same phenomenon in Japan, where many families do not know which Buddhist school they belong to. During my fieldwork there, whenever I was asked what I was researching, conversation would steer toward religious affiliation. Despite my contacts' active participation in the calendrical cycle of Buddhist events such as O-bon (return of the souls of deceased forebears to the *ie,* the household), Higan (spring and autumn equinoxes), and Hatsumōde (New Year shrine or temple visit), many of them were not able to tell me their religious affiliation.

The lack of knowledge about one's specific religious affiliation needs to be understood in the context of the development of Buddhism in Japan from 1635 to 1871. During this period, the *danka seido* system enforced by the Japanese government required all households to register with the nearest Buddhist temple. That was done not to promote Buddhism as the only religion of Japan, but as a means of social control to ensure that no family was Christian or belonged to Nichiren Fuju-fuseha (a Nichiren sect banned in 1669). Registration acquired disclosing the identity, genealogy, residence, occupation, property, and tax obligation of each family member. Registration had to be renewed at the same temple every year and failure to do so was considered a crime.[7] Clearly, this system of affiliation did not imply anything about the belief or faith of the household or individual family members, but rather reflected a reciprocal relationship involving financial support in exchange for mortuary rites.[8]

Although it was formally abolished in 1871, the *danka seido* remained strong "largely because its relationship to the whole ancestral and Japanese socio-religious systems is so deeply rooted that it still continues to be the economic mainstay of Buddhism in the present."[9] Indeed, its consequences are clear among Japanese Brazilian parishioners. A Japanese Brazilian monk at Busshinji told me that it is common for many parishioners from the Higashi and Nishi Hongwanji (Jōdo Shinshū) to come to the Sōtō temple for memorials and vice versa. He did not see any problem in that

> many people don't differentiate between *Nishi, Higashi* and *Sōtō.* For them, if it is Buddhism, it is ok. I know when a family does not belong to Sōtōshū because each school has its own kind of *ihai,* and they bring theirs for the service. I have even seen families that belong to the Seichō-no-Ie[10] come to Busshinji for memorials. The interesting fact is that the Seichō-no-Ie *ihai* is not even a *hotoke*[11] [a Buddha], but a *kami* [deity of the Shinto tradition]. But we don't think of this as a problem. It is fine, really; if the family wants a service we do it.

When I asked him what made people decide at which temple to hold services, he said:

> People call, ask for the price first, and then ask about the hours available for the service. If the price or the time set is not suitable, they may hold their memorial service in another temple. Once I heard a *Nishi Hongwanji* priest say that in the future we shouldn't distinguish Japanese Buddhism in Brazil by schools. We should just call it Buddhism. Maybe he said so because parishioners already do that informally. On the other hand, of course there are parishioners that are very orthodox. Once I went to a town in the countryside that didn't have a *Sōtō* mission. An old man told me he had done the funerary rite for a family member with the *Nishi Hongwanji.* But now because I was there he was doing it all over again with the *Sōtō* since he followed Sōtōshū. He said that for the ancestor it was important that some ritual was performed, better some kind of ritual than nothing at all, isn't it?[12]

The primary importance of rites dealing with death and commemorating ancestors, as Ian Reader has observed in Japan, is that "they should be done, not that they have to be done by a priest of a particular sect."[13] More recently, it seems they do not even have to be celebrated by a real priest. The latest technological addition to the Japanese pantheon of robots is the "robopriest," a robot that can deliver prayers according to the rites of seven different Buddhist sects, Shintō, and two Christian faiths.[14] Japanese Brazilian practices must therefore be understood in relation to and continuity with these types of Japanese practices.

Syncretism, Hybridity, or Creolization?

Keeping these ethnographic cases in mind, I would now like to characterize at greater length the theoretical concepts I have been using. I will evaluate the notions of syncretism, creolization, and then hybridization to show where they overlap and why creolization appears to be the most apt trope in this study of Zen in Brazil. I regard the trope "creolization" as a development of the concept of hybridity, an insight into *how* the process of hybridity takes place.

Although the concept of syncretism has been historically used to analyze religious encounters, I decided not use it here for two reasons. First, even though syncretism has staged a comeback in the analytical literature, it has historically been associated with impurity, understood pejoratively to denote a stage prior to Christian monotheism.[15] In other words, the term was used to evaluate religious blending from the point of view of one of the religions involved. Second, syncretism conveys the image of two clear, autonomous systems overlaid.[16] My analysis of Zen in Brazil complicates this picture by addressing other intersecting influences and negotiations, which in turn created multiple, disjunctive beliefs and practices. Indeed, Brazilian anthropologist Rita Segato has argued that "Brazil has produced a model of multiple interpenetrations usually described as syncretic. I do not think it is enough to use the term syncretism to encompass the meetings and fusions typical of this system. What is significant about it is that plurality continues to be present, although through a particular multicultural mechanism that makes each culture in contact involve, embrace, invoke or simply mark its presence in a much bigger sector of the population than in a specific social group."[17]

The term *creolization* originates from the Spanish *criollo* and Portuguese *crioulo,* both deriving from the Latin verb *creare* (to breed or to create). Until recently, the concept of a "creole culture" was deeply connected to the encounter of African and European culture in the Caribbean. The term was extended to encompass the language spoken by these so-called Creole people, which in turn was regarded as a simplification of the European languages it drew on. Lately, however, linguists have developed a more positive regard for it as they have come to realize that creole languages resulted from superimposing the dominant language's lexicon over the dominated language's syntax, grammar, and morphology.[18] The new language carried a twofold predicament: while it revealed that colonial peoples had yielded and made use of the dominant language by using its lexicon, it also showed that they clung to the inner forms of their own language, which they used as a matrix for this lexicon. Creolization was thus simultaneously domination and a sign of resistance.[19]

Furthermore, contemporary scholars have detached the trope creolization from its Caribbean and linguistic roots and applied the term more broadly to these kinds of processes of cultural encounter and exchange. In the field of anthropology, Hannerz was one of the first to make a strong statement for the concept of creole culture as "our most promising root metaphor" to make sense of the way "two or more historical sources, originally widely different" enter into contact, intermingle, and mix.[20] The itinerary that the terms *creole* and *creolization* have undergone is clearly characterized by Stoddard and Cornwell: "In Trinidad today there is a slippage between the notion of 'Creole' as the African side of the population, the notion of 'Creole' culture being the national culture of Trinidad and Tobago, and the notion of 'creolizing' as the continuous process of intercultural mixing and creativity. It is the latter, extended sense of creolization and *créolité* that cultural theorists appropriate as a synonym for hybridity."[21]

It is this latter sense, inflected by its linguistic history facet, I wish to deploy when analyzing Brazilian Zen. However, before endorsing creolization as a trope to understand the process of cultural mixing in Brazil, it is necessary to examine, first, where creolization and hybridity overlap and second, where both terms have their distinct uses. The concept of creolization as a synonym of hybridity has increasingly gained currency in the past decades in cultural theory, postcolonial studies, and anthropology.[22] Papastergiadis has rightly observed that "hybridity," as with creolization, acknowledges that "identity is constructed through negotiation of difference." Such identity is not a synthesis of the combined elements, but an "energy field of different forces."[23] In other words, identity is not a tidy product, but an ongoing construction through negotiation.

Following Papastergiadis, I suggest that creolization underscores the notion that identity is not a seamless combination, a synthesis of two or more worlds, but a field of energy.[24] Yuri Lotman, a Russian semiotician who defines culture as dynamic rather than a static entity, employs an equally fitting metaphor when he talks about culture as "more like a river with a number of currents moving in different rates and intensities." Culture, in this case would be in a "state of constant 'creolization.'"[25] As much as culture is not a synthetic whole, creolization is not a product but a *process* of interaction and change.

Ultimately all terms are problematic, as they are historically entangled in colonizing processes, but I believe the trope creolization has several advantages over the term hybridity. Hybridity as a metaphor for cultural contact carries with it the resonance of its origin in biological science where it was juxtaposed to racial purity.[26] Hybridity also derives from horticulture and animal breeding practices, which in turn juxtapose it with ideas of sterility and passivity, because hybrid plants and animals do not reproduce. Finally, "hybrids are, by definition, native to nowhere," whereas creole means just the opposite, "to become indigenized, to create a home where one is not at home."[27]

Notwithstanding contemporary attempts to reclaim hybridity as a subversive practice/agency within postcolonial and cultural theory, it still has to grapple with its historical implication in this discourse of race. Creolization as an analytical trope, on the other hand, although it also originated during colonial contact, carries notions of creativity, agency, and innovation by the colonized.[28] Furthermore, the concept of creolization highlights how *the process* of continuous contact and negotiation takes place rather than, as "hybrid" does, the static end product.

Nevertheless, I should mention a caveat before wholeheartedly embracing the term creolization to describe Brazilian Zen. As previously mentioned, the word *creole* derives from the Portuguese *crioulo,* which even today is a derogatory term for Afro-Brazilians in Brazil. Furthermore, the use of this concept may lead some readers to take the history of Brazilian society as more connected with to the Caribbean than it is. In spite of these drawbacks, I maintain that the trope of creolization sheds light onto how Japanese immigrants and their descendants have placed a Brazilian religious vocabulary over a Buddhist matrix while Brazilians of no Japanese ancestry and Catholic Japanese Brazilians have done the inverse process.

Japanese Brazilian Creole Practices: Dealing with the Dead

Since arriving in the country in 1908, Japanese Brazilians have intensively negotiated their religious practices and beliefs. The first obvious sign of it is the ubiquitous creolization between Buddhist and Catholic practices.[29] As noted earlier, all of my informants gave their deceased family members, be they Buddhist, Catholic, or nonreligious, a seventh-day Catholic mass and a forty-ninth-day memorial service, where an *ihai* and a Buddhist name were given to the deceased. For my Japanese Brazilian informants, there was no doubt about the "division of labor" between the Catholic Church and the Buddhist temple concerning how to deal with the dead. Each religion had its mortuary rites that had to be fulfilled.

When I asked why they would have a forty-ninth-day memorial service at a Buddhist temple if they were not Buddhists themselves, my informants gave different answers. Some told me that a Buddhist service would please the deceased (when he/she was a Buddhist) and older family members and friends of the deceased. Conversely, a Catholic mass on the seventh day would please the younger generations who had adopted Catholicism (even when they were not active practitioners). In this case, family members and friends could choose which ritual to attend. Others said that even if the deceased family member was not Buddhist, friends had recommended that they hold a forty-ninth-day Buddhist service, because it was the most important mortuary rite and a traditional custom. Fewer still told me they had a new interest in Buddhism and wanted to use their family tradition to learn more about it. As the many memorial services I took part in revealed—and this is expected from a religion that is sought mostly in time of death—there is very little knowledge of proper behavior on such an occasion. For instance, during the service, the priest took time to explain the school's history, the life of the historical Buddha, the images in the altar, and how to offer incense at it.

Equally revealing is the fact that, according to a monk at Busshinji, 90 percent of deceased Japanese Brazilian people are buried in Catholic cemeteries and only 10 percent are cremated according to Buddhist custom. One reason for this is that there is only one crematorium in São Paulo city; until it existed, the Japanese had no choice but to adopt Brazilian burial customs. However, even though they were buried in Catholic cemeteries, crosses were not placed in the grave. An account of Japanese Brazilian religious practices before World War II given by the Brazilian anthropologist Egon Schaden already revealed strong creolization between Buddhist and Catholic practices. According to Schaden:

> Even before the War there were images of Catholic saints and crosses juxtaposed with Buddhist images in the *butsudan*. There were people who would chant Christian and Buddhist prayers. When a person passed away, flowers, candles, and Japanese incense were set next to the corpse, a Catholic rosary would be put together with a *jyuzu* (Buddhist rosary), and later candles, flowers, incense and food were set on the grave. Sometimes a cross was erected by the *bochiyo,* the Buddhist mortuary pole or stone. Finally, there are people who celebrate the 7th day Catholic mass and on the 49th day after the passing celebrate the traditional *shiju-kunti.*[30]

In the 1970s, Tomō Handa, an Issei who became a journalist and well-known painter, notes once more the compromises made in Brazil to satisfy Issei and Nisei alike: "Funerals are usually conducted in a Catholic style for young people, whilst for the older people it is done according to the Buddhist style. However, there are cases where a Catholic mass is celebrated before burial, but then family and friends go to the cemetery with a Buddhist monk, and bury the body in a Buddhist style."[31]

Furthermore, not only do adherents have creolized practices of maintaining a Buddhist matrix as a basis for a new Catholic vocabulary, but they take also place at the heart of the Sōtōshū institution itself. At Busshinji, although O-bon festivities take place in mid-August (as it is usual in Japan), a similar ritual is held on November 2. This is done to coincide with the Catholic All Souls' Day and in the temple it is called *ireisai* (memorial service ceremony). In the same vein, the Brazilian festivity of Children's Day celebrated on October 15 is also celebrated at Busshinji. However, the festivity is centered on the figure of Jizō, the Bodhisattva who looks after diseased children in Japan. At O-bon, *ireisai,* and Children's Day, both Japanese Brazilians and Brazilians of no Japanese ancestry come to the temple.

Sites of Worship: Locating the *Butsudan*

Another illustration of this process of creolization is the placement of typical Buddhist offerings such as rice, water, flowers, incense, and even treats given by friends at both the *butsudan* and the Catholic altar. The original Japanese Buddhist act of making daily food offerings at the *butsudan* "to the ancestors before the family eats as befits their position as the senior members of the house"[32] worked as a matrix, a grammar, for a new Catholic vocabulary (dealing with a Catholic altar) to be superimposed. The meaning of this gesture was altered when the same offerings were placed before the Virgin Mary. Nícia told me that making offerings was a sign of respect and if the Buddhist altar received all these offerings it would look bad on her mother if she did not take care of her own Catholic altar in the same fashion. More than an object of a particular religion, many Japanese Brazilians that had a *butsudan* at home told me it represented respect and gratitude for the ancestors. In this way, offering practices transcend the practices of Buddhism proper and appear in other settings as well.

A Japanese Brazilian Buddhist monk at Busshinji revealed a similar overlapping of meanings, this time in the way Catholic and Buddhist images found their place on a Catholic altar. His family itself is an embodiment of a hyphenated religious affiliation: whereas his mother is a devout Catholic, his father's family belonged to the Sōtō sect in Japan. In his case, negotiations between his Buddhist practice and his mother's Catholic belief took much more effort on his part. He reminisces:

> My mom is so pious that my name is Francisco Aparecido! She worships the patron saint of Brazil [Our Lady of the Appearance]. So religion is a very serious business for her. We do have *ihai* at home, but it took ages for her to accept them. She has softened a bit now. For instance, the other day I told her: "we have Jizō, that image that protects children, at the temple for sale." She told me: "Oh, well, it is ok. You can buy it and bring it. I'll take care of it." But she asked: "Can I put this Jizō together with the Virgin Mary in the altar?" and I said, "There is no problem, you do whatever you want to do with it." She was really worried about how to take care of the Jizō![33]

Creolization between Japanese and Brazilian practices is also evident in the issue of who is responsible for looking after the *butsudan*. Traditionally in Japan, the *chōnan* (the eldest son), as the head of the *ie*, would keep the altar and tend to it. In contemporary Japan, however, because of the phenomena of urbanization and nuclear families, housewives take care of the *butsudan* as their husbands work long hours outside of the house. The situation in Brazil is equally mixed: The eldest son typically inherits the *butsudan*, but a woman being responsible for the altar is not uncommon. In fact, that is what took place in Nícia's case, where her grandmother, then her mother, and subsequently herself took responsibility for it. Nícia told me:

> When the monk at Busshinji told me that according to tradition the eldest son should keep the *butsudan*, my sister and I called my brother to ask if he wanted to keep it. After consulting with his family he said he didn't want to keep it because he was not Buddhist and neither was his family. So I said I wanted to keep it particularly because of the studies I've been doing. You see, I am learning the Buddhist teachings and practicing meditation.

One Japanese Brazilian, who practices *zazen* under Coen sensei, told me that although he is the *chōnan*, hence the one who should keep the *butsudan*, he was denied this right because he had converted to Zen Buddhism while his family belonged to Sekai Kyūseikyō (Church of World Messianity), a new religious movement (NRM). The altar, therefore, went to his eldest sister when their mother died. He confided that he would have liked to have kept it, but he had fallen from grace when he took up Zen. His mother clearly opposed his religious adherence "because she wanted me to follow the family religion, especially since I was the only man in the house, the heir, the one who should keep family tradition."[34]

Others do not have a *butsudan* to be passed down and are not aware that the eldest son should be responsible for it. One afternoon, when I was at Busshinji, two teenage Japanese Brazilian girls came in. They wanted to buy a *butsudan* at the temple to give to their mother as a birthday present. They thought it would be a good gift because their mother was becoming interested in Buddhism and had no altar at home. They also mentioned it would be a good way to help their mother research the Japanese family tradition that lately she had been interested in. A Japanese Brazilian female volunteer at the temple spent some time with the girls explaining which objects should be placed in the altar and how to care for it.

Contrary to what happens in Japan, where the *butsudan* should either be passed down in the family or be bought at the time of death, here the youngest in the family were buying something for a female member of their immediate family who was still alive, so that she could recollect family history and exercise her interest in Buddhism. I believe the fact that Buddhism is fashionable in Brazil can help us understand new social meanings ascribed to Buddhism. The *butsudan* continued to symbolize ancestor worship, but also became a Buddhist altar (as you would have in other non–Japanese Buddhist traditions) and rather a "cool" object to have at home. As I showed elsewhere, fashion and Buddhism have walked hand in hand in Brazil since the mid-1990s.[35]

Buddhist-Catholic Weddings

In Japan, weddings have historically been a secular rather than religious ceremony. Buddhist wedding ceremonies were created in 1887 using Christian weddings as a model.[36] The Shintō wedding, which now seems traditional, was created even later, dating from the 1900s. In recent years, Christian-style weddings have become extremely fashionable and now account for the majority of wedding ceremonies in Japan.[37] Ian Reader has shown that because of the postwar urbanization and the nuclear family phenomenon, which weakened the bonds between families and Buddhist temples, Sōtōshū Shūmuchō (the head office of Sōtō sect in Tokyo) published and distributed several pamphlets in the 1980s that sought to strengthen the family-temple connection. One of them, the *Ten Articles of Faith (Shinkō Jūkun)*, is an attempt to bring families back to the temple through the marriage ritual. It reads: "Let us celebrate weddings before our ancestors in the temple."[38]

Although some Japanese Brazilians do get married in the Buddhist temple, that does not mean that the ceremony is solely created using Buddhist concepts. Indeed, like funerals, memorials, and the ways in which the *butsudan* is used, wedding practices suggest creolization between Catholic and Shintō/Buddhist practices in Brazil. When writing about Japanese Brazilian customs in the 1960s, Tomō Handa noted: "[Wedding] ceremonies take place in a Catholic church but upon arriving home, there is a Japanese ceremony with *san-san-kudō*,[39] before they go on to the reception. This is certainly done to content the *issei* as well as the *nisei*. One cannot assert things without statistical numbers, but it is only natural that weddings are more and more, year after year, in the Catholic style because of the increasing number of *nisei*."[40]

Handa's prediction certainly came true, and the trend toward creolizing Buddhist and Catholic practices to satisfy Issei, Nisei, *sansei*, and, nowadays, *yonsei* is very much alive, as I have shown throughout in this essay. For instance, the head monk of the Jōdo Shinshū temple of Apucarana (Paraná state), describes wedding ceremonies for Japanese Brazilians during a discussion on Buddhismo-L:

> In Brazil, the wedding rites celebrated by the Jōdo Shinshū School were adapted to our culture, incorporating Western customs. For instance, people frequently get married in Western attire: the groom wears a suit and the bride wears a wedding gown. The couple always insists on adorning the aisle between the pews with flowers and ribbons and having the famous red carpet (which actually can be of any other color). The bridesmaids are almost indispensable and the rings are more often than not part of the rites too. Of course, all this is only cultural accretion, it does not influence the rite per se, which can be celebrated in any place, circumstance, and wearing any attire.[41]

The ceremony itself resembles very much the Catholic one with exchange of vows, rings, and rosaries. In North America, Kashima has reported this kind of creolization taking place in many of the Jōdo Shinshū activities, including weddings. He mentions new features in the American Buddhist wedding ceremony such as a wedding gown for the bride, a tuxedo for the groom, the playing of a wedding march, the exchange of rings, and the witnessing of a wedding license.[42]

Whereas these are moves toward more Catholic or Christian wedding ceremonies performed for Japanese Brazilians, weddings in Busshinji are celebrated for Japanese Brazilians and some Brazilians of no Japanese ancestry who have converted to Buddhism. That itself entails a different approach toward weddings in that the couple is not seeking a Christian analogue. Quite the opposite, converts are usually part of the intellectual elite who have left Catholicism seeking individual responsibility for their "spiritual growth" or enlightenment and are not associated with any institutionalized religion. They praise Zen for its "lack of ritual" and absence of an almighty God. Thus, they expect a different and most of the times less ritualistic ceremony than in the Catholic Church.

Japanese Brazilians Converting to Buddhism: Family History and Spirituality

> Hello! I was surfing in one of the Buddhist websites and realized that because of phonetics the word *dharma* becomes *Daruma* in Japanese. Can anyone tell me if they are both the same for Buddhism? I remember when I was a child my grandparents had a bunch of *Daruma* at home. They were big-eyed, red, bearded dolls that they would paint one eye when they made a wish and they would only paint the other eye when the wish came true.[43]

This message illustrates how some Japanese Brazilians, who have had a little contact with Buddhism through family tradition—in this case the folk practice of appealing to Bodhidharma, the patriarch of Zen Buddhism, for good luck—may suddenly realize that their Japanese heritage was influenced by this religion. For many, turning to Buddhism through an interest in spirituality means also going back to family history.

Indeed, when I asked Japanese Brazilians about their reasons for an interest in Zen Buddhism, many replied they wanted to know more about "traditional" Japanese culture and the "religion of the samurai." The myth of the samurai plays a very important role in the *imaginaire* of the Japanese Brazilians. I gathered from interviews that the samurai is imagined as a powerful figure who lived in traditional Japan and had the world under his command. Some Japanese Brazilians proudly told me their families were descendents of samurai families and not just of peasant farmers. Here, being a samurai descendant is a form of cultural capital and therefore empowerment. Most Japanese who migrated to Brazil were indentured workers and hence, possessed low status in Brazilian society. Although many have ascended to middle class positions, they are still seen by Brazilian upper classes as having little cultural capital.

Furthermore, Japanese Brazilians converting to Zen Buddhism suggests another kind of creolization than we have seen so far: the creolization of the so-called "devotional" practices of ancestor worship and mortuary rites (usually regarded as "immigrants" practices), and the "convert" or "Western" interest in Buddhism (mainly centered on meditation, undertaken by non-Asian groups).[44] First of all, traditional Japanese affiliation with a temple (hence, a Buddhist sect) was organized by household (*ie*); affiliation was not a matter of personal choice or individual faith. By contrast, family affiliation (when known) plays a much smaller role for Japanese Brazilian converts in their choice of sect when it plays one at all. Instead of a family adherence, Japanese Brazilians have adopted individual choice of religion. When I asked a Nisei who practiced *zazen* at Busshinji if his family, who was affiliated to Jōdo Shinshū, was upset because he chose a different school of Buddhism, he replied: "My family does not make this distinction between sects. The distinction you are making is in the realm of the study of Buddhism. My family goes to the *otera* [the temple] just like the *fujinkai* women [women association group] here. They go to the services, but do not differentiate among Pure Land, Zen and so on. They think: 'it is Buddhism, it is *otera,* it is fine.'"[45]

In the same way some Brazilians of no Japanese ancestry seek Buddhism as an alternative to traditional Catholicism—often because they feel the latter does not answer their spiritual needs anymore—Japanese Brazilians, who were mostly Catholic (some practicing and some not), have also been searching for alternative spiritual practices. Members of both groups have explored many religions such as Afro-Brazilian, French Spiritism, and NRM before finding Buddhism. This phenomenon of constant "religious transit" has been well documented in Brazilian society.[46]

Following the North American "Tibetan chic" trend, Tibetan Buddhism is fashionable and very much in the Brazilian print media and popular culture nowadays. As a result of this media exposure, Tibetan Buddhism is usually the Buddhist school seekers start with. It is not surprising then, that when Nícia Takeda became interested in Buddhism she started with Tibetan practice and even undertook a pilgrimage trip to India to meet her lineage's Rinpoche. As with any fashionable trend, teenagers often spot it quickly; her youngest son, the only one who is still living at home, told me about his reading in Tibetan Buddhist literature and his interest in meditation. When Nícia shifted to Japanese Buddhism, it was because of a number of confluent factors: first, her mother's death and her subsequent search for family heritage, second her meeting Coen sensei at her local martial arts school, and finally her decision to quit the other martial arts school (which was affiliated with Tibetan Buddhism) because it was too far away from her home. These factors suggest an understanding of Buddhism as essentially one, and choices about practice may be determined by convenience or accessibility to the nearest temple/Zen-center. More importantly, Nícia chose Japanese Buddhism because she was not only interested in Buddhism itself, but also in her family heritage.

Another telling case is Ryūichi Watanabe, whose wife's forty-ninth memorial service was held at Busshinji. He told me he had no religion to resort to in such a painful time and his Japanese Brazilian golf friends tried to help by saying that he should hold a Buddhist memorial service. Soon afterward, he read an interview with Coen sensei in the Japanese community newspaper and because her words touched him, he decided Busshinji was the right place for the memorial. However, even if he very much appreciated the service and despite holding Coen in high regard, shortly after the memorial he started frequenting a Shambhala Buddhist center where his son and daughter-in-law took him and where he still goes three years after his wife's death. When asked why he had chosen Tibetan over Japanese Buddhism, he said:

> To tell you the truth I was in search of a spiritual practice, not of a religion. I think because my family belonged to Japanese Buddhism, I regarded it as an institution, something connected to the old Japanese community. In Shambhala I use the teachings in daily life. Well, I guess Shambhala meditation is identical to the Sōtōshū's. Following fashion, I am also reading the books by the Dalai Lama.[47]

Here Ryūichi reveals that for him Japanese Buddhism is regarded as a religion because it is associated with his ethnic heritage, which implies social obligations and not an individual choice. On the other hand, Shambhala Buddhism offers him not only a connection to a more cosmopolitan world through fashion, but also with a spiritual practice detached from any ethnic, "old" features.

Other Japanese Brazilians I interviewed also differentiated between religion and spiritual practice. They told me that they do have a religious identification, but seek Zen because it offers meditation practices. One Nisei told me that her family belonged to the Higashi Honganji, but also frequented Seichō-no-Ie. She was baptized, and hence is nominally a Catholic, but also went to Seichō-no-Ie meetings. However, because of personal problems she had been having lately, she sought Zen for its emphasis on meditation. These examples show that Japanese Brazilian spiritual seeking resembles very much the one of Brazilians of no Japanese.[48]

Likewise, books play a crucial role to get them in contact with Zen and to spark their interest. An interest in Japanese history on the one hand, and an interest in philosophy on the other predisposed a Japanese Brazilian Busshinji monk to start going to the Zen temple. As his mother was a devout Catholic, he was raised as a Catholic and studied in a Catholic school. Later in life, he sought out Zen Buddhism after reading D. T. Suzuki and many Western books on Zen. How his ordination took place makes his case especially noteworthy:

> I started going to Busshinji for meditations on Saturdays in the mid-80s. After some time, the monks realized I was diligent in my *zazen* practice and started to ask me about my interest in Zen Buddhism. I said I wanted to study Zen. Then a monk assured me that if I wanted to deepen my knowledge of Zen, *zazen* alone would not be enough. I would have to take a stand in the temple; I would have to become a monk. Only then would I have a commitment to

> Zen. At that time, I did not know what that meant. They obliged me . . . they asked me to come to the temple every Saturday and Sunday. I had no idea what for, and found out it was to help in the rituals. Until then I had never been to a memorial service or any kind of Buddhist rite![49]

This is clearly a case of a Nisei interested in the Western construct of Zen who got into Japanese customs because he was of Japanese heritage. However, this monk made his way back to the so-called "convert" Zen (centered on meditation) and is currently leading the temple's *zazenkai* after many years of conducting memorial services on weekends. He is clear evidence that Japanese Brazilians, being true to their dynamically hyphenated identity, may dwell in both the world of familial-/community-oriented rituals such as mortuary rites and privatized-/individually oriented rituals such as meditation.

Conclusion

In this essay, I have shown that by innovating uses of the *butsudan*, mortuary rites, weddings, and conversion, Japanese Brazilians have a developed a creolized way of "doing Zen." By strategically allowing a Brazilian Catholic lexicon to be superimposed on their Japanese cultural grammar, they were able to maintain their identity in the new country. As noted earlier, this identity is not a static fusion of both Catholic and Buddhist worlds, but rather a field of energy that is always in transition, that is, in a permanent state of creolization.

Furthermore, the many stories I have narrated here show that unlike what has been reported in other Western countries with a Buddhist presence, in Brazil there is no sharp divide between "ethnic" and "convert" practices. Indeed, not only do Japanese Brazilians have devotional practices in the form of funerary and memorial rites and ancestor worship, but some also are interested in Buddhism as meditation and the study of scriptures. To be sure, the fact that currently most Japanese Brazilians are born Catholic also makes it easier for them to have convert interest in Zen. Just like their non–Japanese Brazilian counterparts, they have often wandered through many other religious practices before finding Zen. For both groups, the recent prestige acquired by Buddhism in metropolitan centers and in Brazil suggests an explanation for their conversion. However, unlike Brazilians of no Japanese ancestry, Japanese Brazilians who seek Zen also endeavor to recuperate a sense of their Japanese identity that may have been shorn over generations. Some of them have an opposite attitude, which likens them to non–Japanese Brazilian spiritual seeking: They turn to Tibetan Buddhism instead of Zen because they feel the latter is too laden with institutional religiosity (as their families were once Buddhists) and too little "spirituality."

Notes

This essay first appeared in Cristina Rocha, *Zen Buddhism in Brazil* (Honolulu: University of Hawai'i Press, 2006).

1. Coen is the Portuguese spelling of Kōen, her Buddhist name. A non–Japanese Brazilian, Coen sensei trained at the Zen Center of Los Angeles under Maezumi Rōshi for three years before undergoing training at Aichi Senmon Nisōdō nunnery in Nagoya, Japan, for twelve more years. In 1995, she returned to Brazil to become the head nun of Busshinji in São Paulo city. After a series of conflicts, she lost her position in 2001 and established her own temple. For more on these conflicts, see Cristina Rocha "Zazen or not Zazen: The Predicament of Sōtōshū's Kaikyōshi in Brazil," *Japanese Journal of Religious Studies* 31/1 (2004): 35–66.

2. Although church and state have been separated since the institution of the republican system (1889), in practice the influence of the Catholic Church in Brazilian society has always run deep. Accordingly, conversion to Catholicism was common among Japanese immigrants; some even converted to Catholicism in Kobe, before embarking for Brazil, in order to avoid prejudice upon arrival in the new country. See Stewart Lone, *The Japanese Community in Brazil* (Houndmills, England: Palgrave, 2001), p. 157. Most parents baptized their children after they arrived in Brazil so that they would not be bullied in school, would assimilate into Brazilian society, and would be associated with influential Brazilian godparents (for instance, the farm owner) who would help them achieve social mobility. See Kōichi Mori, "Vida Religiosa dos Japoneses e Seus Descendentes," in *Uma Epopéia Moderna: 80 anos da Imigração Japonesa no Brasil,* K. Wakisaka, ed. (São Paulo: Hucitec/ Sociedade Brasileira de Cultura Japonesa), p. 579; and Takashi Maeyama, "Religion, Kinship, and the Middle Classes of the Japanese in Urban Brazil," *Latin American Studies* 5 (1983): 64. Kojima has pointed out in his M.A. thesis on Japanese Brazilians in Curitiba (Paraná State) that all his interviewees asserted that children had to be Catholic in order to be accepted in Brazilian schools. Shigeru Kojima, *Um Estudo sobre os Japoneses* (M.A. thesis, Universidade Federal do Paraná, 1991). Thus converting to Catholicism strongly contributed to the "Brazilianization" of the immigrants.

3. I decided to use "Japanese Brazilians" instead of nikkei (the more common term to describe Japanese descendents born in the Americas) because the term reflects the dynamics of living in two overlapping worlds that never completely fuse into one.

4. Because of the nationalist government in Brazil and the upcoming war, restrictions were imposed on Japanese immigrants in the late 1930s and early 1940s. These included closing Japanese-language newspapers and Japanese schools and prohibitions against speaking Japanese in public or at home. For more on this see Jeffrey Lesser, *Negotiating National Identity* (Durham, N.C.: Duke University Press, 1999), pp. 129–37; and Lone, *The Japanese Community in Brazil,* pp. 137–44.

5. For more on strategic essentialism see Gayatri Spivak, *The Post-Colonial Critic: Interviews, Strategies, Dialogues* (New York: Routledge, 1990).

6. Ian Reader, *Religion in Contemporary Japan* (Honolulu: University of Hawaii Press, 1991), p. 2.

7. William Bodiford, "Zen and the Art of Religious Prejudice: Efforts to Reform a Tradition of Social Discrimination," *Japanese Journal of Religious Studies* 23/1–2 (1996): 7–8.

8. The *danka seido* was so significant for Japanese Buddhist sects that Duncan Williams has argued that it was one of the reasons why Sōtō Zen became the largest Buddhist school in number of temples (17,548) in eighteenth-century Japan. For more on Sōtōshū and the *danka seido* system, see Duncan Williams, *The Other Side of Zen: A Social History of Soto Zen Buddhism in Tokugawa Japan* (Princeton: Princeton University Press, 2005), chapters 1–2.

9. Ian Reader, "Zazenless Zen? The Position of Zazen in Institutional Zen Buddhism," *Japanese Religions* 14/3 (1986): 18.

10. Seichō-no-Ie is a Japanese NRM of Buddhist, Christian and Shinto inspiration established in 1929. Seichō-no-Ie is the largest Japanese NRM in Brazil, attracting a following of 2.5 million in an inflated estimate given by the movement itself. It is hard to confirm the actual numbers because it falls under the imprecise category "Eastern religions" in the Brazilian census. However, more realistic statistics show that in 1992 Seichō-no-Ie had 75 regional branches in Brazil. See Hideaki Matsuoka, "'Messianity Makes a Person Useful': Describing Differences in a Japanese Religion in Brazil," *Japanese Journal of Religious Studies* 28/1–2 (2001): 77–102; also Leila Basto Albuquerque, *Seicho-No-Ie do Brasil* (São Paulo: Fapesp, Anablume, 1999).

11. In Japan, at the time of death, the Buddhist priest conducts a posthumous ordination to allow Buddhist funeral rites for laypeople. During this ordination, the deceased takes the three refuges, receives a Buddhist name, and becomes a *hotoke*, a Buddha. For more on this see William Bodiford, "Zen in the Art of Funerals: Ritual Salvation in Japanese Buddhism," *History of Religions* 32/2 (1992): 146–64.

12. Unlike what happens in Brazil, Duncan Williams called my attention to the fact that in Los Angeles and many parts of California, parishioners take very seriously the difference between Nishi and Higashi or take pride in being affiliated to Shingonshū. Perhaps the fact that Buddhist schools only sent official missionaries (*kaikyōshi*) to Brazil after World War II can account for the migrants' disconnection over time to the school their families traditionally adhered to.

13. Reader, *Religion in Contemporary Japan*, p. 102.

14. Ben Hills, *Japan Behind the Lines* (Sydney: Hodder & Stoughton, 1996), pp. 46–49.

15. André Droogers, "Syncretism," in *Dialogue and Syncretism,* J. D. Gort et al., eds. (Grand Rapids, Mich.: William Eerdman, 1989), pp. 7–24; Charles Stewart, "Syncretism and Its Synonyms," *Diacritics* 29/3 (1999): 40–62; Charles Stewart and Rosalind Shaw, "Introduction," in *Syncretism/Anti-syncretism,* Charles Stewart and Rosalind Shaw, eds. (London: Routledge, 1994), pp. 1–26.

16. James Clifford, *Routes* (Cambridge, Mass.: Harvard University Press, 1997), p. 7.

17. Rita Laura Segato, "Formação de Diversidade," in *Globalização e Religião,* A. P. Oro and C. A. Steil, eds. (Petrópolis: Vozes, 1997), p. 236.

18. Eve Stoddard and Grant H. Cornwell, "Cosmopolitan or Mongrel?," *European Journal of Cultural Studies* 2/3 (1999): 337.

19. Ibid., pp. 331–53.

20. Ulf Hannerz, "The World in Creolisation," *Africa* 57/4 (1987): 551; Hannerz, *Cultural Complexity* (New York: Columbia University Press, 1992), pp. 264–67.

21. Stoddard and Cornwell, "Cosmopolitan or Mongrel?," p. 340.

22. Hannerz, "The World in Creolisation"; Hannerz, *Cultural Complexity*; Nikos Papastergiadis, "Tracing Hybridity in Theory," in *Debating Cultural Hybridity*, P. Werbner and T. Modood, eds. (London: Zed Books, 1997); Papastergiadis, *Dialogues in the Diasporas* (London: Rivers Oram Press, 1998); Robert J. C. Young, *Colonial Desire* (London: Routledge, 1995).

23. Papastergiadis, "Tracing Hybridity in Theory," p. 258.

24. Ibid.

25. Quoted in Papastergiadis, "Tracing Hybridity in Theory," p. 268.

26. Young, *Colonial Desire*.

27. Stoddard and Cornwell, "Cosmopolitan or Mongrel?," pp. 335, 349.

28. Edward Brathwaite, *The Development of Creole Society in Jamaica 1770–1820* (Oxford: Clarendon Press, 1971).

29. For an analysis of hybridization between Catholicism and Shintō NRMs in Brazil, see Takashi Maeyama, "Japanese Religion in Southern Brazil: Change and Syncretism," *Latin American Studies* 6 (1983): 181–238. For an account of Japanese Brazilians practicing Afro-Brazilian religions see Kōichi Mori, "O Processo de 'Amarelamento' das Tradicionais Religiões Brasileiras de Possessão: Mundo Religioso de uma Okinawana," *Estudos Japoneses* 18 (1998): 57–76.

30. Egon Schaden, "Imigrantes Alemães e Japoneses: Uma Visão Comparativa," in *A Presença Japonesa no Brasil*, H. Saito, ed. (São Paulo: T. A. Queiroz/Edusp, 1980), pp. 144–45.

31. Tomō Handa, *O Imigrante Japonēs: História da sua Vida no Brasil* (São Paulo: T. A. Queiroz, Centro de Estudos Nipo-Brasileiros, 1987), p. 798.

32. Robert Smith, *Ancestor Worship in Contemporary Japan* (Stanford: Stanford University Press, 1974).

33. Personal communication, Busshinji, October 1998.

34. Personal communication, Tenzuizenji, January 2002.

35. See Cristina Rocha, *Zen in Brazil: The Quest for Cosmopolitan Modernity* (Honolulu: University of Hawai'i Press, 2005).

36. Richard Jaffe, *Neither Monk nor Layman: Clerical Marriage in Modern Japanese Buddhism* (Princeton: Princeton University Press, 2001), p. 169.

37. Michael Fisch, "The Rise of Chapel Wedding in Japan: Simulation and Performance," *Japanese Journal of Religious Studies* 28/1–2 (2001): 57–76; and Reader, *Religion in Contemporary Japan*, p. 51.

38. Ian Reader, "Contemporary Zen Buddhist Tracts for the Laity: Grassroots Buddhism in Japan," in *Religions of Japan in Practice*, George Tanabe, ed. (Princeton: Princeton University Press, 1999), p. 497.

39. During the wedding reception the couple sips sake three times each (*san-san-kudō*).

40. Handa, *O Imigrante Japonēs*, p. 798.

41. Buddhismo-L, August 3, 2002. Buddhismo-L is one of six Brazilian Buddhist email

lists. Buddhismo-L is a general list, but there are four others of particular Buddhist traditions (Theravada, Vajrayana, Zen, and Shin) and one for sutra discussion. Available at: http://www.dharmanet.com.br/listas/.

42. Tetsuden Kashima, *Buddhism in America: The Social Organization of an Ethnic Religious Institution* (Westport, Conn.: Greenwood Press, 1977), pp. 129–31.

43. Email sent by a Japanese-Brazilian to Buddhismo-L, April 23, 2002.

44. For more on "ethnic" and "convert" Buddhism in the West, see: Martin Baumann, "Global Buddhism: Developmental Periods, Regional Histories, and a New Analytical Perspective," *Journal of Global Buddhism* 2 (2001): 1–44; Rick Fields, "Divided Dharma," in *The Faces of Buddhism in America,* Kenneth Tanaka and Charles Prebish, eds. (Berkeley: University of California Press, 1998), pp.196–206; Jan Nattier, "Visible and Invisible," *Tricycle: The Buddhist Review* 5/1 (2005): 42–49; Paul Numrich, *Old Wisdom in the New World* (Knoxville: University of Tennessee Press, 1996); Charles Prebish, "Two Buddhisms Reconsidered," *Buddhist Studies Review* 10/2 (1993): 187–206; Charles Prebish, *Luminous Passage* (Berkeley: University of California Press, 1999), pp. 57–75.

45. Personal communication, Busshinji, February 1999.

46. Carlos Rodrigues Brandão, "A Crise das Instituições Tradicionais Produtoras de Sentido," in *Misticismo e Novas Religiões,* A. Moreira and R. Zicman, eds. (Petrópolis: Vozes/UFS/ IFAN, 1994), pp. 25–41; Robert Carpenter, "Esoteric Literature as a Microcosmic Mirror of Brazil's Religious Marketplace," in *Latin American Religion in Motion,* C. Smith and J. Prokopy, eds. (New York: Routledge, 1999), pp. 325–60; José Jorge Carvalho, "Características do Fenômeno Religioso na Sociedade Contemporânea," in *O Impacto da Modernidade Sobre a Religião,* M. Bingemer, ed. (São Paulo: Loyola, 1992), pp. 133–95; and Luis Eduardo Soares, "Religioso por Natureza: Cultura Alternativa e Misticismo Ecológico no Brasil," in *Sinais dos Tempos: Diversidade Religiosa no Brasil,* L. Landim, ed. (Rio de Janeiro: Instituto de Estudos da Religião, 1989), pp. 121–44.

47. Personal communication, São Paulo, November 2001.

48. Like others in the West, Brazilians consider Zen Buddhism a philosophy and many times view meditation as a technique for stress relief (for more on this see Cristina Rocha, *Zen in Brazil,* chapters 3–5). This is a common view of modern Buddhism: Whereas there is no requirement to learn the scriptures or perform other Buddhist practices, meditation is supposed to be the key element that denotes who is a Buddhist. Thomas Tweed coined the term "shoppers" to denote those North American Buddhists who "shop, purchasing a bit of this and consuming a bit of that, but never buying it all" (Tweed, Thomas, "Nightstand Buddhists and Other Creatures: Sympathizers, Adherents, and the Study of Religion," in *American Buddhism, Methods and Findings in Recent Scholarship* Duncan Ryûken Williams and Christopher Queen, eds. [Richmond, U.K.: Curzon Press, 1999], pp. 71–90).

49. Personal communication, Busshinji, October 1998.

2 Bukkyōkai and the Japanese Canadian Community in British Columbia

MASAKO IINO

Many people of Japanese origin in Canada, much like their counterparts on the American West Coast, suffered from the aftereffects of such experiences as forced removal from their homes and incarceration during World War II. Some scholars argue that the mental trauma suffered from the humiliation of being treated as second-class citizens caused many within the Japanese Canadian community to feel ashamed of their Japanese origins.[1] Many tried to distance themselves from anything that reminded them or reminded others of their Japanese origins. However, some Japanese Canadians in this immediate postwar period worked actively to establish Bukkyōkai (Buddhist organizations) in such places as Toronto, Ontario, where they resettled. The Toronto Bukkyōkai, for example, played a central role in the development of the Japanese Canadian community around Toronto.[2] Those Japanese Canadians who built the Toronto Bukkyōkai were open about their Buddhist faith, especially when they faced feelings of antagonism toward Japan and anything related to Japan. Prior to the war, most of these Japanese Canadians had been deeply involved with the Bukkyōkai in British Columbia, where most of the Japanese Canadians lived before World War II. The first Bukkyōkai in Canada, the Honpa Canada Bukkyōkai, was built in 1905 to serve the Japanese Canadian community, not only as religious institutions but also as social network centers. Within thirty years, there were more than ten Bukkyōkai in Vancouver and the surrounding areas.

It has been argued that the mainstream Canadian society saw Bukkyōkai as representing Japanese culture and criticized their members for not assimilating into Canadian culture.[3] Were those Japanese Canadians who were involved with the activities of Bukkyōkai simply nationalistic admirers of Japanese culture who refused to assimilate into Canadian society? This chapter examines the role that Bukkyōkai played in the Japanese Canadian community in British Columbia in the period between the early 1900s, when the first Bukkyōkai was established in Vancouver, and the 1930s, when Bukkyōkai were at their peak. My analysis focuses on the publications of the Young Buddhist Associations (Bussei): *Otakebi* (published by the Fairview Young Buddhist Association, 1930) and *Buddha* (published by the Kitsilano Young Buddhist Association, 1935 and 1940).

Background

The first Japanese immigrant is usually said to have landed in Canada in 1877. It was, however, not until the late 1890s that the number of Japanese, overwhelmingly male, became significant. Until they were forced to move to the interior of Canada during World War II, more than 90 percent of Japanese Canadians lived in British Columbia tending to cluster in the southwest corner of the Lower Mainland area.[4] Like immigrants from other countries, they lived wherever they could find work and where their fellow countrymen were concentrated. They had to bear great instability because most jobs were seasonal or temporary. Their life was hard, consisting of heavy labor, poor living quarters, and both physical and cultural isolation. Under such conditions, most of these male laborers found solace in "gambling, drinking and prostitutes."[5]

As the number of Japanese immigrants increased and their children reached school age, education became a larger issue. In 1902, concerned Japanese consuls and Japanese Christian ministers established a small institution where their children could be educated as a supplement to public school.[6] There was a clear connection between anti-Asian sentiment and the felt necessity for an educational institution in the community. At this point, the Japanese government began to pay attention to this situation. In 1905, Ambassador Plenipotentiary Komura Jutarō visited Vancouver on his way home from Portsmouth, where he had signed the peace treaty between Russia and Japan and contributed $150 to help establish a school for Japanese Canadian children. This led Consul Kishirō Morikawa to make an official proposal to establish a Japanese school that got built in 1906.[7]

At the same time, Buddhist Japanese immigrants began to realize the importance of teaching their children about their Buddhist religion. This was important not just for the religious doctrines, but also because it taught manners and moral education, including loyalty and obedience to the emperor, to their teachers, and especially to their parents. Buddhism was regarded as important for Japanese immigrants because it was a direct link that tied them and their children to their ancestors and Japan. However, because no Bukkyōkai existed in British Columbia, some Issei turned to the established Methodist and Anglican churches as the place to send their children.

Beginning as early as 1892, missionary societies of the various Christian churches provided extensive financial assistance to convert Japanese Canadians. The Christian church was the first Canadian institution to help the immigrants establish a foothold in the new land. Christian ministers served as interpreters, employment agents, and provided legal aid. They helped Japanese women who had arrived in kimonos choose their first Western-style dresses.[8] The following description shows how an Issei woman decided to attend the Christian church in response to a perceived obligation to the Christian missionaries:

The missionary comes to the door and in very polite Japanese invites the Issei mother to a tea at the church. There, she sits around and talks to some of her neighbors. As she is leaving, the missionary politely expresses the wish to see her again. The Issei mother, having accepted his hospitality, feels obligated to attend the church.[9]

In 1896, a mission was established in Victoria and a Sunday school in Vancouver, with a night school and dormitory attached. The church intended not only to teach English but also to introduce Canadian culture to the immigrants. Christianity was considered an integral part of Western civilization and attending Christian church was supposed to help them identify themselves more closely with Canadian society. According to Ken Adachi, "Christian Japanese liked to claim that Christianity was a liberating factor facilitating their adjustment to Canadian life" and they tended to consider themselves more "Canadianized" and "progressive" than Buddhists, who were regarded as conservative.[10] Rev. Gorō Kaburagi, a Japanese United Church minister, ordained in the United States, is often referred to as equating Christianity with civilization in the early 1900s. He criticized Buddhism for being a barbarians' religion and argued that the future acceptance and inclusion of the Japanese in Canada would occur only through conversion and absorption into the "Anglo-Christian" nation.[11] Sending their children to Christian churches was therefore considered by some Issei as a natural method of assimilation into Canadian society as well as a solution to the education problem posed by the dearth of Buddhist institutions. Other Issei did not see it as abandoning Buddhism, but rather as a pragmatic way of conveying at least some form of moral values to their children.

Even seen as expedient, such a move caused much concern among the sincere followers of Buddhism. Community newspapers reported complaints on a regular basis in the early 1900s. The following is one example: "Our compatriots do not like to put funerals in the care of the Japanese Methodist Church . . . [A]s such those who dislike the Japanese Methodist church are increasing in number by the day . . . [B]eing influenced for the worse by the English people's way of thinking destroys the order of our society. It is an extremely improper and dangerous way of thinking . . ."[12]

Without sutra chanting and incense burning, the dead would not be sent to the Pure Land, Issei Buddhists argued. They considered that "most pitiable were the forgotten dead who had been buried ignominiously in shallow, unsanctified graves."[13] These voices of concern became a powerful force toward the establishment of Bukkyōkai. One Buddhist recalls the urgent need for Bukkyōkai as being "provoked by the zealous activities of the Methodist church in the Japanese Canadian community in Vancouver."[14]

Establishment of the Early Bukkyōkai

According to Adachi, even though Christianity made considerable inroads among Japanese Canadians, by around 1910 about 68 percent continued to prefer Buddhism.[15] At first, Buddhism had to be practiced and spread through the community by Buddhist laymen or leaders. Records show that around 1901, in Sapperton near Vancouver, a man called Hatsutarō Nishimura received a portrait of the Buddha on a scroll from Lord Abbot Myōkō of Nishi Hongwanji. He mounted it in a room of a friend's house and every Sunday Buddhist followers gathered in front of the scroll to conduct dharma talks among themselves. In October 1904, some Buddhist laymen and volunteers decided to build a Bukkyōkai and to request a *kaikyōshi* (minister) from Nishi Hongwanji in Japan to provide religious services for the Japanese community in Vancouver.[16]

In 1905, the headquarter temple in Kyoto sent the first *kaikyōshi*. Significantly, this was not a propagation effort on the part of the Japanese Buddhists, but rather an effort spearheaded in Canada, specifically because they felt apprehensive about the evangelistic efforts of various Christian denominations. Paradoxically, the progress of these Christian missions in the Japanese Canadian community served as an impetus for Buddhists to become more formally organized.

On October 12, 1905, Rev. and Mrs. Senjū Sasaki were welcomed by their new congregation in Vancouver. Two weeks later, Rev. Sasaki gave a talk at the civic hall. According to Shinjō Ikuta's *Kanada Bukkyōkai enkakushi* (History of the Buddhist Churches of Canada), "the Dharma talk, heard for the first time in Canada, thundered like the lion's roar to the ears of some 500 persons in the audience. The audience was enthralled by the wisdom of the Buddha."[17] Because there was no Bukkyōkai building where the *kaikyōshi* could hold services, those who requested him sent formed the Foundation Committee, which rented a room at the inn on Powell Street, the Ishikawa Ryokan, in which to hold services. The inn provided a dining room with a statue of the Amida Buddha enshrined. The congregation named the room "the Temple" and declared the foundation date December 12, 1905.

Rev. Sasaki's immediate priority was building a Bukkyōkai, the first in Canada. He and the Foundation Committee members visited every sawmill (the Japanese being deeply involved with the lumber industry) in the Vancouver area to advertise his arrival and to solicit donations. With the help of energetic laymen, the Foundation Committee raised over $5,600 by March 1906.[18] In February 1911, the new building was completed. Although Vancouver was the center of Buddhist activities during this early period, Buddhist groups were also being organized in other communities where Japanese were settling in significant numbers. As in Vancouver, most of these groups began as informal gatherings in homes with occasional visits from the *kaikyōshi* of the Vancouver Bukkyōkai. By 1930, Bukkyōkai were established in New Westminster, Marpole, Steveston, and Mission, British Columbia, and one as far east as Raymond, Alberta.

The growth of these Bukkyōkai was accompanied by a greater concern for organizational independence. During the first three decades of a Buddhist presence in Canada, Bukkyōkai were regarded as part of the Buddhist Mission of North America, which had its headquarters in the United States. In February of 1931, *kaikyōshi* and lay delegates from the various Bukkyōkai in Canada met to discuss their separation from the umbrella organization. As a result of this meeting, the leaders of these Bukkyōkai petitioned Nishi Hongwanji regarding their desire to become an independent missionary district with headquarters in Canada.[19] The request appealed for an independent propagation in Canada and called for the Nisei to become good Canadian citizens and contribute to Canadian culture. By 1934, there existed twelve Bukkyōkai with a total membership of over 1,500, served by six *kaikyoshi.*[20]

The Activities of Bukkyōkai

To the question, "Growing up as children, separated from the *hakujin* (white) community, how important was the Bukkyōkai in your life?" one Nisei man responded:

> It was the only place we could go to and everything was centered around church—all your young associations, Sunday school . . . We would go to public school then to Japanese language school, but strictly academic forms in both. The church was the only place we could get out of academic form and have other activities. As a child you looked forward to various Buddhist days and services, especially the elaborate ones, and visiting to different churches and exchanges of teachers who would tell stories . . . [21]

Another Nisei stated:

> The Buddhist events were very significant to us when we were small children. Because whenever we would have these special services during the year our parents would make lots of food and people coming from other districts would be joining in and having a festive time . . . [I]n Vancouver days during Hanamatsuri [the Buddha's birthday] we have all kinds of things going on at home. In my home it was just like New Year . . . [22]

Thus, before World War II, Bukkyōkai in Canada were community institutions. They played as a significant role in the cultural and ethnic identity of Japanese Canadians. Religious and ceremonial events, especially O-bon (the annual service devoted to the memory of deceased relatives), and monthly memorial services supported the values of filial piety and family continuity. One Buddhist Nisei in Kelowna, British Columbia, who was brought up in Vancouver, emphasizes that the efforts of his parents' Issei generation account for why he became involved in a Bukkyōkai. It was at the temple that he found answers to the questions, "Who am I?" and "What am I?" during his high school days. The temple was a locus for those who reflected deeply on identity: Many found the answer, "I am Japanese and Buddhist."[23]

The *kaikyōshi* of a Bukkyōkai in the Vancouver area described the role of the Bukkyōkai for Issei as not only "a place where they could learn Buddhist teaching," but also "a place where the problems they could not tell others would be solved," "where they were supplied with information," and "where they found relief and comfort." Buddhism for Issei was "something that would fill in the empty part of their heart."[24] Some Nisei who grew up in the 1930s acquired a culture that was completely different from what their parents tried to nurture in them. There were, however, many Nisei who inherited a culture that their parents respected. One ninety-three-year-old Nisei who was brought up in Vancouver, where he once was a leader in a Bukkyōkai stated: "As a young man, I was involved with the Bukkyōkai activities simply because I wanted to please my parents. The more active I became in the Bukkyōkai activities, the happier my parents were."[25] It was against this cultural backdrop that the *Otakebi* and *Buddha* periodicals were born.

Otakebi

In 1930, the Fairview Bukkyō Seinenkai (Young Buddhist Association) published a booklet titled *Otakebi* (A War Cry). Fairview was a district south of Vancouver, where Japanese immigrants who worked in industries such as lumbering, shipbuilding, and ironwork lived. According to *Hokubei kaikyō enkakushi* (History of the Propagation of Buddhism in North America), the Japanese in Fairview, led relatively isolated lives largely because of their lack of English-language proficiency.[26] In 1918, some Buddhist Japanese had decided to invite a *kaikyōshi* there, thinking that what they needed was a Bukkyōkai. The Fairview Bussei was fully organized by 1920 and started to offer various activities, one of which was oratorical contests held at least every couple of months. That these oratorical contests happened so frequently suggests that the temple was a place where Nisei and their Issei parents could discuss the problems that they were facing in Canada.

Otakebi is a collection of speeches delivered by fourteen young Nisei on the occasion of the tenth anniversary of the Fairview Bussei. Although the collection includes some speeches by Christians, the majority are by Buddhists. The fact that all the speeches were given in Japanese—very traditional, formal Japanese—shows that, contrary to the commonly held notion that most Nisei did not learn Japanese, many Nisei who grew up before World War II spoke Japanese and that this was valued by the community. Many Buddhist Nisei report that they learned Japanese in order to communicate with their parents, learning it at Japanese-language schools after regular school hours. More importantly, the speeches in *Otakebi* give us a clear picture of how the Nisei who were involved with Bukkyōkai saw Buddhism, Japanese culture, their ties to Japan, and their place in Canada. In particular, these Nisei reflected on why their Issei parents were being discriminated against and on what they could do to positively contribute to Canada.

One Nisei lists the following reasons for why those of his parents' generation were discriminated against: racism, economic problems, ideological problems, and differences in lifestyle. He further pointed out that "Issei did not make a great effort to understand Canada [and were] unwilling to work together with Canadians—that is, mainstream Canadians." Giving these reasons why Issei Japanese could not become part of larger Canadian society, he asks, "What should Nisei do?" He answers that they should propagate Buddhism in Canada and keep their "Yamato-damashii [Japanese spirit]."[27]

Many of the speeches in *Otakebi* deal with "Yamato damashii" and propose that those who have Yamato-damashii are representatives of Japan, responsible for working, in Canada, for world peace. Many Nisei also express in their speeches their pride in Japanese culture, which is exactly what their parents tried to instill in them. One Nisei claims that it should be the "Nisei's responsibility to cultivate the spirit of repaying obligations and appreciating virtue, to prosper together in peace, and to let white society know the great Buddhist spirit of selflessness, because all of these virtues are disappearing in modern society." Even if "his body might die and decay in the land of Canada," another Nisei wishes, "Yamato-damashii will remain here."[28]

Even though those Nisei express their belief in Yamato-damashii, it is very important to note that this did not mean they were aiming to remain Japanese in Canada. In their speeches, they make it very clear that they consider themselves Canadians and they should strive to be "good" Canadian citizens who would contribute to enriching its culture and to "establish the so-called civilization of the Pacific Era."[29] This, they argued, is what Issei could not accomplish and is left in the hands of Nisei. It is clear that, although the Bukkyōkai was vital to them for representing ties to Japanese culture, they did not intend to remain Japanese Buddhists in Canada. They claimed they were Canadians who happened to be Buddhist.

Buddha

Buddha was a journal published by the West Second Avenue Buddha Club, an organization founded in 1926 affiliated with the West Second Avenue Church in Kitsilano, west of Vancouver. This group changed its name to the West Second Avenue Young Buddhist Association (Bussei) in 1930. In 1931, the West Second Avenue Church changed its name to the Kitsilano Bukkyōkai. The activities of the Kitsilano Bussei ranged from holding meetings to study Buddhism to fundraising for earthquake victims. The group worked together with other Bussei through the Federation of Bussei; records show that some members of the group joined the oratorical contest at the Fairview Bussei. Its journal *Buddha* was first published in 1927. The volume published in 1935 is a special issue commemorating the tenth anniversary of the Kitsilano Bukkyōkai and Bussei; the 1940 issue commemorates their fifteenth anniversary.

Aside from many congratulatory pieces on the tenth anniversary of the Bukkyōkai and Bussei, the 1930 issue of *Buddha* includes a number of essays expressing the aspirations of this community. The title of these essays include: "Responsibility of Nisei," "Be Aware and Reflect!" "Mission of Bussei in Canada," "New Mission of Us Buddhists." The issue also includes the forty-page record of the oratorical contest held by the Kitsilano Bussei in 1935. These young Buddhists, mostly Nisei with a few Issei who had arrived from Japan only a few years back, expressed themselves in a refined and traditional form of Japanese.

A major theme is how Nisei, who were expected to be "builders of tomorrow," might become good Canadian citizens. For example, one Nisei, points out that the Japanese community in Canada is facing a "serious crisis":

> Looking back over the past, since the time they left their home country with great ambitions for success, crossed over the four thousand miles of rough sea and landed in this land, Issei pioneers have suffered from a mistaken sense of superiority and wrong ideas of racism that the white race had toward us, Japanese . . .
>
> Now they, with grey hair on their heads and furrows on their faces, having lost their influence and authority, are departing this life one after another, unable to remove their misgivings about Nisei's future . . . Who should, at this moment, stand up to redress the mortification Issei pioneers experienced . . . and solve such urgent problems as franchise, profession and marriage, the problems which have deeply concerned them? Who should raise themselves to accomplish the mission of our race? . . . You should be aware that now is not the time for discussion, but should be a time to stand up and act.[30]

Another young Nisei from the Mission Bukkyōkai, who was to become a *kaikyōshi* and to actively involve himself with the establishment of the Toronto Bukkyōkai, expresses his ideas eloquently in a speech entitled "Where Do Nisei in Canada Go?" According to him, Nisei should not consider themselves as temporary sojourners as their Issei parents did, but should settle down and set their future course as Canadians of Japanese decent.[31]

For many Nisei, to cherish Yamato-damashii in themselves was in fact vital to becoming good Canadians, as expressed in many speeches in *Buddha*. One such speech advocates the idea as follows:

> We were born with the blood of Yamato race and our personalities cannot be cultivated by the so-called American Spirit. We Japanese should develop ourselves by cultivating "Yamato-damashii" in ourselves and contribute to the world of human beings. It is the mission given to us Japanese youth. [. . .] It is my sincere hope that, in order to become loyal citizens of Canada, Nisei should learn first of all virtue as Japanese. Wake up to realize how valuable "Yamato-damashii" is. This does not at all mean we are disloyal to Canada.[32]

Not only did having Yamato-damashii not conflict with their idea of being good Canadian citizens, but even fighting under the Union Jack as loyal Canadians was only considered possible if they had Yamato-damashii in order to show their bravery.[33] These Nisei voices clearly articulate their wish, in 1935, to be recognized as Canadian citizens in Canadian society, while placing great value on Yamato-damashii, despite the fact that Japan, with Yamato-damashii as a central ethos, was becoming increasingly militaristic.

Nisei awareness of the potential for conflict is expressed still more clearly in an issue of *Buddha* published five years later. In 1940, World War II had already begun and there was an imminent fear that Japan might become involved soon. The Nisei who published the special anniversary issue of *Buddha* in 1940 were keenly aware that they were already confronted with a difficult situation. They felt the urgency of thinking about their place in Canada at a time when the country their parents came from was to fight against it. The preface of *Buddha* emphasizes that they believed Japan, which was preparing for war efforts, as aiming above all "to establish eternal peace in Asia." The preface then encourages Nisei to "be aware of their important responsibility" toward Canada, expressing gratitude to Issei Buddhists who "sacrificed themselves for young Nisei Buddhists"; it reminded them that "the Japanese Canadian community is facing the most difficult period in its history."[34]

Even in such a complicated and difficult period, the Issei and Nisei were still primarily focused on local problems of education, franchise, profession, land ownership, and fishing licenses—the same problems that they fervently discussed in the 1930s. In a speech entitled "The Course as Successors," one Nisei's ideas on their education and professions responded explicitly to Issei criticism of the Nisei in general. According to the speaker, Issei criticize Nisei for their "lack of good manners and respect for their seniors, being selfish, weak-willed, and irresponsible," where in reality, the speaker argues, "they excel in that they are cheerful, frank, and . . . willing to work." While he admits the validity of some Issei criticism, he responds:

> Then, what has made us as we are today? One is the difference of the times, and the other, the result of the social environment that the Issei had created. That is, Issei's adoration of white people led us to weaken our self-esteem, their mistaken idea of freedom and equality led to making us to ignore manners and respect to seniors, their frequent changes of residences and occupations with the sole aim of earning money led to making us restless . . . and their too warm and generous love for us led to leaving us without strong and stable will power.[35]

Then, he asks himself, "What should Nisei do in order to deal with these problems?" His answer is to have "a firm belief." He thinks that Issei pioneers had "a firm, immovable belief" with which they conquered the pain they experienced and the racial prejudice they endured. Nisei should have "a firm belief," or self-esteem, "that they are the ones who were born in Canada with Japanese blood. They should be proud of the fact they are representing Japan."

He claims, moreover, that this faith, this self-esteem, should come from the proper religious faith: Buddhism.

Another Nisei considers explicitly the issue of assimilation in a time of war. Because they have "been taught" to assimilate into Canadian society, Nisei "have definitely acknowledged themselves as being Canadian" both "in their ways of living" and "mentally." The war, however, has created a situation in which white people in this country say to Nisei, "You are a Jap." The fact that he is called "Jap" now makes him admit that he "is certainly Japanese. [He] is of the Yamato race." Unlike the attitude of Nisei found in *Otakebi* in 1930, this Nisei emphasized his identification as a Japanese, at a time when war with Japan was imminent. He once again asks himself, "What is assimilation in the true sense?" His answer is: "Assimilation in the true sense is not to assimilate with the white people who are superior to us, but to stand in a status equal to that of the white, to accept, together with the white, the habits and the values of Canada, and to contribute to Canadian culture." "Whatever words the white people throw at me, my country is not Japan, but Canada where I was born" and he should confront "oppression . . . with the firm faith in [his] blood."[36] He clearly expresses the idea that there is no conflict between the fact that he is a Canadian citizen born in Canada and the pride he feels in being of Japanese decent.

In another speech, entitled "The Goal of Nisei at the Time of War," another Nisei affirms that Nisei are both Canadian and of Japanese origin: "Needless to say, we are Canadian citizens. At the same time we are Japanese. It is natural that we, as Canadian citizens, cooperate in the efforts to lead Canada to win the war. At the same time, as Japanese, we should try not to dishonor our ancestors. Repaying Canada by fighting in the war for Canada, with justice and courage, is to honor our ancestors."[37]

Those Nisei "who make a permanent home in Canada as Japanese Canadians must recognize and appreciate the fact that [they] are members of the Yamato race," the speaker declares, "and advance with white people on an equal stand in Canada, which is what Issei parents have been longing to see." It is clear that these Nisei believe that they can be accepted by Canadian society as Canadians, and are capable of contributing to it not in spite of their Japanese origin, but precisely through their pride in being of Japanese descent, through their Yamato-damashii.

Conclusion

For the Japanese immigrants in Canada early in the 1900s, the Bukkyōkai was an important Issei institution, primarily related to funerary rites. At the same time it represented the symbolic center of their community. The Bukkyōkai was the center of Nisei activities as well, not only serving as a place of worship and religious ceremonies but also offering a variety of youth associations and Japanese-language schools. As one Nisei recalls: the Bukkyōkai was practically "the only place [they] could go to" and "everything was centered around [it]."[38]

To be involved with the activities of the Bukkyōkai was to confirm their ties with their parents and to feel close to their Japanese heritage. Bukkyōkai ceremonies and events such as O-bon and monthly memorial services were thought to teach Nisei obedience and loyalty to the emperor, teachers, parents, and seniors; to support the idea of filial piety and family tradition; and to strengthen the community ties.

The speeches and essays included in *Otakebi* (1930) and *Buddha* (1935 and 1940) clearly show that Japanese Canadians believed that the teaching of Buddhism instilled Yamato-damashii in young Nisei. At the same time, however, Nisei themselves repeatedly insist, in the speeches and essays, that they are Canadians. They were trying to enunciate their identity to the outer world and in doing so they were trying to confirm their own idea of identity. Crucially, Nisei who praised their Yamato-damashii declared that it did not contradict their consciousness of being Canadian citizens. Retaining and cherishing Yamato-damashii did not mean that they were disloyal to Canada. On the contrary, they claimed that in order to become good Canadian citizens, they needed to have pride in the fact that they were of Japanese origin and represented Japan. As Buddhists, Nisei needed Yamato-damashii to believe they were equal to other races. If they lost this sense of ethnic pride, they thought they would be treated as inferior and lose self-esteem both as Canadians and as Japanese.

The Bukkyōkai was important for Japanese Canadians because it symbolized their ties with Japan. Yet, it did not signal a refusal to assimilate into Canadian society. The Bukkyōkai served as vehicle to give them confidence and self-esteem, which was necessary for them to confirm their identity as Canadian. This is clearly shown both in *Otakebi* (1930) and in *Buddha* (1935 and 1940). Between 1930 and 1940, the social background of Canada changed dramatically and so did the situations of the Japanese Canadian community. Yet, in the ideas and faith that Buddhist Nisei expressed in *Otakebi* and *Buddha* in this period one thing was repeatedly emphasized: The Bukkyōkai was important because it gave them the self-esteem that was necessary for them to become full-fledged Canadians, even though the war was to bring a much more difficult and complicated situation, one that every Japanese Canadian would have to face.

Notes

1. See Stephen S. Fugita and David J. O'Brien, *Japanese American Ethnicity: The Persistence of Community* (Seattle: University of Washington Press, 1991).

2. In Canada, the head temple of the Nishi Hongwanji in Kyoto proposed "Buddhist church" as the official term for the newly established "Bukkyōkai." The headquarters sent "kaikyōshi" (ministers) to Canada and Buddhists themselves chose to call their temple in Canada "church." In the 1970s, however, some members of the Buddhist churches started to call their churches "temples," and the recent trend seems to be in favor of "Buddhist temple." See Masako Iino, "Toronto bukkyōkai (TBC) to nikkeijin: Sai teijūki o chūshin ni," in *Kōsakusuru kokka, minzoku, shūkyō: Imin no shakai tekiō,* Muneyoshi Togami, ed. (Tokyo: Fuji shuppan, 2001), pp. 213–42.

3. "New Problems Confronting the Busseis and the Church," *Guiding Light* (December 4, 1959): 3.

4. A substantial amount of research has been done on Japanese Canadians. For example, see Chikako Yamada, *Kanada nikkei shakai no bunka henyō: "Umi o watatta nihon no mura" sansedai no hensen* (Tokyo: Ochanomizu shobō, 2000); Mitsuru Shimpo, *Ishi o mote owaruru gotoku: Nikkei Kanadajin shakaishi* (Tokyo: Ochanomizu shobō, 1996 [1975]); Masako Iino, *Nikkei Kanadajin no rekishi* (Tokyo: Tokyo daigaku shuppankai, 1996).

5. Terry Watada, *Bukkyo Tozen: A History of Jodo Shinshu Buddhism in Canada, 1905–1995* (Toronto: Toronto: HpF Press/Toronto Buddhist Church, 1996), p. 28.

6. Jinshirō Nakayama, *Kanada no hōko* (privately published, 1921), pp. 1334–35.

7. Ibid., pp. 1330, 1338; Tsutae Satō, *Vancouver Nihon kyōritsu gogakkō enkakushi* (Vancouver: Sanwa Press, 1954), p. 55; Consulate General of Japan, Vancouver *Zai-Vancouver sōryōjikan no ayumi* (n.p., 1989), p. 13.

8. Toyo Takata, *Nikkei Legacy: The Story of Japanese Canadians from Settlement to Today* (Toronto: NC Press, 1983), pp. 30–33. Research on the attitudes of Christian churches toward Japanese Canadians in the camps during World War II include Roland M. Kawano, ed., *Ministry to the Hopelessly Hopeless: Japanese Canadian Evacuees and Churches during WWII* (Scarborough, Toronto: Japanese Canadian Christian Churches Historical Project, 1997).

9. Ken Adachi, *The Enemy That Never Was* (Toronto: McClelland and Stewart, 1976), p. 112.

10. Ibid., p. 111.

11. Ryo Yoshida, "The Canadian Methodist Response to the Japanese Immigrants in Canada: The Case of Rev. Goro Kaburagi," paper presented at the conference on the Japanese Canadian Community and Their Christian Church, Doshisha University, Kyoto (1991), p. 20, quoted in Janet McLellan, *Many Petals of the Lotus: Five Asian Buddhist Communities in Toronto* (Toronto: University of Toronto Press, 1999), p. 47.

12. Watada, *Bukkyo Tozen,* pp. 30–31.

13. Ibid.

14. Shinjo Ikuta, *Kanada bukkyōkai enkakushi: Dainiji taisen izen no B.C. shū o chūshin ni* (Toronto: Kanada bukkyō kyōdan, 1981), pp. 16–17.

15. Adachi, *The Enemy That Never Was,* p. 111.

16. Ikuta, *Kanada bukkyōkai enkakushi,* pp. 16–17; Watada, *Bukkyo Tozen,* p. 36.

17. Ikuta, *Kanada bukkyōkai enkakushi,* p. 18.

18. Ikuta, *Kanada bukkyōkai enkakushi,* p. 20; Watada, *Bukkyo Tozen,* pp. 40–41. The Bukkyōkai was not completely monolithic nor without internal conflicts. Both Ikuta and Watada describe how conflict over financial scandals divided Bukkyōkai and how they reached reconciliation. Ikuta, *Kanada bukkyōkai enkakushi,* pp. 34–45; Watada, *Bukkyo Tozen,* pp. 49–70.

19. Ikuta, *Kanada bukkyōkai enkakushi,* pp. 61–66.

20. Ibid., p. 80.

21. Multicultural Historical Society of Ontario, Tape 3581 (1978).

22. Ibid.

23. Author's interview, in Kelowna, August 2001.

24. Author's interview, in Steveston, August 2001.

25. Author's interview, in Vancouver, August 2001.

26. Hōkō Terakawa, ed., *Hokubei kaikyō enkakushi* (San Francisco: Hokubei kaikyō honbu, 1936), pp. 457–65.

27. Fairview Young Buddhist Association, Oratorical Contest Branch, ed., *Otakebi* (Fairview Young Buddhist Association, 1930), p. 76. All the quotations from both *Otakebi* and *Buddha* in this chapter are originally written in Japanese; all translations are my own.

28. Ibid., pp. 60–61.

29. Ibid., p. 80.

30. Kitsilano Young Buddhist Association, ed., *Buddha* (Kitsilano Young Buddhist Association, 1935), p. 52.

31. Ibid., pp. 56–57.

32. Ibid., p. 70.

33. Ibid., p. 57.

34. Kitsilano Young Buddhist Association, ed., *Buddha* (Kitsilano Young Buddhist Association, 1940).

35. Ibid., pp. 11–13.

36. Ibid., pp. 15–16.

37. Ibid., p. 25.

38. Multicultural Historical Society of Ontario, Tape 3581 (1978).

PART 2

Education and Law

To the extent that Buddhism remains confined to ethnic enclaves and does not seek to challenge predominant Judeo-Christian norms and traditions, it has remained virtually "invisible" to the broader civic space of America. Buddhism tends to register in civic space when conflict within or without the community reaches a threshold that engages public institutions such as the legal system, the mass media and such organizations as the military, hospitals, prisons, or schools. For example, Asian Buddhist immigrant temples have in the recent past "made the news" by violating community building standards (the Chinese Hsi Lai Temple in Hacienda Heights, California was viewed as too "garish" when it was first built), zoning laws regulating parking (such as with Vietnamese "home temples" in Orange County, California), or political incidents (such as the Al Gore fundraising scandal with Buddhist monastics). Similarly, Japanese Issei Buddhists were made visible early on in American Buddhist history precisely when they either engaged with or transgressed norms, be they governed by laws or by standards deemed normative by a "moral majority." In these essays by Noriko Asato and Michihiro Ama, we explore how the Buddhism that emerged onto the public stage in newspapers and lawsuits helped it to become a part of the American religious imagination.

As long as Buddhists "cover" (using David Yoshino's term)—for example, by not flaunting monastic robes or shaved heads—their presence in the Americas generally remains invisible to outsiders.[1] Without visible markers of difference to Protestant Christianity—such as the Jewish yarmulke, the Sikh turban, or the Catholic nun's habit—there is no way to distinguish religious difference, though both the Japanese American Buddhist and Japanese American Christian may be seen as racially different. This section explores these markers of difference as they emerge on the public stage in newspapers and lawsuits. Noriko Asato and Michihiro Ama's essays highlight how prewar Issei Buddhists engaged the law and the media in their respective chapters on Buddhist-Christian conflicts in the Japanese language school cases in Hawaii and legal disputes surrounding temple management and religious incorporation laws in Los Angeles.

Asato's essay uses the Japanese language school cases in Hawaii to look at the ways in which prewar Issei Buddhists engaged the law and the media in Buddhist-Christian conflicts. Much as politicians today talk about bilingual education as a threat to American national and cultural identity, a heated debate took place from the 1910s to the 1930s in Hawaii and the West Coast of the United States regarding the role of Japanese language schools. Though many Japanese language schools framed the acquisition of Japanese by the Nisei as a strategy to produce "bridge-builders" who could promote understanding between Japan and the United States, many Americans viewed the language schools as a threat to the core character of America as a nation based on European (or more specifically, Anglo) civilization. From as early as 1906, the Governor of Hawaii blocked Hongwanji's application as a territory-recognized religious body, contending that the Buddhist language schools run by Hongwanji instilled pro-Japanese loyalties. (This objection was overcome in 1907 after vigorous lobbying by Issei Buddhists.)

The Japanese language school issue first developed a religious component after Issei Buddhist parents heard that some schools run by Japanese American Christians had featured anti-Buddhist messages (principals had been teaching children that Buddhism was a "barbaric" religion). In response, they encouraged Buddhist temples to offer their own Japanese-language courses. Japanese Christian leaders such as Takie and Umetarō Okumura began employing the rhetoric of "Americanization" to argue for the adoption of Western clothes, manners, religion (Christianity), and language. Buddhists adapted their curriculum goals accordingly: Instead of seeking to create Japanese subjects, they began to focus on creating Americans with Japanese-language abilities. Buddhists began to argue that it was possible to be an American who also happened to be Buddhist and speak Japanese.

Asato deftly describes how this internal "religious rivalry" exploded onto the civic sphere when a complex coalition of Japanese American Christians, non-Japanese missionary Christians, plantation owners, and prominent members of the Hawaii political system (most particularly legislators such as Territorial Senator Albert F. Judd and Lorrin Andrews) worked to introduce various pieces of legislation that would outlaw or severely restrict Japanese language schools, especially those run by the Buddhists, under the guise of "professionalizing" them. "Sabbath" schoolteachers were explicitly exempted from many of these efforts. The 1919 Federal Educational Survey team's report, serialized in the *Honolulu Star Bulletin* in June 1920, became part of a larger conversation conducted through the media in which language schools were reported to be "if not anti-American, certainly un-American" not only because they did not teach Christianity, but because they purportedly espoused a religion that "regards the Mikado as divine." As it emerged into the civic sphere, the conflict between Buddhists and Christians within the Japanese American community brought to light a fundamental clash of visions between an Anglo-Protestant United States (Anglo in both its linguistic and racial senses) and a pluralistic United States (in which bilingual, Japanese-speaking Buddhists could also be members) that is still relevant today.

Similarly, Michihiro Ama's study of legal cases surrounding a conflict within the community about the ownership of a temple in Los Angeles uses public records to explore how religious authority was defined and refined through conflicting (Japanese versus American; customary versus legal; charismatic versus institutional) sources of power within a community. By focusing on an incident that came out of efforts to consolidating three Nishi Hongwanji temples in Los Angeles, Ama provides an impressive ground-level study of how Buddhist temples changed sectarian affiliations and merged or split over leadership or financial management.

In addition to providing a nuanced look at the creation of what would eventually become the head temple for the Higashi Honganji temple on the U.S. mainland, Ama's study provides an intriguing case study of how Buddhism became defined and refined through competing (Japanese versus American; customary versus legal; charismatic versus institutional) sources of legitimization. He focuses on both who "owns" a temple (as decided in a Los Angeles courtroom) as well as how individual priests, such as of Rev. Junjō Izumida (who "split" or was "expelled" from Nishi Honganji and reaffiliated with Higashi Hongwanji over the conflict over how to merge the three temples) brought libel suits against newspapers who "defamed" him during these heated discussions. What Ama brings to light here is another ongoing debate within the Japanese American Buddhist community about whether and how to maintain ties with sectarian headquarters in Japan (and be subsumed under their authority) and at which point conditions in America (legal, religious, customary) compel Buddhist institutions to cut or minimize ties to their Asian roots.

By employing "conflict" within or without the religious community as their organizing principle, these essays by Asato and Ama access the Buddhist history to be found in legal archives or newspapers (and often excised from official histories written by the Buddhist groups themselves). In addition, Asato's use of Japanese-language sources (and Japanese ethnic newspapers such as the *Shokumin Shinbun* in Hawaii) highlights the necessity for moving beyond English-language material for the study of American Buddhism and its role in this ongoing question of American national, racial, and religious identity. Ama similarly employs a wide range of Japanese-language materials (including extensive use of materials from the ethnic press) and perhaps even more instructively, public records held at the Los Angeles courthouse. In so doing, both Asato and Ama point out new directions for the study of American Buddhism.

Note

1. David Yoshino, *Covering: The Hidden Assault on Our Civil Rights* (New York: Random House, 2006).

3 The Japanese Language School Controversy in Hawaii

NORIKO ASATO

As several essays in this volume demonstrate, the history of Issei Buddhism was much more than a question of theological adaptation or a set of institutional histories. Rather, in many Nikkei communities, Issei Buddhism was part of a larger struggle for survival and Japanese Americans' rights. We can see this most clearly in the power struggle between Buddhist and Christian Japanese language schools in Hawaii. This chapter offers a critical reading of newly unearthed primary sources to shed light on the importance of religious conflict as a key factor behind the emergence of the so-called Japanese language problem.

Hawaii's Japanese language schools were originally established in the 1890s to provide "Japanese national education" to the children of Japanese immigrants while their parents worked as temporary laborers in the territory. Within ten years, these schools—which were mainly administered in the early phases by Christian or Buddhist ministers and their missions—became focal points of conflict in the Japanese community. Within twenty years, as the Japanese increasingly stayed on in Hawaii, these schools became a point of contention in the larger Hawaiian community centered around the role of education in "Americanism," in its linguistic, cultural, and religious senses.

Indeed, by the 1920s, a "Japanese language school controversy" engulfed the Territorial Department of Public Instruction, the legislature, local courts, and eventually expanded into a federal Supreme Court case. This dispute would ultimately end in the 1927 Supreme Court decision favoring the Issei immigrants as having the right to educate *Nisei,* American children, despite the strenuous efforts by the Hawaiian territorial government and their Japanese American Christian allies to abolish the language schools. The five-year suit represented the Issei's battle to establish themselves as members of American society while preserving their heritage.[1] Hawaii's Japanese school controversy is also important because it catalyzed the Japanese language school debate on the West Coast that so influenced Japanese Americans' lives.[2]

The literature on Japanese American language schools in Hawaii (and related fields) reveals the complex social and political background to this controversy.[3] Most of the available studies focus on the period after 1919, when Japanese language school control bills were submitted to the territorial legislature. Few scholars, especially those writing in English, have explored the genesis of Hawaii's long school controversy in the period leading up to 1919. Furthermore, even though the role of religion in Hawaii's Japanese education has been examined by several leading scholars, little of this is available in English.[4] This study is built on these pioneering studies, but reexamines cited and previously unexplored primary materials to uncover the roots of the Japanese language school debate and finds that conflict between Buddhists and Christians to be one of key elements to the debate. This controversy shaped the perception of Japanese language schools as anti-American, which haunted Japanese Americans long after their Supreme Court victory. For example, during World War II, Japanese language schools were brought up as evidence of Japanese Americans' disloyalty to the United States and was offered by the government as a rationale for the incarceration of 120,000 Nikkei, people of Japanese ancestry, in concentration camps—two-thirds of them being Nisei.[5]

In the late-nineteenth century, Japanese Christian and Buddhist priests followed Japanese immigrants to Hawaii. Both struggled to propagate their faith. Christian missionaries struggled to proselytize Issei, who were mostly Buddhists who saw Christianity as a forbidden and foreign religion.[6] Buddhist missionaries arrived shortly after the Christian ones. Among the Buddhists, the Jōdo Shinshū Honpa Hongwanji sect had the most adherents in Hawaii because the majority of Japanese immigrants originally came from the Jōdo Shinshū strongholds of Hiroshima, Yamaguchi, Kumamoto, and Fukuoka prefectures.[7] However, Buddhist priests clearly regarded Christianity as the dominant religion in Hawaii: both whites and many Hawaiians viewed Buddhism as a barbaric cult of idol worship. First Christian and then Buddhist clergy established Japanese language schools and taught Japanese American children while their immigrant parents worked from dawn to dusk in plantations.[8] The schools appealed directly to Issei parents' primary concern—their children's education—and were used by missionaries to attract Nikkei followers. White plantation owners were also key players in the school controversy. Planters initially regarded language schools as incentives for sojourning Japanese workers to extend their contracts. Plantation owners provided land and materials to erect school buildings and sometimes even a salary for teachers. Both Buddhists and Christians thus competed for plantation owner patronage, especially as the missionaries were provided with very modest stipends for their work.

Starting from the first 148 Japanese immigrants, the *gannen mono* (people of the first year of Meiji) were recruited to be sugar plantation contract laborers in 1868, Hawaii's Japanese population steadily increased. During the *kanyaku imin* or government-sponsored period (1885–94), 1,305 Nisei were born in Hawaii.[9] In addition, some children came to Hawaii with their parents, bringing the school-age Nikkei population to 2,000 during this period.[10] Christian missionary Shigefusa Kanda established the first Japanese language school in 1893 in Kohala on the island of Hawaii. Two years later, Methodist Rev. Tamaki Gomi started his school in Maui.[11] Compulsory education for all children from six to fifteen was not mandated in Hawaii until 1896,[12] thus many Japanese children did not receive any formal education unless they went to a local Japanese language school.[13]

Honolulu's first Japanese school, the Honolulu Nihonjin Shōgakkō or Japanese Elementary School (also known as the Nuuanu Nihonjin Shōgakkō) was begun by Rev. Takie Okumura with thirty students in 1896.[14] That year, four hundred Nisei children attended public schools in Hawaii.[15] Japanese parents were concerned with their children's mixture of English, Japanese, and Hawaiian words, called "Hawaii Creole English," commonly called "Pidgin English," and asked Okumura to open a Japanese school.[16] Okumura was born in 1865, the first son of a samurai family in Tosa (Kōchi Prefecture). After failing in several businesses, he studied theology at Dōshisha University and came to Hawaii in 1894 to work with Rev. Jirō Okabe of the Hawaii Evangelical Association.[17] Okumura first started a kindergarten, later opening the Japanese language school in a room within the Queen Emma Hall (originally used as Queen Emma's residence located between Nuuanu and Beretania).[18] The school taught children six years old and older reading, calligraphy, and composition, along with *shūshin* (moral education) and physical education for one to two hours after public school. The curriculum followed Japan's public education system because immigrant parents around that time expected to return home after fulfilling their contracts. The school did not charge tuition from students and was run on donations.[19] Okumura requested that the Japanese Ministry of Education support the school. The ministry sent a copy of the *Kyōiku Chokugo Tōhon* or Japanese Imperial Rescript on Education, national textbooks, and some physical education equipment.[20] In this "sojourner stage," language schools were still tightly affiliated with Japan, celebrating national holidays, such as the emperor's birthday following the pattern established at elementary schools in Japan.[21]

With the increasing number of students, Okumura built a new school building in Nuuanu in 1899. At this time, he was asked by community leaders to shift the administration of the school from a Christian to a nonsectarian, community-run one. According to him, this was an attempt to discourage Buddhist missions from establishing their own schools by using Okumura's "Christian" school as a precedent. Okumura accepted, yielding the school's administration to a committee of thirty-four Japanese members, chaired by Consul General Miki Saitō.[22] Okumura claimed that he discussed his concerns with the leader of the largest Buddhist sect, Hongwanji Bishop Yemyō Imamura and supposedly reached an agreement not to build "Buddhist-run" schools. Despite Okumura's efforts to prevent Buddhists from establishing new language schools, three years later, Hongwanji opened its first school in Honolulu. According to Okumura, this damaged his "secular" school because it lost many students to the Hongwanji Fuzoku Shōgakkō or School Attached to Hongwanji—the enrollment at his school plunged from two hundred to seventy. According to Okumura, Hongwanji promoted purely Japanese education or *chūkun aikoku* spirit (loyalty to emperor and love of the county) and aggressively built schools on every island and plantation, even in communities that already had a Japanese school. This, Okumura claimed, was the origin of Japanese school problem in Hawaii.[23]

Bishop Imamura, however, wrote that the Hongwanji Fuzoku Shōgakkō was built to protect their members' children and to avoid situations such as when a Nuuanu Japanese language teacher criticized Buddhism in a class with many Hongwanji children. The parents claimed that they wished to educate their children under the influence of the Buddha's teaching. Desks and chairs were immediately bought using donations, and teachers, Rev. Hiseki Miyasaki and his wife, were recruited from Japan. The school began with 162 students, who were divided into four classes at the elementary level and two at the advanced level. The curriculum was based on the Japanese national school system, but the school was closed on Saturdays and Sundays. Boys received military training with wooden rifles while girls were taught sewing.[24]

Imamura studied at the Hongwanji Bungakuryō (later Ryūkoku University). Before he came to Hawaii as a missionary in 1899, he studied under Yukichi Fukuzawa at Keiō Gijuku (later Keiō University).[25] Imamura dramatically adapted Buddhism to American society and claimed to have laid the foundation for Hongwanji to prosper during his long service as its second bishop in Hawaii. Imamura announced that his priority was to construct Japanese language schools and Hawaii's main temple or *betsuin*.[26]

Imamura's schools especially thrived after Japanese laborers' strikes at the Waipahu Plantation in 1904 and again 1909 in Oahu. These strikes became an opportunity for Bishop Imamura to foster improved relations with plantation owners. During the Waipahu strike, Consul General Saitō attempted to intervene without success, but Imamura succeeded to convince laborers to return to work.[27] These incidents impressed plantation interests, who saw Imamura's influence and may have thought that "Buddhism tended to enhance the docility of their labor force."[28]

When the Hawaii Hongwanji was designated by the Kyoto headquarters as a *betsuin* for the territory in 1906, Imamura applied to the territory government for a permit recognizing the Hongwanji Mission as a religious body. Governor George R. Carter rejected the application, claiming it would not be beneficial to Hawaii's future. Rev. Okumura contended that the governor thought Buddhist schools instilled loyalty to Japan and the emperor in Japanese children.[29] That rejection, however, did not stop Imamura: When Walter F. Frear became governor in 1907, the Hongwanji Mission was granted official recognition.[30] That year, many children finished the elementary school curriculum and apparently asked for higher education, leading to the establishment of the Hawaii Chūgakkō or Junior High School. For many Issei parents, American education was far from sufficient. They wanted to provide cultural education, emphasizing moral conduct and traditional Japanese values. In this early period, Buddhist schools instilled these parents' perspectives and provided the special education they wanted for their children.

By 1910, Hongwanji had established twenty-seven schools, the largest number among sectarian language schools, with over six thousand students in Hawaii.[31] Other religious organizations also saw the benefit of running Japanese schools. For example, the Jōdo sect established eleven schools with eleven teachers, the Congregational Church ran six schools taught by ten teachers, and as did the Methodists with two schools and two teachers. There were also thirty-three secular schools, many of which were run by local Japanese communities. These independent schools reflected some Japanese parents' hope to divorce religious influence from their children's education. Some parents also wanted these independent schools because religious competition created multiple schools in one area, causing enormous financial burden on the Japanese immigrant community. Whenever a school expanded, moved, or needed to construct a new building, the community was asked to contribute. Donations for such "public activities" were considered the members' obligation; if people refused to contribute this "tax," they were regarded as not fulfilling their civic responsibilities.[32] During the 1919 Oahu strike, Japanese laborers listed the cost of maintaining Japanese language schools as one of their reasons for needing higher wages.

In 1910, Hawaii's Japanese vernacular daily *Shokumin Shinbun* called on Bishop Imamura to separate religion from language school education.[33] Ever since the newspaper's first issue in 1909, education for Japanese immigrants' children was one of the main concerns of its publisher, Kazutami Eguchi, a former Christian missionary, who implicitly labeled Buddhist schools as problematic in his editorials. He condemned clergy for running schools as side businesses and praised Consul General Saitō's efforts to cut off religious influences from the Honolulu Nihonjin Shōgakkō, which Eguchi called a model school.[34] Eguchi argued that Japanese school problems existed everywhere on the eight islands and warned that they were derived from the problem of mixing religion and education. This situation would only be solved by their separation, he claimed.

When the Honolulu Nihonjin Shōgakkō was about to add a junior high school in March 1910, it requested an appropriate principal recommendation from the Japanese Ministry of Education.[35] Bishop Imamura learned of his rival school's expansion and wrote directly to Vice Foreign Minister Kikujirō Ishii, requesting him not to endorse Okumura's school, which was supported by mostly Christian Nikkei. In his letter, Imamura pointed out Hongwanji's achievement to establish its junior high school, the Hawaii Chūgakkō in 1907. He claimed that he had invited excellent teachers and produced an English prospectus, explaining its purpose and inviting anyone to apply. He claimed it received strong support from Nikkei and even from outside the ethnic community, resulting in an enrollment of 91 male and 32 female Nikkei students. According to Imamura, the Honolulu Nihonjin Shōgakkō immediately countered by offering its own junior high school–level class to compete with his school, which soon closed because of low enrollment. Imamura claimed that Christian parents then sent their children to his school, agreeing that all children, despite religious differences, can learn under the professionally trained teachers in his school.

Imamura was upset that the Honolulu Shōgakkō now announced it was opening a junior high school and used its connection with former Consul General Saitō to request a principal and subsidies from the Japanese Ministry of Education. Imamura explained that unlike present Consul General Sen'ichi Ueno, Saitō unfairly favored the Honolulu Shōgakkō over his, thus provoking Buddhists and creating more competition. Imamura argued that the Christians' activities damaged his efforts toward communal harmony and should not be tolerated.[36] In spite of Imamura's appeal, the Honolulu Nihonjin Gakkō opened its junior high school and a women's school in 1910, changing its name to the Hawaii Chūō Gakuin or Central Institute.[37]

The rivalry between Imamura and Okumura is a well-known part of this history, but there were other scenes of conflict. For example, in 1911, a Japanese school controversy on the Papaikou plantation on the Big Island, drew in the entire Japanese community. Papaikou Nikkei were very proud of having developed their community with autonomy and cooperation, and without religious influence. The Papaikou Japanese School was a manifestation of this independent community spirit. However, Buddhists accused Papaikou Japanese School Principal Hiroshi Tahara of teaching children that Buddhism was a barbarian and unrespectable religion. The Papaikou Hongwanji Temple had just opened the previous December, and Hongwanji Rev. Kenshō Kagō demanded that the school fire the principal and replace him with one that he would invite from Japan. The school's education committee tried to reconcile the parties, but no compromise satisfied everyone, and the Hongwanji temple announced plans to establish its own school. Newspapers editorialized that the entire controversy was Rev. Kagō's ploy.[38] The *Shokumin Shinbun* wrote that the Hongwanji temple was planning to take over the school as a means of extending its power; it was no longer a secret that the headquarters of the Hongwanji and Jōdo sects in Japan assigned the running of schools as a part of the job description of overseas' missionaries.[39]

The same day, the *Shokumin* published a front page article entitled "School Thieves Are Not Only Buddhists." According to the article, Japanese members of the Hawaiian Evangelical Association (HEA) tried to take over a secular school, the Pahoa Nihonjin Shōgakkō in Puna, Hawaii. Revs. Kan Higuchi of Hilo, Shirō Sokabe of Honomu and Takeshi Ban of Olaa, offered the school authorities $20 monthly support if the school employed a new teacher these priests appointed for the presently vacant position. The newspaper found these ministers' offer inappropriate because the Pahoa Shōgakkō had enough resources to remain independent. The paper argued that the HEA wanted to expand its influence in the area—where they had no churches—by controlling the school.[40] Throughout this time, the *Shokumin* continuously focused on the Japanese school debate, often with articles that were more emotional appeals than objective reports. All of this illustrates that Hawaii's Japanese language school problems were deeply rooted in religious conflict, as individual Nikkei communities became active participants in the struggle.

"Another similar incident to Papaikou" took place in Lihue in Kauai.[41] The problem began with a quarrel between Lihue Nihonjin Shōgakkō teacher Takeda and Mrs. Tsuji, who was another teacher and the wife of Rev. Mitsutarō Tsuji who ran both the church and the Shōgakkō.[42] Because of the quarrel, Takeda resigned and Rev. Tsuji brought in a replacement from Honolulu. However, Tsuji's action displeased some of the Nikkei community, who accused him of not consulting with them.[43] Although the school was established by the church, the community members pointed out that they also made monetary contributions to the school. Supporters of Takeda and the plantation owner had a meeting at which they resolved that they did not want to keep Rev. Tsuji, and they sent their resolution to the HEA.[44] In response, Rev. Okumura rushed to Lihue to resolve the problem.[45] He agreed to make the Lihue Nihonjin Shōgakkō independent by yielding it to the community upon the condition that the school's education committee would include a Christian priest and would consult with him regarding the selection of a new teacher. He insisted that neither the teacher invited by Rev. Tsuji nor the one Lihue Buddhists recruited from the Waipahu Hongwanji School should take over the school. According to Okumura, his reasonable offer was rejected because of unrelenting resistance of the opponents.[46] Rev. Tsuji and his wife eventually resigned from the Lihue Church and were replaced by Rev. Kakichi Okamoto, but the school debate remained unsolved and the two schools operated independently.[47]

Three months later, on August 7, 1911, the Lihue school conflict was supposedly resolved through an accord between HEA superintendents Revs. Orramel H. Gulick and Frank Scudder, and Lihue Lutheran Church pastor Rev. Hans Isenberg. Rev. Isenberg was also the youngest brother of Paul Isenberg, the former president of a sugar plantation agency Hackfeld and Company (which later became American Factors). Hans was "active in the business affairs of Hackfeld and Company and Lihue plantation."[48] The HEA board agreed to transfer the Lihue Japanese School to the Lihue plantation and make it an independent school, free from the influence of any religious organization and governed by a committee composed of both white and Japanese residents.[49] This agreement seemed very generous to the HEA, which expressed its wish that "all Japanese schools [be] established on a non-sectarian basis."[50] However, the new independent school now belonged to the planter, which, according to the HEA proposal, had the power to select white committee members. The Japanese section of the HEA, through Rev. Isenberg and the plantation, could thus exert influence on the administration of the Lihue Shōgakkō. This was the HEA's new strategy for dealing with school controversy: they gave up the official name to claim the schools as well as the need to subsidize them, but maintained their actual control through school committee members. Because Okumura and his Christian colleagues publicly announced their stance that Japanese language schools should be secular, blaming Buddhist schools for the rising public opinion against language schools, Christians could not publicly argue for their control over schools. Their new creation of "independent schools" would prevent schools from becoming owned by Buddhists, while allowing Christians to manipulate schools to achieve their objectives.[51]

The HEA also tried to hamper Buddhist schools by appealing to local authorities. The superintendents of the HEA Japanese section Orramel Gulick,

John Gulick, and Perley L. Horne petitioned Hawaii's Department of Public Instruction (DPI) regarding the use of a Waialua public school building. The petition accused Buddhists of using their Japanese schools to expand control over the Japanese population in Hawaii. The petitioners argued that Buddhist schools opposed the Americanism that Hawaii's public schools promoted. They proposed Japanese language instruction be offered within the public school system. This, they argued, would help sever the connection between Buddhists and language schools and simultaneously counter anti-Americanism among Japanese.[52]

Reporting this incident to the Japanese foreign minister, Consul General Sen'ichi Ueno claimed that this petition was exaggerated and suggested the DPI simply deny the request. Ueno explained that in the earlier period, Japanese were unorganized and had to rely on clergy to care for children's education. However, he continued, Japanese slowly became independent and no longer needed the clergy for this. Ueno added that some of the Hongwanji schools became independent from the mission, but many of them remained with Hongwanji. Ueno continued that the petitioners' official goal was to make all Japanese schools secular and to silence anti-American factions; in reality, he was convinced, this was a strategic move in the feud between Christian and Buddhist missionaries. Ueno clarified that the petition was supposedly submitted by American missionaries, but that it was actually part of the Japanese Christians' plan to eradicate their opponents' schools.[53]

Saburō Kurusu who was Honolulu deputy consul general in 1912 recalled that there "always were problems about Japanese language schools, . . . one plantation had two or three denominations' schools which never conceded to each other." According to Kurusu, planters thought it was easier to give money to the Japanese consulate, rather than directly to a particular school, and looked to the consulate to resolve the problems.[54] The Hawaiian Sugar Planters' Association (HSPA) secretly contributed $1,000 annually to the consulate from 1907 to 1920 to underwrite language schools.[55] In 1914 alone, for example, there were conflicts between schools in more than fifty locations throughout the islands.[56] There was competition not only between Buddhist and Christian schools, but also between schools of competing Buddhist sects.[57] Neighbors also fought over where to build local schools.[58]

In July 1914, Hongwanji-affiliated schools, including twenty-nine elementary and three junior high schools (accounting for 25 percent of all students attending Japanese schools in Hawaii), announced a major change in educational policy.[59] The Hongwanji Education Committee explained that "Japanese language schools were seen by some as confronting American public schools, imbuing Japanism, and hindering Americanization."[60] They declared that the original purpose of the schools was to foster Japanese citizens in order to equip children for public education in Japan; however as Issei's perspectives changed to settlement, the goal of Japanese education should shift to cultivating children as American citizens. Realizing this change, Hongwanji school officials decided to modify their role to become an "educational home" and offer themselves as a means to connect Nikkei families with public schools. To reflect this, Hongwanji changed the name of its schools (*gakkō*) to *gakuen* (institutions) or "educational homes." The reason, it announced, was to remove public suspicion. The statement explained that at Hongwanji schools, language teaching is limited to one hour a day and focuses only on reading and writing. Japanese history and geography were still taught, but only within the context of teaching vocabulary that would enable the students to carry on conversations with their parents. Moral education was only taught for one hour per week and was now not based on Japanese nationalistic legends, but rather was intended to benefit the children's lives in America. This statement was released both in Japanese and English and sent to the DPI and other school officials.[61]

In February 1915, the Hawaii Japanese Education Association, Hawaii's central Japanese teachers organization, was established. That year, Japanese Americans made up almost one-third of the public school's population, and the number of Japanese language schools came close to equaling that of public schools.[62] As Hongwanji sensed growing public suspicion, Japanese teachers in the islands perceived a need to unify the schools and to communicate the purpose of Japanese schools in order to eliminate misunderstandings outside the community. The language schools drew public scrutiny partially because Nisei possessed dual citizenship. Nisei born in the U.S. territory were American citizens and also received Japanese citizenship based on parentage until the Japanese government changed the law in 1924.[63] Another issue for the new association became the task of creating a new textbook series to replace Japan's national textbooks. Concerned by religious conflicts and lack of cooperation between schools, Hongwanji Shōgakkō Principal Tamie Ōuchi approached Makiki Shōgakkō Principal Ryūhei Mashita about unifying Japanese schools in Hawaii and compiling textbooks appropriate for Nisei. They immediately agreed and approached other principals, Tetsuzō Takamura (Palama Hongwanji Shōgakkō), Masashi Masuda (Kakaako Nihongo Gakkō), and Takashi Uzawa (Chūō Gakuin). They proposed organizing a central teachers' association within the local Honolulu Japanese Education Association, which led to the creation of the Hawaii Japanese Education Association. In the midst of religious battle, some principals were seriously concerned with the future of Japanese education.[64]

At the association's special meeting in August 1915, Japanese teachers also changed their schools' names from "*Nihonjin shōgakkō*" (Japanese elementary schools) to "*Nihongo gakkō*" or Japanese language schools following the Hongwanji schools' example. Consul General Hachirō Arita argued that the previous name suggested that they their mission was equivalent to that of public schools in Japan: raising Japanese subjects. He insisted that Japanese schools should no longer provide national education, but simply provide language education. He emphasized that Hawaii was becoming a more important place politically, drawing more American public attention. Therefore, he argued Japanese should embrace educational policy appropriate for Nisei who are American citizens.[65]

In 1917, America entered World War I, causing the Americanization movement to become more intense. In July, five Japanese teachers were denied permission to disembark in Hawaii. Four of them were teachers invited by Hongwanji schools. Although some priests or educated persons in a local area taught in the schools, more often experienced teachers were recruited from Japan. Immigration officials argued they were contract laborers and violated a 1917 law.[66] This was shocking news for Hawaii's Japanese teachers who took it as evidence of growing public hostility. This measure obviously made it harder to recruit new qualified teachers from Japan.

Two years later an even more traumatic incident occurred, which terminated the mutually beneficial relationship between Buddhist clergy and planters. In 1919, Japanese plantation laborers revived the dormant higher wage movement. Bishop Imamura and priests from several other Buddhist sects requested the HSPA to yield to the workers' demands.[67] This crisis eventually worsened into total confrontation as negotiations fell through, leading eventually to the 1920 Oahu sugar plantation strike. Japanese language schools became integral players in this struggle; their buildings were used as strike meeting sites and shelters for workers booted off plantation houses.[68] Several Buddhist teachers and leaders of Hongwanji Young Men's Buddhist Association also played prominent roles in the six-month strike.[69]

Amid this turmoil, former Territorial Senator Albert F. Judd launched a Japanese school control law campaign on January 4, 1919, in the *Pacific Commercial Advertiser*.[70] Judd editorialized on the need for a bill that would require public and private school teachers to obtain a certificate from the DPI. The DPI would issue teachers such a certificate upon passing a test to ensure that teachers possess "ideals of democracy and have a knowledge of the English language, American history, and methods of government."[71]

Understandably, Japanese language educators strongly opposed this, because if enacted, it would mean the end of most of their schools, as few Japanese teachers spoke fluent English. When the Judd bill was introduced, there was a rumor that Okumura's son, Umetarō had a close relationship with Judd, and the father and son were the source of the bill in order to retaliate against Hongwanji schools.[72] Okumura denied involvement with Judd's measure, but was called a traitor or betrayer of the Japanese because he supported Judd's idea. Okumura argued that these requirements for teachers were understandable because their work was to promote Americanization and to raise future American citizens. In response to strong Nikkei opposition to the measure, Okumura explained that this would only deepen Americans' suspicion and misunderstanding.[73] The HEA tried, however, to request that the Board of Education make their priest-teachers exempt from the examination requirement and automatically grant them teaching licenses.[74]

In response to Judd's attack, Imamura tried to do his best to defend Hongwanji schools to the wider community. For example, Imamura wrote a letter to the *Honolulu Star Bulletin* editor that appeared on February 27, 1919, admitting that Hongwanji indeed practically controlled Japanese education for Japanese children born in Hawaii, but emphasizing that their "control is not with the object of blocking the Americanization of the Japanese children, but rather as an assistance thereto." Imamura emphasized "Buddhism taught by the Hongwanji mission is not to foster Mikadoism," as his opponents had argued; the mission's main objective, is "not for the control of the Japanese community through a religious hold," but rather to help these children communicate with their parents, many of whom are illiterate.[75]

The ethnic community conducted a campaign against Judd's proposal, as the territorial legislature began its session in March. Contrary to public anticipation, it was Republican Lorrin Andrews, an influential descendant of an old Hawaii missionary family, who proposed in the house the licensure of all private schools by the DPI. He also proposed the appointment of an inspector of foreign language schools.[76] While Andrews' bill was still in the house, the Chairman of the House Education Committee Henry Lyman revived the bill that Judd had originally outlined on March 20; on April 11, he introduced an additional bill to restrict the operating hours of language schools.[77] Facing strong protests from the Japanese community and perhaps cognizant of the federal State Department's warning to California legislators to halt their exclusion movement, the territorial legislature passed neither Andrews' nor Lyman's bills.[78] After these school control bills failed in 1919, the legislature passed a more modest act authorizing Governor Charles McCarthy and Superintendent of Public Instruction Vaughan MacCaughey to request the U.S. Bureau of Education to conduct a survey of education in Hawaii.[79]

On October 10, 1919, the Federal Educational Survey team, appointed by the commissioner of the Bureau of Education, arrived in Hawaii. The survey's official mission was supposedly to examine Hawaii's entire education system and propose educational reform. However, it was directed to especially scrutinize the Japanese language schools.[80] Provoking public outrage, Honolulu's daily, the *Pacific Commercial Advertiser,* claimed that not only did Japanese schools not teach Christian religion, but that they taught a religion that "regards the Mikado as divine." The *Advertiser* asked, "Can we afford to have future American citizens brought up in the belief that the ruler of a foreign land is superior to the government of this country?"[81] After two months of study, the team concluded that the language schools are "centers of an influence which, if not distinctly anti-American, is certainly un-American." It recommended that "all foreign-language schools to be abolished."[82] The report was serially published in the *Honolulu Star Bulletin* throughout June 1920.[83] The study was extremely influential and encouraged many organizations to endorse school control measures.[84]

Christian priests did not waste this chance to attack Buddhist schools. In July 1920, the Japanese section of the HEA publicly announced a resolution objecting to HSPA's support for Buddhist organizations. Committee members who signed the statement included John P. Erdman, Lloyd R. Killam, Vaughan MacCaughey, Theodore Richards, Orramel H. Gulick, Arthur L. Dean, Takie Okumura, and Teiichi Hori. MacCaughey at that time was DPI superintendent. Louise H. Hunter, who studied Buddhist-Christian conflict in Hawaii, wrote, "with the exception of Takie Okumura, probably no one was more opposed to foreign language schools (the Buddhist in particular) than Vaughan MacCaughey."[85] The resolution stated that if the HSPA continued to subsidize non-Christian religious organizations, it would harm people's welfare and the Christianization and Americanization of foreigners in Hawaii. The Japanese section explained that this statement was finally authorized by the HEA, but the idea itself was not new. The committee had been making appeals of this kind to the HEA board, but the board still hesitated to deal with this matter out of fear it would be perceived as religious retaliation.[86]

The Japanese section pointed to the Buddhist involvement in the plantation strikes as subversive both to America and Christianity. However, the HEA did not take any drastic action to suppress Buddhist ministries. This could be in part because some members of the HEA were related to HSPA leaders, because many members of both groups included descendants of missionaries who came to Hawaii in the early-nineteenth century. If their relatives' sugar plantation underwrote Buddhist temple's activities in order to control Japanese laborers, it would not be an easy decision to support something that would terminate this cooperative relationship.

Rather than further aggravating hostile legislators by defending Japanese language schools, a group of Japanese leaders drafted a compromise school control bill.[87] Endorsed by Honolulu's Chamber of Commerce, it easily passed at a special session of the Hawaii legislature and was immediately signed by Governor McCarthy on November 24, 1920.[88] Act 30, as it became known, followed the guidelines recommended by the Federal Survey with only a few modifications. The effect of the federal report was not limited to the islands. After the vehement resistance of Japanese in Hawaii was suppressed, a school control bill modeled after Hawaii's was passed "without strong opposition from the Japanese" in California.[89] This would eventually encourage the exclusionists' attack on Nisei's rights of American citizenship on the false premise that language school attendance was evidence of "disloyalty" to the United States.[90]

Conclusion

We have examined the origin of the Japanese language school controversy in Hawaii. Japanese language schools were first established as temporary institutions until immigrant families returned to Japan. However, Issei changed their perspectives to settlers in Hawaii, and Nisei born in Hawaii were entitled to American citizenship. In addition to public school education, parents wanted to provide Japanese education and invested their precious wages into these language schools. Both Christian and Buddhist clergy understood this and exploited their hopes as an opportunity to do mission work. The largest Buddhist sect in Hawaii was Honpa Hongwanji. In 1920, it had 75,000 adherents, 60 churches and substations, 30 Young Men's Buddhist Associations, 40 Young Women's Buddhist Association chapters, and 42 Japanese language schools, embracing some 7,100 children and 155 teachers in the territory alone.[91] With such strong support from its members, Hongwanji controlled much of Hawaii's Japanese school situation; this power, however, was used by others to arouse public suspicion. Christians were the first to establish schools and their schools provided robust competition with Hongwanji. Although the HEA was involved with language schools, unlike Hongwanji, their schools were much smaller and sustained mainly by priests' individual efforts. Buddhist and Christian rivalry over schools created countless religious battles in Japanese communities throughout the islands. These internal community conflicts were later used as the political means to control Hawaii's Japanese situation. Later, the anti-Japanese school movement migrated to West Coast states and became a political instrument to solve local "Japanese problems." Despite the 1927 court decision, these battles pitting Buddhists against Christians continued during the 1930s and early 1940s, until their total closure during World War II.

Notes

I would like to thank Kanani Reppun of the Mission Houses Museum Archives for locating documents about the Hawaii Evangelical Association. I also am grateful to archivists DeSoto Brown, Judith Kearney, Patty Lei, and Ron Schaeffer of the Bishop Museum for their knowledgeable assistance. I appreciate the efforts of Honpa Hongwanji Bishop Chikai Yosemori to locate Hongwanji documents. I am also deeply indebted to Dr. Duncan Ryûken Williams for his encouragement to focus on Buddhism as part of my research on Japanese language schools.

1. Issei could not become American citizens until 1952, but Nisei who were born in the Territory of Hawaii after its annexation to the United States in 1898 were American citizens.

2. See Noriko Asato, *Teaching Mikadoism: The Attack on Japanese Language Schools in Hawaii, California, and Washington, 1919–1927* (Honolulu: University of Hawai'i Press, 2005) for the effects of Hawaii's Japanese language school controversy on Japanese language school problems in California and Washington.

3. Ann L. Halsted, *Sharpened Tongues: The Controversy Over the 'Americanization' of Japanese Language Schools in Hawaii, 1919–1927* (Ph.D. diss., Stanford University, 1989); Yoshihide Matsubayashi, *The Japanese Language Schools in Hawaii and California from 1892 to 1941* (Ph.D. diss., University of San Francisco, 1984); Noriko Shimada, "Wartime Dissolution and Revival of the Japanese Language Schools in Hawai'i: Persistence of Ethnic Culture," *Journal of Asian American Studies* 1 (June 1998): 121–151; and Asato, *Teaching Mikadoism.* For studies on California's Japanese language schools, see Toyotomi Morimoto, *Japanese Americans and Cultural Continuity: Maintaining Language and Heritage* (New York: Garland, 1997) and Teruko Kumei, "'The Twain Shall Meet' in the Nisei?: Japanese Language Education and U.S.-Japan Relations, 1900–1940," in *New Worlds, New Lives: Globalization and People of Japanese Descent in the Americas and from Latin America in Japan,* Lane Ryo Hirabayashi, Akemi Kikumura-Yano, and James A. Hirabayashi, eds. (Stanford: Stanford University Press, 2002), pp. 108–25.

4. Louise H. Hunter, *Buddhism in Hawaii: Its Impact on a Yankee Community* (Honolulu: University of Hawai'i Press, 1971); Yukuji Okita, *Hawaii nikkei imin no kyōikushi: Nichibei bunka, sono deai to sōkoku* (Kyoto: Minerva shobō, 1997); Sadanobu Washimi, "Hawaii Jōdoshū to Nihongo gakkō," in *Bukkyō kyōka kenkyū,* Mizutani Kōshō Sensei Koki Kinenkai, ed. (Kyoto: Shibunkaku, 1998), pp. 481–96; Tomoe Moriya, *Amerika bukkyō no tanjō: Nijū seiki shotō ni okeru nikkei shūkyō no bunka henyō* (Tokyo: Gendai shiryō shuppan, 2001).

5. Peter Irons, ed. *Justice Delayed: The Record of the Japanese American Internment Cases* (Middletown, Conn.: Wesleyan University Press, 1989), p. 39.

6. Christianity was illegal in Japan until 1873. The passport belonging to Tomisaburō Makino, one of the *gannenmono,* contained the line, "Never convert to another religion," showing that the centuries-old custom of prohibiting Christianity continued into the first wave of immigration. See Hawaii Nihonjin Iminshi Kankō Iinkai, ed., *Hawaii Nihonjin iminshi* (Honolulu: Hawaii Nihonjin rengō kyōkai, 1964), p. 226.

7. Yemyo Imamura, *Hawaii kaikyōshi* (Honolulu: Honpa Hongwanji, 1918), pp. 26–27, 29.

8. For Japanese immigrants' plantation life, see Hilary Conroy, *The Japanese Frontier in Hawaii, 1868–1898* (Berkeley: University of California Press, 1953); Ronald Takaki, *Strangers from a Different Shore: A History of Asian Americans* (New York: Penguin, 1989); Gary Y. Okihiro, *Cane Fires: The Anti-Japanese Movement in Hawaii, 1865–1945* (Philadelphia: Temple University Press, 1991); Masayo Umezawa Duus, *The Japanese Conspiracy: The Oahu Sugar Strike of 1920* (Berkeley: University of California, 1999).

9. Gijō Ozawa, *Hawaii Nihongo gakkō kyōikushi* (Honolulu: Hawaii kyōikukai, 1972), p. 14.

10. There might have been more children born in Japan during the *kanyaku imin* period. See Alex Ladenson, *The Japanese in Hawaii* (Ph.D. diss., University of Chicago, 1938), p. 132.

11. Hawaii Nihonjin Iminshi Kankō Iinkai, ed., *Hawaii Nihonjin iminshi,* p. 247.

12. Lawrence H. Fuchs, *Hawaii Pono: A Social History* (New York: Harcourt, Brace & World, 1961), p. 270.

13. Ozawa, *Hawaii Nihongo gakkō kyōikushi,* p. 14.

14. Ibid., p. 21; Okita, *Hawaii Nikkei imin,* p. 104.

15. Ozawa, *Hawaii Nihongo gakkō kyōikushi,* p. 14.

16. Eileen H. Tamura presents an insightful treatment relevant to Hawaii in *Americanization, Acculturation, and Ethnic Identity: The Nisei Generation in Hawaii* (Urbana: University of Illinois Press, 1994), p. 96. Also see John E. Reinecke, *Language and Dialect in Hawaii: A Sociolinguistic History to 1935* (Honolulu: University of Hawai'i Press, 1969).

17. Fusa Nakagawa, *Tosa kara Hawaii e* (Kōchi, Japan: 'Okumura Takie to Hawaii Nikkei Iminten' Jikkō Iinkai, 2000), pp. 56, 65.

18. Takie Okumura, *Taiheiyō no rakuen* (Kyoto: Naigai shuppan, 1930), p. 168.

19. Hawaii Japanese Education Association, *Hawaii Nihongo kyōikushi* (Honolulu: Hawaii Education Association, 1937), p. 6. In 1902, the Honolulu Nihonjin Shōgakkō began collecting tuition from students due to the expenses to expand the school building. Tuition for students in the regular course was 30 cents, and the advanced course was 50 cents per month. *Yamato Shinbun,* February 13, 1902.

20. Hawaii Japanese Education Association, *Hawaii Nihongo kyōikushi,* pp. 4–5.

21. Ibid., p. 5.

22. Okumura, *Taiheiyō no rakuen,* pp. 221–22.

23. Okumura, *Seventy Years of Divine Blessings* (Honolulu: n.p., 1940), p. 41; Okumura, *Taiheiyō no rakuen,* pp. 222–23.

24. Imamura, *Chōshōin ibunshū* (Honolulu: Hawaii Honolulu Hongwanji, 1937), p. 160.

25. Chie Honda, "Dainiji sekai taisenmae no Hawaii ni okeru Jōdo Shinshū Honpa Honganji no Nihongo gakkō," in *Amerika no nikkeijin: Toshi, shakai, seikatsu,* Yanagida Toshio, ed. (Tokyo: Dōbunkan, 1995), p. 193.

26. Imamura, *Hawaii kaikyōshi,* p. 42.

27. Imamura, *Hawaii kaikyō shiyō* (Honolulu: Honpa Hongwanji Hawaii kaikyō kyōmusho bunshobu 1918), p. 37.

28. Hunter, *Buddhism in Hawaii,* p. 71.

29. Okumura, *Taiheiyō no rakuen,* p. 227.

30. Moriya, *Amerika Bukkyō no tanjō,* p. 109.

31. Letter, Bishop Yemyo Imamura to Vice Foreign Minister Kikujirō Ishii, April 11, 1910. The Diplomatic Record Office, Japanese Foreign Ministry, Tokyo (hereafter DRO) 3.10.2.10–3.

32. *Nippū Jiji,* July 14, 1911.

33. *Hawaii Shokumin Shinbun,* September 16, 1910; also cited in Okita, *Hawaii Nikkei imin,* pp. 122–23.

34. *Hawaii Shokumin Shinbun,* August 20, 1909; also cited in Okita, *Hawaii Nikkei imin,* p. 114. Kazutami Eguchi was a pseudonym for Sadajirō Okumura.

35. Letter, Consul General Senichi Ueno to Foreign Minister Jutarō Komura, March 18, 1910. DRO 3.10.2.10–3.

36. Letter, Hongwanji Bishop Yemyo Imamura to Vice Foreign Minister Kikujirō Ishii, April 11, 1910. DRO 3.10.2.10–3.

37. Okita, *Hawaii Nikkei imin,* p. 143.

38. *Hawaii Shokumin Shinbun,* April 19, 21, 26, 28, 1911; *Nippū Jiji,* April 21, 1911.

39. *Hawaii Shokumin Shinbun,* April 21, 1911.

40. *Hawaii Shokumin Shinbun,* April 14, 1911.

41. *Nippū Jiji,* May 11, 1911.

42. *Nippū Jiji,* April 20, 1911. Rev. Tsuji came to Hawaii in July 1898 and was assigned in Lihue in 1905. Okumura, *Hawaii dendō sanjūnen ryakushi* (Honolulu: n.p., 1917), pp. 12, 16.

43. *Nippū Jiji,* April 20, 1911.

44. *Nippū Jiji,* May 24, 1911.

45. *Nippū Jiji,* April 22, 1911.

46. *Nippū Jiji,* May 11, 1911.

47. *Nippū Jiji,* May 6, 11, 1911.

48. Edward Joesting, *Kauai: The Separate Kingdom* (Honolulu: University of Hawai'i Press and Kauai Museum Association, 1984), pp. 224, 227.

49. *Nippū Jiji,* August 8, 1911; Minutes of the Japanese Committee, August 29, 1919. Hawaii Evangelical Association Collection, Hawaii Mission Houses Library Archives (henceforth, HEAC).

50. Minutes of the Japanese Committee, August 29, 1919. HEAC.

51. *Hawaii Shinpō* editor Sometarō Shiba (written "Sheba" at that time) reported that the Lihue school problem was settled on August 17, 1911. Issues of the *Hawaii Shinpō* from that year are no longer available even on microfilm, but the minutes of the Japanese section of the HEA indicates that they discussed Sheba's article and his role in the settlement. According to Sheba's article (from the minutes), after the agreement was reached between the HEA superintendents and Rev. Isenberg, Sheba escorted him to the Lihue Japanese community. They apparently reached an agreement under the following terms:

1. Apply to the Consul for a teacher, upon whose arrival the school shall be transferred to the School Committee.
2. The School shall be governed and maintained by a Committee elected by parents.
3. One Christian shall be elected as a member of the Committee.
4. The contributions from white people shall be continued as heretofore.
5. Messrs Isenberg and Wilcox shall be advisors.
6. The progress of the School shall be satisfactory.

This agreement between Isenberg and the Lihue Nikkei was much more detailed than the one that appeared on the *Nippū Jiji* or the HEA minutes. It specifies more clearly Christians' involvement in the school committee. The HEA Japanese section discussed Sheba's article because Rev. Scudder claimed to be unfamiliar with these terms, so he wrote Isenberg to find out whether or not these terms were actually discussed with the Japanese people. Isenberg replied to Scudder that he was aware Sheba had met with the Japanese, but that unlike what the previously cited article claimed, he did not actually meet them in person. The question remains how Sheba determined the terms. However, before Sheba became a newspaperman, he was a Christian priest in 1890 in Koloa, eight miles from Lihue. According to Okumura's history of Christian missionary work, Koloa and Lihue were covered by one priest when one of these places had no residing priest. The reason Sheba was chosen (probably by Rev. Isenberg) as a "messenger" might be his connection to Lihue. Minutes of the Japanese Committee, August 29, 1919. HEAC; Okumura, *Hawaii dendō sanjūnen ryakushi,* p. 5.

52. *Nippū Jiji,* June 5, 1911.

53. Letter, Ueno to Komura, July 25, 1911. DRO 3.10.2.1.

54. Hawaii Nihonjin Iminshi Kankō Iinkai, ed., *Hawaii Nihonjin iminshi,* p. 234.

55. Letter, Hawaii Consul General Hisakichi Nagataki to Foreign Minister Nobuaki Makino, March 6, 1913. DRO 3.10.2.10.

56. Hawaii Nihonjin Iminshi Kankō Iinkai, ed., *Hawaii Nihonjin iminshi,* p. 234.

57. Washimi, "Hawaii Jōdoshū," p. 489.

58. Okita, "Maui kyōikukai no chōwa seishin to Nihongo gakkō," in *Hawaii Nikkei shakai no bunka to sono henyō,* Yukuji Okita, ed.(Kyoto: Nakanishiya shuppan, 1998), p. 7.

59. Imamura, *Hawaii kaikyōshi,* p. 55. In 1915, there were 122 Japanese schools in Hawaii. Ozawa, *Hawaii Nihongo gakkō kyōikushi,* pp. 31–33, 49–50.

60. Imamura, *Hawaii kaikyōshi,* p. 54.

61. Ibid., pp. 54–57. *Nippū Jiji,* July 30, 1914.

62. Ozawa, *Hawaii Nihongo gakkō,* p. 70.

63. In 1924, the Japanese government changed the law, requiring for parents to register with the Japanese consulate in order to obtain a Japanese citizenship for their children. Brian Niiya, ed. *Japanese American History: An A-to-Z Reference from 1868 to the Present* (New York: Facts On File, Inc., 1993), p 129.

64. Hawaii Nihonjin Iminshi Kankō Iinkai, ed., *Hawaii Nihonjin iminshi,* p. 233. Principal Mashita was originally sent by the Japanese Education Ministry to be principal of Okumura's school in 1902. Ozawa explained that the Maui Education Association initiated the movement to organize the Hawaii Education Association and sent a proposal to other local Japanese teacher's associations—Honolulu Education Association, Oahu Island Education Association, Kauai Island Education Association, Hawaii Island Education Association, Hawaii Island Education Study Group, Kau Education Association, Kona Education Association. Mashita, Takamura, Ōuchi, Masuda, and Uzawa were appointed as board members at the first meeting. Ozawa, *Hawaii Nihongo gakkō kyōikushi,* pp. 56, 70.

65. Hawaii Japanese Education Association, *Hawaii Nihongo kyōikushi,* pp. 62, 70, 76; Ozawa, *Hawaii Nihongo gakkō kyōikushi,* pp. 72–73.

66. Imamura successfully challenged their detention in 1920 after several court battles. Ozawa, *Hawaii Nihongo gakkō kyōikushi,* p. 79.

67. See Tomoe Moriya, *Amerika Bukkyō no tanjō,* p. 97, for her insightful analysis of Imamura's change in attitude toward Japanese strikes.

68. Halsted, "Sharpened Tongues," p. 69.

69. Okihiro, *Cane Fires,* pp. 130–31.

70. Judd was a lawyer who had served as a representative of the Hawaiian Sugar Planters' Association in its 1906 effort to secure Filipino laborers. He served in the Hawaiian Senate from 1911 to 1913, but he was not a legislator when he campaigned for the Japanese language school measure. John William Siddall, *Men of Hawaii* (Honolulu: Star Bulletin, 1917), p. 155.

71. Judd's definition of "teachers" also included administrators in "all schools in the Territory," except "Sabbath" schools. *Honolulu Advertiser,* January 4, 1919.

72. Hawaii Japanese Education Association, *Hawaii Nihongo kyōikushi,* p. 168; Report from Hawaii, attached to telegram, Consul General Rokuro Moroi to Foreign Minister Yasuya Uchida, March 13, 1919 (DRO 3.10.2.1). Hunter, who studied Okumura's personal papers, did not find evidence of Okumura's direct involvement with the bill. She concluded, however, "his peripheral activities and his later 'projects' for Americanizing the local-born Japanese were motivated by the desire to liquidate Buddhism and all Buddhist institutions." Hunter, *Buddhism in Hawaii,* p. 113.

73. Four months later, Judd denied the rumor that Rev. Okumura was behind his proposal and insisted that he wrote it alone and was solely responsible for the idea. Okumura, *Taiheiyō no rakuen,* pp. 256–58.

74. Minutes of the Japanese Committee, August 9, 1921. HEAC.

75. *Honolulu Star Bulletin,* February 27, 1919.

76. Halsted, "Sharpened Tongues," pp. 93–95. A consular report from Hawaii on March 20, 1919, suggests that Andrews solicited a bribe from the Hawaii Japanese Education Association, but did not receive it. The anonymous author of the report assumed that this was the motive behind his bill (DRO 3.10.2.1).

77. Ozawa, *Hawaii Nihongo gakkō kyōikushi,* pp. 97–106.

78. John Reinecke, *Feigned Necessity: Hawaii's Attempt to Obtain Chinese Contract Labor, 1921–1923* (San Francisco: Chinese Materials Center, 1979), p. 52. Secretary of State Robert Lansing sent a cablegram to the California legislature, requesting "no anti-Japanese action" in 1919. Roger Daniels, *The Politics of Prejudice: The Anti-Japanese Movement in California and the Struggle for Japanese Exclusion* (Berkeley: University of California Press, 1962), p. 82. This was reported in Hawaii's newspapers.

79. *Honolulu Star Bulletin,* April 30, 1919; cited in Matsubayashi, "The Japanese Language Schools in Hawaii and California," p. 111.

80. For details on the Hawaii's Federal Education Survey, see Asato, "Mandating Americanization: Japanese Language Schools and the Federal Survey of Education in Hawaii, 1916–1920," *History of Education Quarterly* 43 (2003): 10–38.

81. *Pacific Commercial Advertiser,* November 6, 1919.

82. U.S. Department of the Interior, Bureau of Education, *A Survey of Education in Hawaii* (Washington, D.C.: Bulletin 1920, No. 16, Government Printing Office), p. 134.

83. Halsted, "Sharpened Tongues," p. 82.

84. Hunter, *Buddhism in Hawaii,* p. 127.

85. Ibid., p. 108. MacCaughey took office in March 1919.

86. *Hawaii Hōchi,* July 12, 1920

87. Halsted, "Sharpened Tongues," pp. 95–96.

88. Ibid., p. 97.

89. Reginald Bell, *Public School Education of Second-Generation Japanese in California* (Stanford: Stanford University Press, 1935; reprint, New York: Arno Press, 1978), p. 20.

90. U.S. Congress, House Committee on Immigration and Naturalization, *Japanese Immigration Hearings. 66th Congress, 2nd session, 1921* (Washington D.C.: Government Printing Office, 1921; reprint, New York: Arno Press, 1978), p. 240.

91. U.S. Department of the Interior, p. 111.

4 The Legal Dimensions of the Formation of Shin Buddhist Temples in Los Angeles

MICHIHIRO AMA

"Reverend Izumida is a Traitor," read the headline in *Rafu Shimpo* on September 11, 1917. This was the beginning of the public bashing of this minister in the Los Angeles Japanese press. Attacks on Izumida continued on September 14 and 15 with such headlines as "Clean Up the Place Where a Demon Hides: Throw out Izumida Junjō . . . Save the Buddhist Mission of Los Angeles," "Advice to Reverend Izumida," and "Izumida Junjō: Reverend of Traitors and Lost Faith." These newspaper articles chronicled Izumida Junjō's protest against the consolidation of three Japanese Buddhist churches in Los Angeles. After an incident in which the Nishi Honganji headquarters tried to consolidate the Rafu Bukkyō-kai (the Buddhist Mission of Los Angeles), the Nanka Bukkyō-kai (the Buddhist Mission of Southern California), and the Chūō Bukkyō-kai (the Central Buddhist Mission) without success, it excommunicated Izumida, who later joined Higashi Honganji.

This chapter examines how two kinds of authority, as defined by American legal institutions as opposed to the power exercised by a Japanese organization, were negotiated in a Japanese American Buddhist institution when a minister from Japan came to the United States and built a Buddhist church. A case in point is the incident involving the dispute between Nishi Honganji clergy and laity in Los Angeles centering around Izumida Junjō (1866–1951). Nishi and Higashi Honganji are two major denominations of Jōdo Shinshū (a.k.a Shin Buddhism, a school of Japanese Pure Land Buddhism).

A Master Narrative

The history of Nishi Honganji on mainland United States begins in San Francisco. In 1897, Hirano Nisaburō, a devout Japanese Buddhist who had immigrated to California, temporarily returned to Japan and visited the Nishi Honganji headquarters in Kyoto. He requested ministers to be sent to San Francisco, because there was no Buddhist church despite the increasing number of Japanese immigrants in California. In the following year, the headquarters sent Honda Eryū and Miyamoto Ejun to investigate the immigrant's situations, which Nishi Honganji later considered its beginning of the propagation on the mainland. In September of the following year, it further sent Sonoda Shūye (1863–1922) and Nishijima Kakuryō (1873–1942) to San Francisco as Buddhist "missionaries" (*kaikyōshi*) with the former given the title of first superintendent (*kantoku*).[1] Subsequently, Nishi Honganji Buddhist churches came to be established in San Francisco, Sacramento, and San Jose.

Izumida Junjō (1866–1951) played a major role in establishing a Buddhist group in Los Angeles. He was born in 1866 as the second son of Izumida Hōjō, the resident minister of Anyūji, a Nishi Honganji temple in Nagasaki prefecture, and later moved to Shōrenji in Saga prefecture. Junjō was ordained in 1893 and became a full-fledged minister in 1897. A year later, he taught at Bungaku-ryō (present-day Ryūkoku University) in Kyoto operated by Nishi Honganji. In 1902, Izumida traveled to San Francisco on the recommendation of an administrative minister, Akamatsu Renjō, who later held the highest academic position at the headquarters (*kangaku*). Inspired by the propagation centers in San Jose and Sacramento, he decided to stay longer on the Pacific coast. He returned home in 1903 and convinced his family and members of Shōrenji of his leaving Japan again. In the following year, he returned to the United States and arrived this time in Los Angeles.[2] In 1905, there were roughly 15,000 Japanese in Los Angeles and the population grew yearly until 1917. Due to this rapid increase, a Buddhist church became necessary to serve the immigrants' needs for funerals, memorial services, and spiritual guidance. In September 1904, Izumida formed a nonsectarian Buddhist group called the Rafu Bukkyō-kai on 229 East Fourth Street. Later, its first building was constructed on South Savannah Street in the city's Boyle Heights district.[3]

Records show that soon afterward, two more Buddhist organizations related to Nishi Honganji emerged in Los Angeles. Nanka Bukkyō-kai appeared on Jackson Street in October 1905 and Chūō Bukkyō-kai on 508 Turner Street in October 1912. The Nishi Honganji headquarters appointed Uchida Kōyū (1876–1960) as the acting head minister of the Nanka Bukkyō-kai in 1905. He then succeeded Sonoda and two other interim superintendents and became the fourth superintendent (*kantoku*) in San Francisco. Uchida organized the propagation of Nishi Honganji as the Buddhist Mission of North America (BMNA) and became its first bishop (*sōchō*). In the meantime, Kawakami Teishin and Haraguchi Shinjō established the Chūō Bukkyō-kai.[4]

It took a lot of effort for Nishi Honganji to unite the three Buddhist churches. Although efforts to unify them had begun earlier, the first major attempt took place after September 1916 when the Rafu Bukkyō-kai split into two—those for and against Izumida.[5] On this occasion, Sonoda Shūye, who had moved to Europe and returned to the headquarters in Japan, made a proposal to consolidate the three churches. Although ministers at these churches initially agreed, Izumida later opposed it for unknown reasons. As a result, Nishi Honganji excommunicated Izumida while completing the consolidation in September 1917. Nevertheless on October 4, the Chūō Bukkyō-kai went back on their decision and withdrew from the consolidated organization. In the meantime, the Nanka Bukkyō-kai's congregation and the anti-Izumida group from the Rafu Bukkyō-kai joined together and organized the Honganji Bukkyō-kai (present-day Honpa Honganji Los Angeles Betsuin, also known as Nishi Honganji Los Angeles Betsuin). Later, the Executive Council of the Nishi Honganji in Los Angeles, headed by Sonoda, dismissed Haraguchi from the Chūō Bukkyō-kai, causing this organization to lose its connection with Nishi Honganji headquarters and join the Honganji Bukkyō-kai.

The aforementioned description is often found in the early history of the Japanese immigrants in Los Angeles. Using newly available legal and Buddhist church documents as well as personal records and newspaper articles, this study, however, tries to develop a somewhat more complex picture of the early establishment of these Buddhist churches.

A Close Analysis of the Consolidation of the Three Churches

There was an incident called *Butsuzen chinuri sōdō* (lit. a bloody fight in front of the Buddha) at the Rafu Bukkyō-kai on September 17. This broke out among the board members when they were discussing the resignation of Izumida, who was the president of the organization at that time. Jisōji Tetsugai (1888-?), the associate minister, presided over the meeting in which it was said that Izumida had mismanaged and embezzled church funds and had presented different financial records to the board and the superintendent of the BMNA. He was also said to have made financial reports without proper signatures. At the meeting, some pro-Izumida members, upset by these accusations, physically attacked the accusers, Messrs. Matsuba and Nakamura. Both sides eventually came to some kind of reconciliation, even though these two individuals initially planned to take Izumida and other members to court. It was also said that other ministers formed the Nanka Bukkō-kai because of the argument over the recipient of the donations between them and Izumida.[6] Bishop Uchida, in charge of the BMNA office, seized the opportunity of the split in Rafu Bukkyō-kai to push for consolidation of the three churches that he had planned for some time.

The Nishi Honganji headquarters in Kyoto supported Uchida's decision. On May 1, 1917, he visited Los Angeles and persuaded the leaders of these churches to merge, though without success. The headquarters, therefore, sent Sonoda Shūye, the former superintendent of the BMNA, to Los Angeles on June 26, 1917. Sonoda, interviewed by the *Rafu Shimpo,* said Nishi Honganji had too many missions (three) in Los Angeles and suggested that it would be better to consolidate to minimize financial and ministerial difficulties. Further, he pointed out the decline in the quality of the ministers.[7]

The *Rafu Shimpo* then reported that under the guidance of the Executive Council headed by Sonoda the three churches approved the consolidation. On September 4, representatives of each made proposals including unifying the three churches and making just one large organization, after which membership would be increased and the teaching propagated more efficiently; choosing the best location for the new building in the Japanese community in Los Angeles and promoting the teaching, charities, and various other social activities on behalf of the members; combining the current assets and debts of each church and reorganizing management; appointing Uchida as the head minister of the consolidated church and reshuffling all other ministers working at the three; and selecting ten members from each church to form a consolidation committee.[8] Prior to this agreement, the ministers of the BMNA, on August 13, 1917, had decided on consolidating the churches simultaneously, sending Izumida back to Japan and removing Haraguchi from Los Angeles, appointing Uchida as acting head minister of the consolidated church, appointing Kudara Toryū as minister of the San Francisco Bukkyō-kai to replace Uchida, eliminating the board system and appointing ministers as presidents of the churches, thereby giving Sonoda exclusive authority over the ministers, asking Japan's Foreign Ministry to stop giving out visas to ministers not authorized by the Nishi Honganji headquarters, and sending regular reports of propagation activity directly to Sonoda in Japan.[9]

The documents filed with the Los Angeles Superior Court, however, reveal that the Rafu Bukkyō-kai's decision for consolidation was not unanimous.[10] Although the proposal for consolidation was presented to Rafu Bukkyō-kai's first general meeting on September 9, 1917, the majority of members rejected the motion and Izumida respected their decision. After the meeting, those who were for it banded together and tried to discredit Izumida as president of the church. The Executive Council accused him of taking church property and money with an alleged investigation of his conduct. The pro-consolidation members called a second general meeting on September 16, 1917. Previous to that, however, they had persuaded fifty people to apply for church membership, and at least twenty-one of them attended the said meeting. Although thirty members voted against consolidation, the majority, including these twenty-one, espoused the motion and voted Izumida out as both the church's president and minister. But for the addition of the new members, neither the proposal for consolidation nor the one to remove Izumida would have passed because the bylaws of the church stated that the president, Izumida himself, had to first approve new membership applications.[11] Despite this conspiracy, the Executive Council dismissed him from his two positions and ordered him to leave his residence and return to Japan.

Izumida had his own reasons for protesting Sonoda: Izumida had formed the Rafu Bukkyō-kai before the Nishi headquarters recognized it; the headquarters had never appointed him as the minister; he continued religious services even after his dismissal by the Executive Council because the bylaws of the Rafu Bukkyō-kai did not specify its exact relationship with Nishi Honganji; he strongly showed his sympathies toward the members who opposed the consolidation; and finally he did not take any money from the church. Izumida, who disagreed with Sonoda's decision, reluctantly admitted that he was disobeying orders from the headquarters and would await a reprimand.[12]

Because of Izumida's refusal, those for consolidation took a legal action. The anti-Izumida group filed a petition for an injunction on October 4, 1917, to stop him from continuing as a minister of the Rafu Bukkyō-kai and president of the organization. The next day, the court issued a temporary restraining order against Izumida based on an affidavit from T. Hirata, who complained that Izumida was continuing services and receiving money even after his dismissal as well as causing great embarrassment to the church and the Japanese community as a whole. The court later rescinded this order on October 16, 1917, after Izumida provided evidence showing that he had never been under the jurisdiction of Nishi Honganji.[13]

After several court sessions, the case went to trial (the jury was waived) and the trial judge L. N. Valentine gave decision on October 4, 1918. He found that neither Izumida nor the Rafu Bukkyō-kai was under the jurisdiction of Nishi Honganji; hence, the Executive Council could not remove him as minister of the church or president of the organization. The court also found that Izumida did not act in a manner, which had caused great embarrassment to the church or to the Japanese community, and ruled in his favor, awarding him all but $3.00 of his requested costs ($148.10).[14]

In the meantime, Izumida himself filed a lawsuit involving the defamation of his character on December 7, 1917.[15] On September 15, 1917, the *Rafu Asahi shinbun* (*The Los Angeles Morning Sun*) reported on the efforts to consolidate the three Buddhist churches in Los Angeles, stating that there were good reasons for doing so, despite Izumida and his followers' opposition. The article called the opposition the "pro-Izumida gang" and cited Izumida's dishonesty as the basis for his opposing consolidation. It further accused him of embezzling offerings and labeled him a person of low repute and character. The article went on to say that "no further statement is necessary; to be guided by a person with such a character probably there will be no way but to be led to hell."[16] Izumida sued the *Rafu Asahi shinbun* and editor (Tanaka) on December 7, 1917, in the Los Angeles Superior Court and contended that the article not only ruined his reputation but also led people to discredit him. Izumida asked for $30,000 in compensatory damages and $20,000 in punitive damages. Tanaka and the *Rafu Asahi shinbun* denied that the article was defamatory.[17]

From June 26 to August 15, 1918, the judge, without a jury, examined the case that also involved the controversial handling of offerings. The embezzling of money was described as the cause of the contention between Izumida and Asayoshi Ryūun, who, because of it, left the Rafu Bukkyō-kai and started the Nanka Bukkyō-kai. On August 16, the *Rafu Shimpo* reported on the last debate between the attorneys of both parties. The respondent's counsel pointed to Izumida's unfair practices and criticized the way he had borrowed money to finance the church, as it did not follow the guidelines of nonprofit organizations. But the plaintiff's counsel argued that financial problems were common to a start-up church in need of operational expenses and that Izumida used the money for "debit and credit" and not for his personal gain.[18]

After the trial, Judge Hewitt sided with Izumida, recognizing that the Rafu Bukkyō-kai was "the largest and most influential and best known Buddhist Mission in the State of California, having a very large congregation and membership composed of persons from the City of Los Angeles, County of Los Angeles, and other surrounding counties, and from other districts throughout Southern California"; hence, the flagrant remark concerning Izumida's mishandling of offerings caused substantial harm to him. On September 24, 1918, Hewitt awarded him $300 in compensatory damages and $279 in costs in the suit.[19]

Although Izumida survived two *causes célèbres,* the Nishi Honganji headquarters was unsatisfied with the two verdicts and decided to defrock him. It ordered him to appear before the Kyoto headquarters twice, but he refused to appear. Without his presence, it held an internal investigation on December 12, 1918, and finally went ahead to disrobe him.[20] In August 1919, the *Rafu Shimpo* reported that Izumida was no longer a Nishi Honganji minister, quoting from the reports of "Internal Circulation" (*Honzan rokuji*) issued on June 30.[21] Izumida was reprimanded under Article 7, Section 1 and Article 13, Section 6 of the "Regulations of Disciplinary Punishment" (*chōkai jōki*), which the headquarters applied to a minister who was disrespectful to the dharma and dealt with defrocking. But under Chapter 12, Articles 35 and 36 of the "Constitution of Nishi Honganji's Detailed Rules" (*jihō saisoku*), the headquarters could reduce these sentences and exonerate the minister, if he regretted his wrongdoing. To put it differently, the headquarters *did* consider reinstating Izumida. Later, Inoue Tokumei, the Director of the Propagation Department (*fukyō-bu*) at the headquarters sent a letter to Masuyama Kenju (1887–1969), the sixth bishop of the BMNA on January 16, 1931, mentioning Izumida's possible return to Nishi Honganji.[22]

Not all the ministers were against Izumida. Nakai Gendō (1877–1945), who had served as resident minister of the Seattle Church between 1902 and 1907, sent a letter of protest to the headquarters, while advising Izumida to accept the punishment and wait for exoneration.[23] These two had known each other before coming to the United States. Izumida taught at the Bungakuryō, when Nakai was the student editor of the Buddhist journal, *Hansei zasshi* (or *Hanseikai zasshi*). Nakai once wrote an article criticizing the Kyoto City officials for tolerating prostitution. In response, Izumida was indicted because he was the editorial supervisor. Luckily his attorney succeeded in defending Izumida.[24] Because of Izumida's involvement in his case, Nakai had felt indebted to him. But Nakai's protest did not make much difference at headquarters.

After being excommunicated from Nishi Honganji, Izumida contacted a Higashi Honganji priest. His memoirs, which describe the whole affair in Los Angeles, include his final decision:

> Although the punishment of the Nishi Honganji headquarters was not just, I avoided further contention. For the propagation of Buddhism, I decided to become independent, as Shinran Shōnin had demonstrated being "neither monk nor layman." Nevertheless, by the request of the members and in my own interest, we asked Fujimoto, a Higashi Honganji priest, to take all the judicial records to the Higashi Honganji headquarters. Then we made a formal request to Higashi Honganji to hire me as its minister, if they found no fault on my side. After evaluation, the headquarters sent me a telegram permitting me to set up a Higashi Honganji propagation center (*fukyōsho*) in the Rafu Bukkyō-kai.[25]

Izumida consoled himself by regarding his situation as similar to Shinran's exile. It is unclear who Fujimoto was, when and how Izumida contacted him, or what made Izumida interested in Higashi Honganji. At any rate, the Rafu

Bukkyō-kai became affiliated with Higashi Honganji in December 1919.[26] In June 1920, the Higashi headquarters sent Abe Genryō (later, the second president of Kōka Joshi Daigaku in Kyoto—Kōka Women's College) to the Rafu Bukkyō-kai. His records state:

> In the autumn of 1919, Fujimoto conveyed Izumida's message to the Higashi Honganji headquarters. Izumida showed his desire to join our order because he had been defrocked by Nishi. Otani Eijō, our chief administrator at that time, accepted his offer and decided to mark Izumida's affiliation as the beginning of the Higashi Honganji propagation in North America. In the following year, I was appointed as minister serving in North America and left Japan at the end of June. After arriving in San Francisco, I met with the bishop of the BMNA, Uchida Kōyū, Izumida's brother-in-law, and heard his side of the story, then I moved to the Rafu Bukkyō-kai.[27]

Abe's mission was to supervise the setting up of a Higashi Honganji propagation center at the Rafu Bukkyō-kai and recognize Izumida's transfer from Nishi to Higashi; however, the exchange between Abe and Uchida remained unknown.

The Higashi Honganji headquarters swiftly affiliated Izumida to its order. It ordained him (*tokudo*) on May 27, 1921, after registering him at Tokushōji in Kyoto. Izumida became a full-fledged minister (*kyōshi*) on June 1, 1921.[28] The Rafu Bukkyō-kai came to be known as Higashi Honganji Los Angeles Betsuin on March 20, 1921, and the Superior Court of Los Angeles County recognized it on October 4 in the same year.[29] The headquarters appointed Izumida as *rinban* (custodian of a *betsuin*) of the said *betsuin* (regional temple) on May 25, 1922, and Kurita Ejō and Tsufura Shōsetsu began their ministerial service in Southern California.[30] Izumida, representing the Rafu Bukkyō-kai and Abe Esui, the chief administrator representing the headquarters, exchanged signatures agreeing with the establishment of the Higashi Honganji Los Angeles Betsuin and its bylaws. From that time on, the property of the Rafu Bukkyō-kai was placed under the abbot of Higashi Honganji in Japan. On August 25, 1922, Izumida became the first bishop of the Higashi Honganji Mission in North America.[31]

Whereas Higashi Honganji began propagation in Los Angeles, Nishi Honganji completed its consolidation. The merger between the Nanka Bukkyō-kai and the anti-Izumida group of the Rafu Bukkyō-kai led to the birth of the Nishi Honganji Bukkyō-kai in December 1917.[32] The ministers including Uchida, Jisōji, and Asayoshi who got rid of Izumida, placed a statue of Amida Buddha in the building and officiated at the inauguration service. The Chūō Bukkyō-kai, which remained independent, received an image of

Amida Buddha from the Kyoto headquarters and organized its own women's association sometime in 1919,[33] though it later joined the Nishi Honganji Bukkyō-kai. After witnessing the emergence of the Higashi Honganji Los Angeles Betsuin, Uchida asked his headquarters on November 10, 1922, to elevate his *bukkyō-kai* in Los Angeles to *betsuin* status. In September 1931, his request was granted.[34]

Conflict over the Americanization and Japanization of Church Management

The attempts to consolidate three Japanese Buddhist churches in Los Angeles illustrate the democratization of a Buddhist institution in the United States, but simultaneously reveal the headquarters' desire to Japanize them. The failure to consolidate not only represented a shift in authority within a Japanese Buddhist organization in the United States, but also demonstrated the impossibility of applying Japanese customs to the American legal system. In Japan, the headquarters of a Buddhist organization (*honzan*) had the power over its affiliating temples and could suppress heretics (*ianjin*) often with the threat of the judicial system. The Nishi headquarters seemed to have applied this Japanese custom in the United States, although Izumida was merely disloyal to his headquarters.[35] At the same time, the headquarters failed to understand how the legal authority functioned in the United States. According to the bylaws of Rafu Bukkyō-kai in English (amended in January 1917), the president was defined as "chief missionary" (Article VII). There was no reference to the name "Nishi Honganji" at all. However, in the Japanese edition of these bylaws (*Rafu Bukkyō-kai kaisoku*), a *kaikyōshi,* indicating a minister appointed by the headquarters, was regarded as the president.

Although neither the Kyoto headquarters nor the BMNA office directly took Izumida to court, their prestige was damaged, as Uchida stood behind the anti-Izumida group headed by Jisōji Tetsugai. The BMNA reported the lawsuit in the *Beikoku bukkyō,* its monthly journal, and justified the headquarters' position by denouncing Izumida's misconduct: "This incident was caused by the Rafu Bukkyō-kai itself, thus, it had nothing to do with the Kyoto headquarters and the Department of the Superintendent [the BMNA's bishop's office]. During the reviewing process in court, however, the relationship between Izumida and the headquarters/Department of Superintendent was questioned, and chancellor Sonoda and superintendent [bishop] Uchida were summoned to appear. Unfortunately, because of their involvement, this event was seen as contention between Izumida and headquarters . . ." [36]

While accusing Izumida of mismanagement of the Rafu Bukkyō-kai, the BMNA denied the involvement of its headquarters in the lawsuit. But Uchida was inconsistent over his treatment of Izumida and Haraguchi, who was dismissed but not defrocked. In court, when Izumida's counsel asked Uchida why Haraguchi was still working in the same capacity as before at the Chūō Bukkyō-kai, Uchida could not give a definite reply.[37]

The consolidation of the three churches also suggests a debate over the authority of the board of trustees. As mentioned earlier (at the BMNA Ministers' Meeting on August 13, 1917), Sonoda and Uchida came up with the idea of terminating the board system and giving more power to the ministers as presidents of the churches. The headquarters attempted to bring to the United States the Japanese style of temple management, in which resident ministers had much more authority. On the other hand, the bylaws of the Rafu Bukkyō-kai stated: "Directors and Representatives shall supervise this institution and decide on important matters of this institution" (Article VIII).

It is, however, unclear how much Izumida understood the significance of the board system, because there seem to be other factors to explain the collisions between Izumida and Sonoda/Uchida. Izumida's excommunication was based on his conduct and had nothing to do with his understanding of the doctrine. First, Izumida held double standards regarding his relationship with the Nishi Honganji headquarters and BMNA. When Izumida came to San Francisco in 1902, he worked for the BMNA. The youth group and women's association of San Francisco Church welcomed him as a *kaikyōshi*. In 1903, he became the chief editor of *Beikoku bukkyō,* to which he often contributed articles.[38] After returning to Japan in 1904, Izumida proposed the establishment of a Los Angeles propagation center to the Nishi Honganji administrators. The headquarters, however, could not appoint him as *kaikyōshi* at the time because of the need for more priests on the Asian continent and the support given to the Japanese army during the Russo-Japanese War. Thus, Izumida came to California without official assignment (he was officially given the title of *kaikyōshi* in 1908).[39]

In Los Angeles, Izumida showed an ambivalent attitude to the BMNA office. On one hand, he continued to report his activities to the *Beikoku bukkyō* right up to the time of the Rafu Bukkyō-kai's split. He also participated in the BMNA Ministers' Meeting as late as July 1914. In the meantime, BMNA office paid him a monthly stipend of $25 for two years, in exchange for his reports on the activities of the Buddhist churches in Southern California. His stipend was afterwards reduced to $17.50 a month and eventually stopped altogether. Izumida was said to donate all the money he had received from the BMNA office to the Rafu Bukkyō-kai.[40] Despite his involvement with the BMNA, Izumida avoided establishing a Buddhist church affiliated with Nishi Honganji in Los Angeles. At the turn of the twentieth century, there was no Japanese Buddhist organization in Southern California. If the church's denomination had been strictly defined, it would have prevented Izumida from pursuing his objectives, namely to serve all immigrants by disregarding their affiliation to any Buddhist sect that they had held in Japan.

The second factor, which caused Izumida to collide with Sonoda, Uchida, and Jisōji, was their differences of commitment in the propagation of Buddhism in the United States. Because of Izumida's decision for permanent settlement in Los Angeles, he might have become conservative concerning his local position as president of the Rafu Bukkyō-kai and in the negotiations with the Executive Council. Izumida died in Los Angeles in 1951, whereas the latter group of ministers, who had graduated from prestigious universities in Japan and stayed in the United States for a while, returned home and became elite ministers. In other words, coming to the United States paved their way to the top of the administrative echelon. Sonoda became head of Bungaku-ryō (present-day Ryūkoku University) in 1905 and held the position of *kangaku* in 1911. Uchida stepped down as bishop in 1923 because of ill health, but served as the Director of Education and Propagation at the Kyoto headquarters between 1925 and 1935. Jisōji resigned from the BMNA in 1919 and later became a professor at Ryūkoku University.[41]

Third, Izumida's personality might have been the source of internal rivalries. Records show that the Rafu Bukkyō-kai's split had something to do with Izumida's character. On one hand, he hardly got along with the other ministers. He also lacked social skills and rarely complimented anyone.[42] Tsufura Shōsetsu who later worked at the Higashi Los Angeles Betsuin also had a difficult time with him.[43] On the other hand, the immigrants from Saga prefecture supported Izumida, because he also came from Saga. When various newspapers made derogatory statements about him, Matsumoto Honkō and other Issei pioneers from Saga stood by him.[44]

Although the evaluation of his character varied, Izumida tried to avoid legal settlements. On the advice of Fujii Sei, president of the *Kashū Mainichi shinbun* (*California Daily Newspaper*), who supported him during the lawsuit, Izumida visited the plaintiffs and asked them to nullify their court action.[45] Contrary to the accounts of the *Rafu Shimpo* and *Los Angeles Morning Sun,* Fujii displayed a different image of Izumida in his eulogy (printed in the *Kashū Mainichi*):

> Old master Izumida finally passed away at county hospital. He came to Los Angeles fifty years ago and started organizing a Buddhist gathering. On East

> Second Street, Mr. Kunita from Hiroshima had a restaurant where about ten elderly immigrants gathered and listened to Izumida's hopes for propagating Buddhism in America. This was the beginning of the Rafu Bukkyō-kai. They still remember that the first small building was built on East Fourth Street, which was later moved to Boyd Street. A couple years later, a bigger church hall was built between South Savannah and Second Street. While attending college, I often helped Izumida with translating Caucasian's lectures. The present Higashi Honganji Betsuin was founded much later. A carpenter from Saga was very kind to Izumida, and built the magnificent building at a low price, to which many of us gave him thanks. Through the years, the old master Izumida had a difficult life and I felt sorry for him. I knew for a long time that he couldn't buy food or take the train. Being at the age of eighty, he still suffered a lot from not having the daily necessities. Tears often blurred my eyes when I thought of him on a rainy morning or stormy evening. The achievements of the old master were never recognized and he died as if forgotten at county hospital. However, I should be happy for him because he fulfilled his life . . .[46]

Fujii was the one who advised Izumida to affiliate the Rafu Bukkyō-kai with Higashi Honganji; hence, his perception may have reflected favorably on Izumida.

The clash between the authority of the American legal institutions and that of the Nishi Honganji headquarters led to the establishment of Higashi Honganji on the mainland. After breaking away from Nishi Honganji, Izumida sought affiliation with Higashi Honganji, because it was difficult for the Rafu Bukkyō-kai to remain completely nonsectarian. By that time, other Japanese Buddhist schools had started their propagation in Los Angeles. Aoyama Shutai began to propagate the Shingon doctrine in the fall of 1912; Asahi Kansei held the first gathering of Nichiren believers in May 1914; and Isobe Hōsen started the Sōtō Zen mission in May 1922.[47] With all these new organizations maintaining sectarian affiliates, Izumida must have felt compelled to become part of a denomination, otherwise the Rafu Bukkyō-kai would not have been able to survive.[48] As a result, the opportunity for the eastward transmission of Jōdo Shinshū came as a surprise for Higashi Honganji, because it had not intended to advance to mainland United States yet.

Conclusion

This chapter has examined the cross-cultural experiences of Japanese Buddhist immigrants in the United States. The case study of Izumida Junjō brings out two points. First, the Issei Buddhists were not as harmonious as we have been led to believe by past scholarship. Conflicts between the clergy and laity and among Buddhist churches suggest that they were different in terms of vision and cultural practices that they had brought over from Japan and prefectural backgrounds, though these differences did not relate to doctrinal understanding. Second, this case study demonstrates the Japanese authority's ignorance of the American judicial system in the early history of Japanese American Buddhism. Izumida's winning the case not only set a stage for the Nishi Honganji headquarters to concede the autonomy of Buddhist churches in the United States, but also illustrated a new, modern development of Japanese Buddhism, such as the democratization of organizational management and the incorporation of a local body under the laws of a modern nation state.

Notes

This essay was initially presented in Section A215 (Asian North American Religion, Culture, and Society Group) of the 2003 Annual Meeting of American Academy of Religion held in Georgia, Atlanta, November 22–25. For assistance on this research, I thank Naomi Yamada, Shin'ichi Nishikawa, Shigeki Izumi of Otani University, the late Yūji Ichioka of University of California, Los Angeles, Junki Izumida, Nobuyuki Izumida and his wife, Bishop Akinori Imai, Shōju Okamoto and all other ministers, staff members of the *Rafu Shimpo*, and the Japanese American National Museum Research Center staff. For his helpful comments, I thank Brian Hayashi of Kyoto University.

1. Buddhist Churches of America, ed., *Buddhist Churches of America: A Legacy of the First 100 Years* (San Francisco: Buddhist Churches of America, 1998), pp. iii-v. For the personal record of Sonoda, see Sonoda Kōkun, ed., *Sonoda Shūye Beikoku kaikyō nisshi* (Kyoto: Hōzōkan, 1975).

2. Izumida Junjō, "Zaibei gojūnen no kaiko 1," *Kashū Mainichi shinbun*, April 8, 1949; "Zaibei gojūnen no kaiko 2," April 9, 1949; "Zaibei gojūnen no kaiko 3," April 11, 1949.

3. According to Izumida's memoirs, he held the first gathering at a Japanese restaurant on 115 East Second Street in early August 1904 ("Zaibei gojūnen no kaiko 4," *Kashū Mainichi Shinbun*, April 12, 1949). In January 1907, plans were made to purchase some land and build a Buddhist church on a budget of $25,000 ("Zaibei gojūnen no kaiko 28," May 10, 1949). On July 3–4, 1911, Izumida officiated at the church's inauguration ceremony on South Savannah Street ("Zaibei gojūnen no kaiko 46," June 1, 1949).

4. *Hompa Hongwanji Los Angeles Betsuin 1905–1980* (Los Angeles: Hompa Hongwanji Los Angeles Betsuin, 1980), pp. 37–38; *Minami kashū nihonjin nanajūnen shi: A History of 70 Years* (Los Angeles: Japanese Chamber of Commerce of Southern California, 1960), p. 242; *Buddhist Churches of America*, p. 239.

5. Kudō Etatsu from Sacramento and Ichimura Manjō from Fresno had already attempted consolidation before 1916 (*Hompa Hongwanji Los Angeles Betsuin*, pp. 37–38).

6. "Ranbō rōzeki naru rafu bukkyō-kai yakuin kai," *Rafu Shimpo*, September 19, 1916; "Rafu bukkyō-kai no chōsa," September 22, 1916; "Bukkyō-kai soshō jiken chōtei," September 27, 1916; "Bukkyō-kai soshō iyoiyo rakuchaku," September 29, 1916.

7. "Gōdō ni kanshite," *Rafu Shimpo*, August 25, 1917.

8. "Shinshū shozoku san bukkyō-kai gōdō kettei," *Rafu Shimpo*, September 5, 1917. However, the Chūō Bukkyō-kai was reluctant to consolidate ("Chūbutsu no rinji sōkai," *Rafu Shimpo,* August 14, 1917), though the Rafu Bukkyō-kai accepted ("Sanbutsu gōdō mondai," *Rafu Shimpo*, August 21, 1917). In the following week, the Nanka Bukkyō-kai also agreed, though not unanimously ("Nanbukkai no sōkai," *Rafu Shimpo*, August 28, 1917).

9. The minutes of the 1917 Ministers' Meeting was initially found in P3 Box 4. According to the new classification at the BCA Archives, the minutes are most likely found in Subject Files, Box No. 1.03.01, which contains the minutes of the annual Ministers' Meetings.

10. The dispute at the Rafu Bukkyō-kai was brought to the Los Angeles Superior Court as two cases: *Jisōji v. Izumida* (1918) and *Izumida v. L.A. Morning Sun* (1918). The first lawsuit appeared as Case # B55497. The plaintiffs were T. Jisōji, T. Hirata, J. Okamoto, N. Tōyama, Y. Hirai, S. Shigaki, and R. Suenaga. The plaintiffs' counsels were L. V. Stanton and Evans, Abbott, and Pearce. The respondent was Izumida and his counsel was J. Marion Wright. The lawsuit was filed on October 4, 1917, and the trial judge, L. N. Valentine, handed down the verdict exactly one year later.

11. Affidavit of Chiji'iwa Seidō on October 11, 1917.

12. Sonoda's "Records of Izumida's Examination," filed under Case #B55497.

13. The petition for writ of injunction was filed on October 4, 1917. Based on an affidavit on application for injunction pendente lite made by T. Hirata, the court issued an order to show cause and interlocutory injunction on October 5. Hirata made an affidavit upon application for order citing defendant for contempt on October 8. He requested the punishment to be meted out to Izumida because Izumida continued to perform religious duties. Kiyoshi Ono, one of the board directors of the Rafu Bukkyō-kai and who defended Izumida, made the affidavit on October 10. Izumida Suma, Izumida's wife, Mr. Shirahama, another member of Rafu Bukkyō-kai board of directors, and Izumida himself made the affidavits on October 11 to verify that Izumida had not acted against the court order issued on October 5. Chiji'iwa Seidō made the affidavit on October 11. Both parties agreed upon the stipulation to be set for trial on October 11. The court issued the vacating temporary restraining order on October 16 to remove the previous order released on October 5, which had prohibited Izumida from performing any religious duties. Izumida made the answer to respondent to petition for writ of injunction Izumida on October 17. Hirata made the affidavit for subpoena duces tecum on October 29 and submitted the financial records and documents kept during the second general meeting of the Rafu Bukkyō-kai to the court. The original trial date was set for November 8, 1917. In the trial, Fujii Sei, president of the *Kashū Mainichi Shinbun,* made the affidavit on November 19. The plaintiffs made an amendment to complaint on March 5, 1918, stating that the Executive Council fired Izumida on September 16, 1917, and in his place, Jisōji Tetsugai became the president of the Rafu Bukkyō-kai. The respondent made the answer to amendment to complaint on March 18 and rejected such a complaint. The plaintiffs made the second amendment to complaint to conform to proof on June 5, 1918, and stated that Izumida lacked the qualities and credibility of a minister; Izumida caused confusion to both the Rafu Bukkyō-kai and the Nishi Honganji headquarters; and the Executive Council fired Izumida from the presidency of the Rafu Bukkyō-kai. The respondent made the answer

to the second amendment to complaint on June 7 and rejected the amendment, because Izumida had not been under the authority of the Nishi headquarters. The Los Angeles Superior Court made the final judgment on October 4, 1918, but the *Rafu Shimpo* featured a headline on June 11, 1918, saying Izumida had won the case.

14. Conclusions of Law, 10.

15. The second lawsuit appears as Case #B57794. The plaintiff was Izumida himself and his counsel was J. Marion Wright. The respondent was the *Los Angeles Morning Sun*, Mr. H. Tanaka and his counsel, E. J. Fleming and B. F. Woodward. The trial judge, Leslie R. Hewitt, handed down judgment on September 24, 1918.

16. Quoted from the file of Case #B57794. For the entire translation of the newspaper article, see Findings of Fact, III in Appendix 2, "Time of the Downfall of the Anti-Consolidation Party."

17. Based on the summons and complaint for libel filed by Izumida against the *Los Angeles Morning Sun* and H. Tanaka, the defendant claimed the notice of exception of sureties and demand to justify in December 1917. Tanaka made a contract with a third party just in case he would lose this lawsuit and pay compensation. The court recognized Tanaka's action on December 24. Both parties agreed upon the stipulation to be set for trial on January 21, 1918. The notice of motion was delivered to Izumida on June 18, 1918, in which the respondent requested the examination of the minutes of the Rafu Bukkyō-kai board meetings, its financial records and the records of death certificates (*kakochō*), and donation envelopes given to Izumida. On the same day, the respondent made an affidavit under Section 1000 of the Code of Civil Procedure and stated that these records were also necessary to defend himself. The court delivered the notice of taking deposition to Izumida and Shirahama and requested them to report the financial situation of the Rafu Bukkyō-kai to the court by June 21, 1918 (order directing subpoenas to issue).

18. "Ihōsha no songai yōkyū hitoshi," *Rafu Shimpo*, August 16, 1918. The trial was held on June 26, 27, and 28, July 31, and August 1, 2, 5, 6, 12, 13, 14, and 15. Because the process of the trial is not recorded in the file, it is worth reading articles of the *Rafu Shimpo*. For instance, Izumida showed his anger at Asayoshi who had spread the rumor that Izumida was embezzling offerings ("Izumida hibō saiban," June 29, 1918). The newspaper reported on the testimonies of two individuals, Ono and Yamamoto, who defended Izumida, saying that there were no guidelines for ministers' receiving offerings ("Gogo kara no higi jiken kōhan," August 2, 1918). In the next day's edition, the *Rafu Shimpo* reported that three individuals, Tanimoto, Shigaki, and Nakamura, testified that Izumida had embezzled the offerings given to Asayoshi, after which Asayoshi decided to start the Nanka Bukkyō-kai ("Omoshirokatta gogo no kōhan," August 3, 1918).

19. Findings of Fact, IV in Appendix 2. Jacob Marion Wright, who defended Izumida in both cases, was known as the attorney for the Southern California Nikkei plaintiffs and defendants. He was the leader in their quest for civil rights and equality in the United States. For discussion of his work, see Bruce Allen Castleman, *The California Alien Land Laws* (M.A. thesis, University of San Diego, 1993), p. 57.

20. "Izumida sōseki hakudatsu," *Rafu Shimpo*, January 7, 1919.

21. "Sōseki hakudatsu tsūchō," *Rafu Shimpo*, August 6, 1919.

22. "Chōkaijōki dai shichijō, ichi" and "Chōkaijōki dai jūsanjō, roku," *Honzan rokuji* (July 15, 1912), pp. 115–6. "Jihō saisoku dai jūni shō dai sanjūgojō/dai sanjūrokujō," *Honzan*

rokuji (April 13, 1898), p. 84. The correspondence to Bishop Masuyama, dated November 16, 1931 (BCA Archives, Correspondence Files, Box No. 1.02.05, Folder 1931).

23. "Sonoda shi no hōkoku," *Rafu Shimpo*, February 24, 1918.

24. Izumida, "Zaibei gojūnen no kaiko 43," *Kashū Mainichi Shinbun*, May 27, 1949. After returning to Japan because of illness, Nakai continued to propagate Buddhism in English. He was outspoken and critical of the headquarters' efforts to transplant the style of Japanese temple management in the BMNA. See Gendō Nakai, "Beikoku bukkyō-kai no kiki," part 1, *Chūgai Nippō*, September 10, 1925; ibid., part 2, September 11, 1925. Immediately after World War II, Nakai refused to use the black market, only accepting food as part of the ration system, and collapsed. See, Kokusai bukkyō bunka kyōkai, ed., *Nembutsu seizan: Oshū nembutsu denpa shōshi* (Kyoto: Nagata bunshōdo, 2000), p. 17.

25. Izumida, "Zaibei gojūnen no kaiko 74," *Kashū Mainichi shinbun*, July 2, 1949.

26. "Rabutsu nishi kara higashi e utsuru," *Rafu Shimpo*, December 13, 1919.

27. Higashi Honganji internal file, "Reports from Overseas Propagation, including China, Taiwan, South Pacific, etc."

28. From the record of Izumida Junjō's registration, filed at Higashi Honganji.

29. The statement, attached to the bylaws of the Higashi Honganji Buddhist Church, amended on January 17, 1963.

30. *Shūhō* 235 (May 1921); 8, reprint, *Shūhō* vol. 11, p.464; *Shūhō* 237 (July 1921): 12, reprint, *Shūhō* vol.11, p.516; and *Shūhō* 248 (June 1922): 10–11, reprint, *Shūhō* vol. 12, pp.164–5 (Kyoto: Higashi Honganji, 1997).

31. Izumida, "Zaibei gojūnen no kaiko 79," *Kashū Mainichi shinbun,* July 9, 1949.

32. "Sakan naru honganji bukkyō-kai nyūbutsu shiki," *Rafu Shimpo*, December 9, 1917. In September 1917, the three Buddhist churches (the anti-Izumida group was seen as representing the Rafu Bukkyō-kai) agreed to consolidate and decided that (1) the consolidation committee would announce the merger of the three churches and designate the Nanka Bukkyō-kai as the tentative office of the three; (2) six selected committee members would calculate the debts of these three churches; (3) three committee members and Sonoda would draft new bylaws; and (4) Sonoda would have the authority to relocate ministers ("San bukkyō-kai gōdō seishiki ni seiritsu su," *Rafu Shimpo*, September 30, 1917). However, the members of the Chūō Bukkyō-kai suddenly opposed the plan, though the anti-Izumida group of the Rafu Bukkyō-kai and the congregation of the Nanka Bukkyō-kai went ahead. The Nishi Honganji headquarters eventually dismissed Haraguchi from the Chūō Bukkyō-kai, after the reconciliation between these two failed. He also resisted Sonoda's orders to leave the church ("Chūō bukkyō-kai no gōdō hantai kettei," *Rafu Shimpo*, October 6, 1917; and "Haraguchi-shi kaishoku saru," October 10, 1917). The displacement of Haraguchi from the position of *kaikyōshi* occurred on October 9, 1917, see *Honzan rokuji* (February 29,1918), p. 8.

33. "Chūbutsu butsudan tōchaku," *Rafu Shimpo*, March 27, 1918; "Chūbutsu fujin kaigi," May 19, 1918.

34. The eight-page letter of request kept in the BCA Archives, P3 Box 4. When the Higashi Betsuin in Los Angeles was established on February 24, 1919, the Nishi Honganji headquarters sent a letter to Uchida, encouraging him to expand his propagation territory to compete with Izumida. This letter was initially found in the BCA Archives, P2 Box1.

35. Within Nishi Honganji, the incident known as the "Turmoil over Three Kinds of

Religious Acts" (*sangō wakuran*) between the late-eighteenth and early-nineteenth centuries exemplifies the practice of its headquarters, which shows "the overriding concern with social stability and orthodoxy exercised by both the state and temple authorities during the Tokugawa period and the willingness of the temple to employ its bureaucratic apparatus to determine and suppress dissent." Dennis Hirota, *Toward a Contemporary Understanding of Pure Land Buddhism* (Albany: SUNY, 2000), p. 12. James Ketelaar depicts the incident of Ohama in Mikawa in the early Meiji period. A local Higashi Honganji priest, Ishikawa Tairei, was said to have instigated a riot, involving three to four thousand peasants and fifty-one priests, by opposing local bureaucrats who forced Shinto practices upon Shin Buddhists. Two priests, Tairei and his friend Hoshikawa Hōtaku, disagreed with the headquarters' suggestion to work with the local authorities. Eventually, the headquarters distanced itself from the Mikawa priests, and when the local authorities suppressed the riot, Tairei was executed. James E. Ketelaar, *Of Heretics and Martyrs in Meiji Japan: Buddhism and Its Persecution* (Princeton: Princeton University Press, 1990), pp. 77–86. Sixteen years after his execution, each priest was granted an imperial pardon and elevated to the status of martyr by the headquarters.

36. "Rafu Bukkyō-kai soshō jiken ryakuhō," *Beikoku bukkyō* 19/7 (1918): 17.

37. "Izumida kōhan," *Rafu Shimpo*, June 5, 1918.

38. For instance, "Beikoku bukkyō," *Beikoku bukkyō* 4/5 (1903): 21; "Rafu bukkyō-kai kaihō," *Beikoku bukkyō*, 12/3 (1911): 28–9.

39. Izumida, "Zaibei gojūnen no kaiko 3," *Kashū Mainichi shinbun,* April 11, 1949.

40. Izumida had further solicited financial help from headquarters, which instead gave him the honorary title of *shinju santō* on December 9, 1915 (BCA Archives P2 Box1). The affidavit of Ono Kiyoshi on October 10, 1917, testifies that Izumida came to Los Angeles alone without a letter of appointment by the Nishi Honganji headquarters. Ono's testimony includes Izumida's relationship with the BMNA.

41. Sonoda and Uchida graduated from Tokyo Imperial University, present-day Tokyo University, and Jisōji from Kyoto Imperial University, present-day Kyoto University (*Buddhist Churches of America*, pp. iv-v).

42. Matsumoto Honkō, "Ikeru Izumida Junjō-shi no omoide 3," *Kashū Mainichi shinbun*, December 4, 1951.

43. Telephone interview with Tsufura Satoru, the third son of Tsufura Shōsestu, on July 11, 2006.

44. Matsumoto Honkō, "Ikeru Izumida Junjō-shi no omoide 2," *Kashū Mainichi shinbun*, December 3, 1951; "Ikeru Izumida Junjō-shi no omoide 3."

45. Izumida, "Zaibei gojūnen no kaiko 79," *Kashū Mainichi shinbun*, July 9, 1949.

46. Fujii Sei, "Watashi no ran," *Kashū Mainichi shinbun*, November 27, 1951.

47. For the early propagation of Shingonshū in Los Angeles, see Richard Payne, "Hiding in Plain Sight: The Invisibility of the Shingon Mission to the United States," *Buddhist Missionaries in the Era of Globalization*, Linda Learman, ed. (Honolulu: University of Hawai'i Press, 2005), pp. 101–22.

48. A story that has been passed down in the Higashi Honganji Los Angeles Betsuin. This account is from the late Hirosumi Tsuyoshi, who served as its minister in Southern California for more than forty years.

PART 3

Race and Print Culture

The question of how Buddhism is presented and represented to the larger American public has been a concern of Buddhists from the beginning. This was, in part, because of an increasing awareness among Issei Buddhists that Euro-American audiences often became sympathetic (if not actual converts) to Buddhism through what Thomas Tweed has called "book Buddhism," or an encounter with Buddhist ideas through print rather than through Buddhist individuals. Representations of Buddhism thus became a central concern fairly early on. Bishop Yemyo Imamura of the Nishi Hongwanji writes in his preface to Ryusaku Tsunoda's 1914 book on Shin Buddhism: "[W]hat we have been teaching in our church and school is so little known, or, rather, to my great regret, has so often been grossly misrepresented to the public, that some of them often speak slightingly of our faith as if it were a form of superstitious idolatry, and our educational work as a system of bigoted nationalism that lays a stumbling block on the way of Americanizing our people."[1]

Other broad-minded Issei Buddhists shared Imamura's intense wish to convey the message that Buddhism was not a "superstition" but rather a "universal" world religion equal in stature and influence to Christianity. By so doing, they wanted to assert that Buddhism was not "anti-American," but rather in accord with certain progressive lines of American thought.

The two essays in this section deal with representations of Buddhism in the publishing world, especially as found in Buddhist periodicals, magazines, and books at the turn of the century and in the first decades of the twentieth century. They also address how such representations became crucial to the transmission of the religion, not only to the larger public, but also to American-born Nisei.

Buddhist cosmopolitanism—"Buddhist modernism" as Lori Pierce dubs it—coincided with the rise of periodical culture throughout the United States. Literacy rates were growing, and magazines had become cheaper to distribute. It was in this context that journals such as the *Light of Dharma,* which Pierce takes up in her chapter, and *Beikoku Bukkyō* and *Berkeley Bussei,* which Tomoe Moriya discusses, became central to defining Buddhism in the United States.

Pierce notes that not only were Issei Buddhists at the forefront of Buddhist scholarship (e.g., attempting to counter Orientalist European scholarship that denigrated Japanese Buddhism as a corruption of "original" Indic forms of Buddhism), they also pioneered publications that sought to portray Buddhism in a positive light. In this latter capacity, as Pierce notes, they began the effort "to engage in theological conversations with other Buddhists around the world, and to use the medium as a casual and inviting forum for the dissemination of their faith."

The cosmopolitan outlook of these Issei Buddhists meant that they advocated a "universal" Buddhism: in other words, the promotion of Buddhism as a world religion open to all people. They believed this to be true not only vis-à-vis Christianity, but also vis-à-vis particular Japanese sects. The journals that they published were influential: They "were circulated to individual subscribers as well as to public and private libraries, churches, and other Buddhist institutions creating a self-reinforcing and self-referential audience and cadre of experts who could be called upon to interpret Buddhism for beginners."

According to Pierce, *Light of Dharma,* edited by Nishi Hongwanji leaders Nishijima and Sonoda, was especially critical to the larger project of including Japanese Buddhism in scholarly, intellectual, and religious discourses about Buddhism in the modern world, and of promoting a vision of a "universal" Buddhism. (Although the editors of the *Light of Dharma* were Nishi Hongwanji leaders, they published virtually nothing on the sect or its founder Shinran.) *Light of Dharma* was also able to participate in a broader, global discussion of Buddhism because, unlike other more Japanese-specific periodicals, it was an English-language journal that featured and referenced other English-language journals published in South Asia or Britain.

Such periodicals helped to promote and to foster a growing number of what could be called "Buddhist intellectuals" among the Issei Buddhists. Tomoe Moriya takes up two such individuals—Yemyō Imamura and D. T. Suzuki—in her study of publication culture among the Issei and Nisei. She suggests that these intellectuals held five perspectives in common: (1) nonsectarianism, (2) a relative evaluation of any ethnic culture (an identification as Buddhist first, and ethnicity or nationality second), (3) internationalism, (4) interests in Buddhist ethics and social justice, and (5) a tendency toward Americanization. These Issei understood that publications served as the public "face" of Buddhism that would "transmit" the dharma as part of a new, global civilization in which Japanese Buddhists were critical for a non-European presentation of the religion. As such, they became leaders in "translating" Buddhism (both literally and figuratively) to the world.

Given this global outlook, the need to find language that could help transmit Buddhism in both sectarian and nonsectarian contexts became a vexing problem for Issei Buddhists. Moriya notes how D. T. Suzuki found in Zen to have a "universal" quality—suggesting in one of his writings that whereas Jōdo Shinshū and the Nichirenshū demonstrate "the creation of the Japanese religious mind," Zen was not essentially restricted to any particular culture and applicable to all circumstances. Although this view of Zen can be critiqued, it does point to an effort by early intellectuals to find elements of Buddhism that could transcend sectarianism, which was seen as an obstacle to true "universalism." Even journals such as *Beikoku Bukkyō* (Buddhism in America) that had a majority Jōdo Shinshū constituency, found it necessary to proclaim in its mission statement, "We believe that Śākyamuni Buddha is the incomparable person who discovered the Truth"—aligning itself with an universal Buddhism, rather than emphasizing faith in Amida Buddha, the core of its sectarian faith.

A major motivating factor for this kind of approach to Buddhism seems to have resulted from prejudices toward "Orientals" and "heathens" encountered by the Issei. Moriya notes how, especially after World War I and the plantation strikes, Imamura sought to address contemporary political and social issues in his books on Buddhist democracy and peace (1918) and on religious freedom (1920). In these books, Imamura drew on ideas of Buddhist "universality," "ethics," and "democracy" to suggest that Euro-American Christian civilization was not the only source for understanding "Americanism." Instead, Imamura defined Americanism as open religiously, ideologically (in the line of the pragmatism of William James and John Dewey), and culturally (as a mixed experience of many, rather than as a "pure" culture).

At the same time, Euro-Americans were starting to become more than just consumers of Buddhist publications; they were also becoming active producers of a new Buddhism. The growth of this neo-Buddhism, created by so-called English departments within Hawaii and mainland U.S. Japanese American Buddhist missions, suggests that the line between "ethnic" and "convert" was not as sharp as one might suppose.

As these essays by Pierce and Moriya help to show, Buddhist modernism was just as much a part of the Issei Buddhist universe and discourse as ethnic- and sect-specific temples. The study of these Buddhist periodicals and publications that, as Pierce suggests, "helped to disseminate [Buddhism's] particular form and ideology," can thus be seen as an essential aspect of the study of Buddhist modernism, one that shows the role that Issei Buddhist intellectuals played in establishing a transnational culture of Buddhist representation capable of serving multiple agendas, including the further "Americanization" of Buddhism.

Note

1. Yemyō Imamura, introduction to *The Essence of Japanese Buddhism*, Riusaku Tsunoda, ed. (Honolulu: The Advertiser Press, 1914), pp. 5–7.

5 Buddhist Modernism in English-Language Buddhist Periodicals

LORI PIERCE

In April of 1901, Kakuryō Nishijima published the first issue of the *Light of Dharma.* It began life as a bimonthly journal and was, according to its editor, a "religious magazine devoted to the teachings of the Buddha." The first issue commemorated the Japanese festival of Hanamatsuri and was designated as the "Buddha Birthday number." The cover recorded 1901 as the Buddha Year 2444. The front matter included an image of the Daibutsu, the large Buddha statue in Kamakura, famously painted in 1887 by the water color and stained glass artist John Lafarge. The title of the journal deliberately evoked Sir Edwin Arnold's best-selling paean to the Buddha, *The Light of Asia.* The mission of the journal was stated simply: to make known the dharma as the "universal law of nature." "The divine light of dharma will guide every suffering mortal to the Realm of Immortality and Peace."[1] Writing for an exclusively English-speaking and predominantly American audience, Nishijima informed his readers that "[i]t is a fact, now recognized by religious and scientific students in America and Europe, that the knowledge of this Divine Law is slowly, but surely, penetrating and permeating the sincere, deep-thinking minds of the West, and the time has now come for the Buddhists from the so-called Buddhist countries of the Orient to meet with the intellectual and spiritual demand of the Occident of the present age."[2] This statement, flattering to American readers but challenging to Asian readers, demonstrated the editor's vision that *Light of Dharma* would be a vehicle through which the dharma could be effectively spread from East to West.

The journal, published from 1901 to 1907 by the North American Buddhist Mission in San Francisco, appealed to a very specific audience: a small but growing number of Europeans and Americans who considered themselves to be Buddhists or who were sympathetic to Buddhism.[3] Nishijima's declaration, the image on the frontispiece, and the title of the periodical would have resonated deeply with an audience of white Buddhist sympathizers who were—by the early-twentieth century—a generation after Buddhism had been "discovered" by Western Orientalist scholars quite familiar with these tropes. Journals such as *Light of Dharma* had become a popular method of disseminating the tenets of the faith, philosophy, and practice to an enthusiastic, albeit perhaps naïve Western audience. *Light of Dharma* and other English-language Buddhist periodicals played an unusual role in the dissemination of Buddhism to the West. They propagated a peculiar hybrid faith—what I would call a "Buddhist modernism" that relied on the iconographic reiteration of the image and life of the Buddha, content that stressed doctrinal unity through a common catechism, the use of English as the vernacular, and an emphasis on the textual authority of Orientalist scholarship. The Buddhist modernism expressed in the pages of these periodicals can be understood as an attempt to lay out a common set of principles that could facilitate dialogue and discussion among Buddhist sects and between Buddhists and other religionists. Buddhist modernism de-emphasized sectarian difference by focusing on the life of the founder, the important texts, and the search for authentic religious impulse. Buddhist modernism was the search for common ground, the creation of a hybrid form of the religion that "existed everywhere and nowhere," but could be recognized by any member of the faith.[4]

Light of Dharma was not the first Buddhist journal in the English language. In 1888, Angarika Dharmapala began publishing a supplement to *Sarasavi Sandaresa* in English called the *Buddhist.* Nor was *Light of Dharma* the first Buddhist periodical published in the United States: The *Buddhist Ray* was published from 1888 to 1894, in Santa Cruz, California. In fact, between 1888 and the onset of World War II, more than a dozen English-language Buddhist periodicals were published in Europe, Asia, and North America. The most well-known of these enjoyed an extensive if not voluminous circulation throughout the United States, Asia, and Europe as they were read and exchanged within the small community of English-speaking Buddhists and Buddhist sympathizers. At least six were long-lived, relatively sophisticated in their presentation and appearance, and influential enough to garner the attention and contributions of well-known Orientalist scholars and Buddhist reformers and teachers.

As Thomas Tweed has suggested, the popularity of Buddhism in the United States can be measured by the "public conversation" that was carried out in periodical literature of the era. The rise of Buddhist periodicals was part of a larger increase in the numbers of periodicals published in the United

Table 5.1. English-Language Buddhist Periodicals, 1888–1941

Journal Title	Editor	Dates	Location	Other
Buddhist Ray	Hermann Vetterling/Philangi Dasa	1888–1894	Santa Cruz, California	First "Buddhist" publication in the United States
*Buddhist**	Anagarika Dharmapala Theosophical Society in Ceylon	1888–1892	Ceylon/Sri Lanka	English-language supplement to "Sarasavi Sandaresa"
*Buddhist: The English Organ of the Southern Church of Colombo**	Buddhist Theosophical Society	1888–1901	Ceylon/Sri Lanka	
*Buddhist**	Jinarajadasa (?) Young Buddhist Association	1901–1907	Ceylon/Sri Lanka	YMBA of Colombo
*Maha Bodhi Journal**	Angarika Dharmapala	1892–1933	Ceylon/Sri Lanka	Succeeded by *Journal of the Maha Bodhi Society*
Bijou of Asia	M. Matsuyama Buddhist Propagation Society (Kaigai Senkyokai)	1888–1899	Kyoto, Japan	Noted received by H. Vetterling in Nov. 1888† Merged with the *Orient* in 1899.
Buddhism: An Illustrated Review	Allan Bennett/Ananda Metteya	1903–1908	Rangoon, Burma	Assisted by J. McKechnie/Silacara
Zen: A Buddhist Magazine	Dwight Goddard	19**–?	Thetford, Vermont	
Light of Dharma	K. Nishijima Buddhist Mission of North America	1901–1907	San Francisco, California	
Buddhist Review	Buddhist Society of Great Britain and Ireland	1909–1922	London, England	First Buddhist journal in England; A. Metteya/Bennett served as editor for several volumes.
Buddhist Lodge Monthly Bulletin	A. C. March	1925–1926	London, England	The Buddhist Lodge was formed by a subset of "Buddhist minded" Theosophists. See C. Humphreys, *Sixty Years*.

Table 5.1. Cont.

Journal Title	Editor	Dates	Location	Other
Buddhism in England	"Journal of the Buddhist Society" (1924–1955)	1926–1943	London, England	Succeeded by Middle Way in 1943.
British Buddhist	Angarika Dharmapala; British Maha Bodhi Society	1926–1935	London, England	Succeeded by the *Wheel* in 1935.
Young East	International Buddhist Society	1925–1941	Tokyo	
Dōbō	The Organ of the Hawaii Federation of Young Buddhists' Associations	1900–1941	Honolulu, Hawaii	English-language copies of 1932 (February–July), 1933 (January) –1934 (March), and 1941–42 only.
Bhratri	Young Buddhist Association California	1932–1934?	California	
Berkeley Bussei	Young Buddhist Association California	1939–1960	California	
Buddhist World	The United Young Men Buddhists' Association of Hawaii; English section editor—Ernest Hunt (Bhikkhu Shinkaku)/Japanese section—T. Ono	1924–?	Hilo, Hawaii	Japanese title *Bukkyo no Sekai.*

This list is not exhaustive; rather it contains a rough chronology of Buddhist periodicals published primarily in English before World War II. It does not include periodicals that were strictly academic (*The Journal of the Pali Text Society*, for example); nor does it include journals that were more Theosophical or merely sympathetic to Buddhism as one of many spiritual paths or philosophical outlooks (for example, the *Monist*).

*These journals were most likely successors to one another that underwent name and editorial changes based on the shifting affiliations between the Buddhist and Theosophical societies in Sri Lanka.

†Richard Jaffe describes the *Bijou* as the "Arnold inspired, bimonthly, English language journal. Devoted to the spread of Buddhism in other lands." See footnote ten in Richard M. Jaffe, "Seeking Sakyamuni: Travel and the Reconstruction of Japanese Buddhism," *Journal of Japanese Studies* 30/1 (Winter 2004): 69.

States. Between 1865 and 1885, the number of periodicals published in the United States rose from 700 to 3,300; between 1885 and 1900 that number increased to 5,500.[5] Changes in postal rates made magazines cheaper to distribute, the expansion of the economy increased the size of the middle class, with disposable incomes for magazines, and literacy rates continued to rise. Tweed contends that the Buddhist vogue that overtook popular culture in the late-nineteenth century began with the publication of a translation of the Lotus Sutra from French that appeared in the Transcendentalist journal the *Dial* in 1844. Other Buddhist texts became available, translated from Pali, Sanskrit, and Tibetan by Orientalist scholars such as Brian Hodgson, Eugene Burnouf, and T. W. and Caroline Rhys-Davids. These articles stimulated a lively discussion about Buddhism as a "world religion" in popular European and American general-interest periodicals such as the *North American Review* and the *Atlantic Monthly.*[6] By the end of the nineteenth century, Orientalist scholarship had produced translations of Buddhist texts into English, French, and German in serial publications such as Frederick Max Mueller's *Sacred Books of the East.* Because texts were becoming so widely circulated, Buddhism was becoming more widely known outside of scholarly circles. Sir Edwin Arnold's *Light of Asia* (1879) was an international best seller, giving ordinary Europeans and Americans some access to Buddhist beliefs. Buddhism could now be the subject of lively discussions in daily American newspapers such as the *Brooklyn Eagle,* where in a twenty-three-year period a remarkable 287 articles and notes appeared on Buddhism.[7]

English-language Buddhist periodicals were a part of this trend. Many of the earliest periodicals with Buddhist content were the product of academic organizations, especially those interested in philology and translations, the Asiatic Society of Bengal's *Asiatic Researches* (1784), for example. The progress of research on Buddhist texts and traditions spawned academic organizations devoted to exclusively to Buddhism, most notably The Pali Text Society founded by Thomas Rhys-Davids (1882). These journals reproduced carefully crafted research monographs, and, even though they had Buddhist texts as their primary subject matter, they did not advocate or advance a specific theological or doctrinal position.

Light of Dharma and other Buddhist periodicals from the era were distinct from these scholarly journals because they were deliberately attempting to represent Buddhism in a positive light; they engaged in theological conversation with other Buddhists around the world; and they used the medium as a casual and inviting forum for the dissemination of their faith. These periodicals were produced by Buddhists for sympathetic audiences who were interested in expanding their understanding of the faith. *Light of Dharma* was unique among these because it was produced in the United States and because it was published and edited by the Nishi Hongwanji—Japanese Jōdo Shinshū Buddhists. Typically we imagine that religious institutions in immigrant communities primarily functioned to help immigrants adjust and acculturate. This theme certainly dominates the historiography of ethnic religiosity in the United States as well as the scholarship of Japanese American history.[8] Whereas it is certainly the case that Japanese Buddhist institutions in the early-twentieth century were centers of Japanese American communities, providing aid, assistance, and comfort to immigrants and their children, there is a neglected and more complex set of factors reflected in an enterprise such as the publication of *Light of Dharma.* In spite of the expense and difficulty of publishing a periodical, Kakuryō Nishijima and Shūye Sonoda, the two superintendent missionaries at the Nishi Hongwanji, undertook this unique venture. Why?

Perhaps the better question is why not? If the intention was to convert Americans to Buddhism, their efforts make perfect sense. After all, Christian missionaries had been plying their trade in Japan and other parts of Asia for generations. Why *wouldn't* Buddhists missionaries attempt to make converts in addition to caring for their countrymen and women? But was that the intention of *Light of Dharma?* Was its sole audience mainstream white Americans whom they thought might be potential converts? Perhaps *Light of Dharma* was an attempt to reach out to an American audience not to convert them, but to educate them about this new religion in their midst. Well aware of the American proclivity for racial exclusion and sometimes violent discrimination, many Japanese were anxious to cultivate good relations between white Americans and Japanese immigrants. *Light of Dharma* could then be seen as an attempt on the part of Buddhist leaders to educate Americans about Jōdo Shinshū Buddhist worship, practices, and belief. Yet, in the entire seven-year run of *Light of Dharma,* there is only one article on Shin Buddhism, and no more than a handful focused on particular aspects of Japanese culture or religious practice.

It is difficult to say why Nishijima and Sonoda took this task upon themselves, especially immediately after arriving in the United States. Based on what is known about the course of Buddhist modernism in Japan, South Asia, and North America at the time, I speculate here that Nishijima and Sonoda inaugurated the publication of *Light of Dharma* as part of the larger project of including Japanese Buddhism in the scholarly, intellectual, and religious discourses about Buddhism in the modern world. By the turn of the nineteenth century, new forms of Buddhism were emerging as the result of the interactions between Asian Buddhists and European scholars and sympathizers. European colonialism in the form of Orientalist scholarship meant that Buddhist texts previously unknown to the Western world were being uncovered and translated, revealing to non-Buddhists a new religion, which was as historically grounded and philosophically sophisticated as Christianity, Judaism, and Islam. For many Asian Buddhists the recovery and valorization of ancient Pali texts served as an impetus toward reform of moribund local institutions and forced them to think of Buddhism in universal rather than parochial terms. But Orientalist scholarship also meant that Buddhism was being redefined by non-Buddhists. What was starting to count as authentically Buddhist reflected the particular intellectual biases of European scholars. With an eye toward understanding "true Buddhism," they favored expressions of Buddhism that best reflected the life and words of the founder, Siddartha Gautama. Orientalist scholarship offered Asian Buddhists a two-edged sword: Textual translations and a focus on the life of the Buddha made Buddhism imminently comprehensible to Westerners who defined religion as practice and belief based on founders and texts. If Buddhism was an ethical doctrine articulated by a moral founder, then Buddhists were not heathens who engaged in immoral, idolatrous worship. In fact, Buddhist theology presented quite a sophisticated ethical program that could compete with Christianity, and because it appeared not to be overly concerned with superstitions such as heaven, angels, or miracles, was compatible with the scientific rationalism of the modern world. The positive attention Buddhism received by scholars and sympathizers helped Westerners accept and affirm Buddhism as a legitimate faith. However, this modernist approach undermined the spiritual authority of Asian Buddhists and denigrated the philosophical underpinnings of the entire body of Mahayana philosophy that was perceived to be a later and therefore less authentic expression of "true" Buddhism.

In Ceylon, Thailand, Burma and Japan, Asian Buddhists had to come to terms with a situation in which they both benefited from and were potentially harmed by their association with Western Orientalist scholars and sympathizers. The Jōdo Shinshū missionaries who arrived in San Francisco (and prior to that, in Hawaiʻi) were steeped in the progressive ethos of "new Buddhism" (*shin bukkyō*) and reform in Japan. They were understandably eager to add their voices to the global conversation that was taking place about their religion. Their participation in activities that were crucial to the construction of a modernist interpretation of Buddhism—youth-oriented organizations such as the Young Buddhist Association, intellectual projects such as *Light of Dharma*, and, more generally, the project of evangelizing America—suggests that this faction of Issei Buddhists were willing to grapple with the dilemmas presented by engagement with the West.

Buddhist Modernism in Japan

Buddhist modernism emerged in Japan at a time of remarkable change. The infusion of Western values, beliefs, and practices represented both a threat and an opportunity to revitalize moribund, insular thinking. While Japan struggled with modernization, Westernization, and Christianization, Buddhist leaders struggled to redefine the role that religious institutions would play in this new era. The Meiji revolution, which restored the emperor, began an era of religious reform and revival. Shintō, Buddhist, and Christian groups attempted to redefine religious roles and identities for a modern nation. Meiji religious leaders also contested which religion was the most appropriate for Japan, and which beliefs best expressed Japan's national spirit. Japanese Buddhist leaders were buffeted about. One decade they were defending themselves against charges of corruption by Shintō rivals; the next decade they were making a serious effort to defend themselves against Christianity, which was gaining converts and social respect as it established social service missions and supported reform movements. Pure Land sects survived the anti-Buddhist *haibutsu kishaku* campaign, but they had to accommodate themselves to this new modern Japan. This era of Japanese Buddhist history produced a number of reform societies and political groups, many modeled after Christian organizations, especially those in Tokyo and other urban centers. Intellectual groups debated the degree to which Western political ideologies should be allowed to influence Japanese society. Social reform movements at large stimulated the reform movements within Buddhism, some stressing interdenominational cooperation, whereas others pursued doctrinal purity. Buddhist groups thus also sponsored hospitals, ministered to prisoners, and provided disaster relief.[9]

Early in the Meiji era, Buddhist priests and scholars began to study Western philosophy and the relationship between Christianity and the state in Western nations. A few Buddhist priests studied abroad in Europe under the tutelage of Orientalist scholars and others undertook pilgrimages to South Asia, China, and India in order to reconnect Japanese Buddhism with its Asian lineage. In *Presenting Japanese Buddhism to the West,* Judith Snodgrass traces the network of connections that were established by these traveling monks, particularly those who represented Japan at the World's Parliament of Religion in Chicago in 1893. Snodgrass traces the growth of Buddhist modernism in Japan, arguing that Japanese religionists (such as the delegation sent to Chicago) were explicitly attempting to defend Japan and Japanese religion against Christianity and Western imperialism. These traveling Buddhists made important contacts with Buddhist sympathizers and Orientalist scholars. Bun'yū Nanjō, the first Buddhist priest from the Nishi Hongwanji was sent to England in 1876 to study with Max Mueller, helping to catalogue the Chinese Tripitika. Kōzen Gunaratna was sent to study Pali in Ceylon and made contact there with Dharmapala and the Theosophical Society. Henry Steel Olcott's famous journey to Japan in 1889 was instigated at the request Kinzō (also known as Kinza) Hirai. In spite of Olcott's perception of the trip—that it was part of his mission to unify the Buddhist world—Snodgrass argues that young Buddhist reformers used Olcott's trip and the work and attention of other Western Buddhist sympathizers to demonstrate "their shared concern with the value of the West in authorizing local initiatives."[10] In other words, Japanese Buddhists engaged in the work of reform and revival were interested in the international conversation about Buddhism insofar as Western Buddhist sympathizers were able to lend a certain amount of credibility to their reform agenda. The external force of Orientalist scholarship was as important as the internal forces in Japan in forging a *shin bukkyō,* Buddhist modernism in a Japanese idiom, an "Eastern Buddhism . . . a philosophical, rationalized, and socially committed interpretation of Buddhism."[11]

Yemyō Imamura was an exemplar of this modernist Buddhist outlook. Educated by these "New Buddhists," he was born and raised during these years of change eventually becoming a missionary in the West, serving over thirty years as the bishop of Hawaii Hongwanji. Yemyō Imamura was born in May 1867 the son of a Shinshū Buddhist priest.[12] After his mother's death, his father remarried Satomi Masao, also the child of a traditional Shinshū family. According to Tomoe Moriya, Imamura's education in Japan reflected the new sensibilities of the Meiji era. Nishi Hongwanji schools had adopted a liberal arts curriculum and even began educating nonministerial students. Many schools also adopted the study of Christianity and the English language.[13] Imamura attended Kahōkan, a private Buddhist school headed by his uncle, Ama Tokumon. Ama had studied a variety of Buddhist traditions and was among the Buddhist leaders to meet with Henry Steel Olcott during his trip to Japan with Anagarika Dharmapala. The school and the mix of students from a variety of Buddhist sects reflected his ecumenical outlook and broad philosophical idealism. There, Imamura was involved with progressive temperance and youth movements. He joined the Hanseikai, a temperance organization and helped to inaugurate the *Hanseikai Magazine.* The movement and magazine were independent, iconoclastic, and youth-oriented. They criticized Buddhist leadership, and as early as 1888, Imamura called for an organization of young Buddhists that would be nonsectarian and democratic and that would promote relationships between sects and independence of thought. "Buddhism is really a common property belonging to all of us, clergy and laity. . . . Instead of leaving preaching and propagation in the hands of the priests, we hope to see the rise of followers who are able to preach Dharma even while discussing politics which deals with the supreme power of the entire nation, and also while educating and propagating freely among men and women working with broomsticks and plows."[14]

Imamura attended Keiō University, a progressive educational institution founded by Fukuzawa Yukichi with the help of Arthur May Knapp, a Unitarian minister.[15] After graduating, instead of returning to his home temple to take over from his father, he taught school until his uncle persuaded him to become a missionary and join him in Hawaii, where Imamura continued his work with youth-oriented Buddhist groups. In 1898, he took up the leadership of the Young Buddhist Association. In June of 1900, the Young Men's Buddhist Association began publishing a periodical, *Dōbō.*

Imamura promoted the progressive spirit of modern Buddhism, including an effort to reach out to Euro-Americans in Hawai'i who were interested in Buddhism. As a prominent member of the largest ethnic group in Hawai'i, he cultivated personal relationships with his Hawaiian and white neighbors, inviting prominent citizens to Buddhist events. In 1921, Imamura established an English section of Hawai'i Hongwanji. The English department served the dual purposes of promoting Buddhism among Euro-Americans and English-speaking Nisei. The English department employed the services of white Buddhist sympathizers Ernest and Dorothy Hunt, who enjoyed a long association with Imamura at Nishi Hongwanji.[16]

Through the English department, Hawaii Hongwanji expanded its outreach on an international level as well. In 1929, after the visit of the reform-minded Chinese Buddhist monk Tai Xu, Imamura and Hunt founded the Hawaii branch of the International Buddhist Association.[17] Under its auspices, they published two journals, *Navayana* and the *Hawaiian Buddhist Annual.* These periodicals had a limited circulation but drew a variety of Buddhists into conversation with one another. The *Hawaiian Buddhist Annual* reproduced essays from prominent scholars and personal reminiscences from Japanese American students. *Navayana* published letters from anonymous "bhikshus" and the well-reputed Buddhist scholar Caroline Rhys-Davids.[18] These journals accomplished one of the goals Imamura set for himself when he began to write for the *Hanseikai Magazine*—promoting a modern progressive religious faith by organizing Buddhists from diverse backgrounds and facilitating their dialogue in print.

Buddhist Periodicals

Buddhist periodicals were an essential aspect of Buddhist modernism in that they helped to disseminate its particular form and ideology. More than that, these periodicals became the primary way in which Buddhist sympathizers could gain access to the theological conversations and debates that were helping to define Buddhism in its modernist form. Buddhist periodicals connected a global community of Buddhists, underlining their common identity. They appealed to lay practitioners, professional religionists and intellectuals alike because they often brought together a wide variety of materials, from poetry and sermons to sutras. These periodicals made English the lingua franca of global Buddhism, which in turn deepened the allure of Buddhism among English speakers. Buddhist periodicals were circulated to individual subscribers as well as public and private libraries, churches, and other Buddhist institutions. This created a self-reinforcing and self-referential audience and cadre of experts who could be called upon to interpret Buddhism for beginners. The periodicals are an important historical and research resource because they present one of the few points of access still available into the thinking of Buddhists in this era. They also delineate the intricate webs of interactions between Western and Asian Buddhists who formed the basis of neo-Buddhist movements emerging in Asia, Great Britain, and North America.

Not surprisingly, most of the English-language Buddhist periodicals issued at this time were published in the British Empire. The connections among British Orientalists, Asian informants, and Buddhist monks generated a wave of publications by Asian Buddhists such as Dharmapala and white Buddhist organizations such as the Buddhist Society of Great Britain and Ireland (1907–1926). Dharmapala's influence on international Buddhism in the early-twentieth century needs no reiteration here.[19] Buddhism in the modern era was nearly entirely dependent upon Dharmapala's ceaseless travel and advocacy. Long after the influence of Helena Blavatsky and Henry Steel Olcott had receded, Dharmapala continued his charitable and educational work in South Asia by constantly working his network of supporters in the West. He befriended Buddhists in nearly every corner of the world; his long-standing philanthropic friendship with Mary Foster, a part-Hawaiian heiress, scandalized some members of her conservative Protestant family.[20] His relationship with Japanese Buddhists studying in Ceylon was responsible in part for Olcott's speaking tours through the country. He was also well known to many of the prominent Orientalist scholars, garnering their respect in spite of his early association with Theosophy.

Dharmapala published the first English-language Buddhist periodical in Ceylon in 1888. Having come under the influence of the Theosophists, he worked for the society publishing and distributing their newspaper, *Sarasavi Sandaresa.* In 1888, he collected some money from friends, enlisted the help of a native English speaker and began publishing the *Buddhist.*[21] It was only published for a few years, but it was the direct predecessor of the longest continually published Buddhist periodical, *Maha Bodhi.* Founded as the *Journal of the Maha Bodhi Society, Maha Bodhi* was the model for all subsequent English-language Buddhist publications. The journal reproduced speeches, textual translations, and sermons; reported on news of the Buddhist world; and solicited contributions from an eclectic mix of Asian Buddhists and Western Buddhist sympathizers. Dharmapala's extensive international contact among lay practitioners, Buddhist monks, and Orientalist scholars made it possible for *Maha Bodhi* to publish material by everyone from Thomas Rhys-Davids to D. T. Suzuki.

Dharmapala's prominence and the centrality of Ceylon for Theosophists and other Buddhist sympathizers meant that Westerners who converted to Buddhism often ended up in Ceylon in search of the company of monks and monasteries. The earliest exemplar of this convention was Allan Bennett, or Allan Bennett Macgregor (1872–1923).[22] Bennett became interested in magic and esoteric practices as a young man. After reading *Light of Asia,* he traveled to Ceylon where he studied yoga and then to Burma where he studied Pali. He became a bhikkhu and took the name Ananda Metteya. While in Rangoon, Bennett followed the example of Dharmapala and founded the International Buddhist Society. He was especially interested in founding an order of English-speaking Buddhist monks who, after being trained in South Asia, could be sent back to England as missionaries. Bennett began publishing *Buddhism: An Illustrated Review* in 1903, only three years after he left England for Asia. The journal was a one-man operation and without staff support and adequate funding, and with an inefficient local postal service, the project was difficult. He harangued his subscribers to send in contributions and complained about the postal regulations that made the distribution of his journal in the United States so difficult. Through his contact with Charles Lanman, a professor of Sanskrit at Harvard and a member of the Pali Text Society, he hired an agent, Albert Edmunds, also a fellow Buddhist sympathizer, to help promote and distribute the journal in North America. Bennett enjoyed a great deal of prestige as a white European Buddhist convert living in South Asia. Dharmapala was a frequent contributor to the journal, as was Paul Carus. He regularly ran news of the Buddhist world including updates on the work of Japanese Buddhist missionaries in the United States. Eventually the strain of the work proved to be too much for Bennett. Even after enlisting the help of J. F. McKechnie, another British expatriate and Buddhist convert who was given the dharma name Silacara, Bennett eventually gave up on the review and returned to England. The International Buddhist Society in Rangoon continued on without him and for many years published another English-language Buddhist periodical, *Young East* (1925–1941), which enjoyed wide distribution in Asia.

Bennett returned to England as a highly regarded "expert" on Buddhism. His personal experience gave him a certain degree of cultural cache—the Buddhist name, the robes, the actual experience of living in Burma and Ceylon, and his knowledge, however limited, of Pali. He made frequent contributions to many Buddhist periodicals, especially in the form of sermons, and later compiled a book, *An Outline of Buddhism, or Religion of Burma.* Bennett was also a principal inspiration to the founders of the Buddhist Society of Great Britain and England (1907–1926), the first Buddhist promotion society in England, which went on to publish the first English-language Buddhist periodical in Great Britain, the *Buddhist Review.* Bennett may have been an inspiration, but T. W. Rhys-Davids, the Orientalist scholar and translator, gave the group a degree of gravitas. The division between those who approached Buddhism from the distance of scholarship and those who were more interested in some form of Buddhist practice or belief accounts for the formation of several splinter groups and their attendant newsletters, bulletins, and magazines.[23]

As with Bennett's earlier *Illustrated Review,* the *Buddhist Review* (which Bennett also helped to edit) traded on the contacts between members of Buddhist circles around the world and published and reprinted articles by Paul Carus, the Rhys-Davids's Dharmapala, D. T. Suzuki, and paid special attention to news of the Buddhist world, particularly work in Europe and the British Empire. The review published extensive scholarly book reviews, adding to the knowledge base of sympathizers and converts by digesting the latest scholarly works. It tended to reflect a more scholarly approach to Buddhism, as well as some of the academic prejudices of Orientalist scholarship. Its statement of purpose functioned as a no trespassing sign: "No encouragement is given to the practice of occultism, mystery or thaumaturgy. Buddhism is a world religion, the guiding philosophy of one-third of the human race. It is simple, easily comprehended, and appeals to all mankind, high or low."[24] Theosophists and other New Thought devotees would find little to their tastes in the pages of the *Review.*

A review of Ryūsaku Tsunoda's monograph *The Essence of Japanese Buddhism* (introduction by Yemyō Imamura) revealed another strong Orientalist bias. The review dismissed the book as follows:

> The above quotations may suffice to give some idea as to what this Japanese cult really means. The Buddha has become a deity to be worshipped; there is a sort of heaven where the dearest saint unites with him very briefly, and then returns to earth on a mission of mercy; light and mercy are constantly flowing into the world from the Buddha's personality . . . All this is very interesting, and is told us with much of the well-known Japanese charm and sweetness. It may, as a system of culture, produce much that is worthy and beautiful. But assuredly it is not Buddhism.[25]

The review notes and praises the work of Japanese Buddhist missionaries and monks, but it gives special attention to efforts to "reform" Buddhism. "Count Otani, the *Times* informs us, the Abbot of the West Hongwanji Monastery at Kyoto, is attempting to restore Buddhism to its ancient purity, and to place it on an ethical rather than a doctrinal basis. An extensive propaganda is going on, not only in Japan, but in Korea and China."[26]

Obviously the review reflected the reigning stereotypes about the Mahāyāna as a later and therefore less authentic form of Buddhism. Orientalist scholarship had determined that which was retained in Pali texts was pure and authentic and remained a more credible source for understanding the "essence" of Buddhism. Buddhist periodicals reinforce this approach; this was not insignificant given the role that *Light of Dharma* was to play in an ongoing conversation both scholarly and practical and designed to appeal to a modern audience.

Light of Dharma

Light of Dharma was preceded by the *Buddhist Ray* as the first English-language Buddhist periodical in the United States. The *Buddhist Ray* was the brain child of one Hermann Vetterling who wrote as "Philangi Dasa," a name that can only be considered a "buddhonym," a Buddhist or Buddhist-sounding pseudonym used to give the writer an air of authenticity or to indicate special access to Buddhism or Buddhist cultures.[27] Vetterling was a former New Church minister and devotee of the teachings of Emanuel Swedenborg. Vetterling had either an overdeveloped sense of his own importance or a prescient view of the future of Buddhism in the United States. When he conferred upon the Newberry Library a entire run of the *Buddhist Ray*, he made clear that he understood the importance of his bequest: "I have refused a fancy price for this, wishing it to become the property of your library." Everything about the *Buddhist Ray* reflected Vetterling's idiosyncratic approach to life, religion, and publishing. The journal he vowed to publish alone for seven years was "devoted to Buddhism in general and the Buddhism in Swedenborgians in particular." The *Buddhist Ray* digested the news and articles from other Buddhist periodicals, but the largest share of the journal was often taken up with reprints of Vetterling's own *Swedenborg, the Buddhist.* The title notwithstanding, Vetterling's enterprise was not limited to, or even primarily about, Buddhist topics or ideas. It was a digest of a wide range of ideas on everything from vegetarianism and vivisection to vampirism. More Buddhist-tinged than Buddhist, the *Buddhist Ray* is nonetheless a significant milestone in the history of Buddhism in the United States. It coexisted with Dharmapala's earliest publishing venture and draws our attention to periodicals, events, and people little remembered or discussed in histories of Buddhism in the modern era. Vetterling received correspondence of thanks from the king of Thailand and his son after he forwarded them a copy of his journal. Chulalongkorn (Rama V 1868–1910) was well known for his efforts at modernizing Thailand and was very interested in the work of Buddhists in other countries. Vetterling also recalls an early English-language periodical, *Bijou of Asia,* "devoted to foreign correspondence regarding Buddhism."[28]

Light of Dharma was a remarkable publication for a number of reasons. Given the pressures of establishing a new institution, the fact that Sonoda and Nishijima took on such a time-consuming and expensive task suggests that they saw it as essential to their vision of Buddhism in the United States. *Light of Dharma* was a "powerful instrument in the modern field of religious thought, to the end, that mankind may be helped to higher levels of moral excellence and intellectual force."[29] When Tetsuei Mizuki, the second superintendent of the Buddhist mission, returned to Japan, Nishijima lauded him and his accomplishments by noting his two goals for the North American Buddhist Mission: "In San Francisco, Mizuki . . . labored to accomplish two ends—first to supply Japanese Buddhist with not only a religious home, but a social home for Japanese boys . . . and second to preach the gospel of the Buddha to English speaking people, with the hope that the ethics and philosophy of the founder of Buddhism might find lodgment in their hearts and minds."[30]

In order to accomplish the goal of preaching the gospel of the Buddha to the English-speaking world, *Light of Dharma* focused on a very specific set of ideas and doctrines. The content of each issue was meant to instruct English-speaking Americans and other Buddhist sympathizers about the basics of Buddhism and to inform them about the progress of Buddhism around the world. Many of the articles were reprinted from other sources; Nishijima and Kentoku Hori and other priests associated with the North American mission wrote articles specifically for the *Light of Dharma,* but the majority of the articles were translated from Japanese sources or were reprinted sermons, speeches, or articles originally published in other journals. This was a common practice in much of magazine publishing at the time; it was also common in the Buddhist periodicals. Articles reprinted in *Light of Dharma* were drawn from *Open Court* and Theosophical Society journals from around the world, Young Buddhist Association journals and newsletters, and *Maha Bodhi.*

The editors of *Light of Dharma* tended to reprint articles that focused on a relatively narrow range of Buddhist theological topics. As an educational text, *Light of Dharma*'s students would have learned a Buddhist catechism that stressed the Four Noble Truths and the Eightfold Path, ethical behavior from a Buddhist point of view, and a very general explanation of Buddhist sectarianism. Contributors to *Light of Dharma,* particularly Buddhist sympathizers and converts, stressed the importance of the Buddha and retold the story of Buddha's path to enlightenment in sermons and speeches. The Buddha was frequently compared with Christ; readers were instructed that both were men who had rejected the common wisdom of their time and struck out on their own path. The Buddha's path to enlightenment was not a miraculous legend; a reasonable person could expect to follow the Buddha's example and become enlightened as well. There were no miracles, no vision, nothing extraordinary or extrasensory. Unlike salvation, enlightenment was a rational, achievable experience.

Each year, the April issue was designated "the Buddha number," a commemoration of the Japanese holiday of Hanamatsuri that honors the birth and life of the Buddha. At least in print, the celebration is never associated with Japanese rituals. Instead, readers of *Light of Dharma* were instructed that the holiday commemorates the birth of the Buddha, just as Christmas commemorates the birth of Christ. The Buddha's birthday became an occasion for community celebration and gathering in many modernist *sanghas;* in London, in 1911, the Buddhist Society of Great Britain and Ireland hosted a gathering of 300–400 people on the occasion of Buddha day.[31]

Readers of the *Light of Dharma* would not have garnered a very thorough understanding of the content of Mahāyāna doctrine; only two articles attempted to explain the subtleties of Mahāyāna philosophy or the history of philosophy necessary to understand it. D. T. Suzuki described the Mahāyāna as part of the natural course of development of Buddhism as it moved out of India and began to "assimilate all the other religious systems which it might come in contact, and which were worth assimilating because they answered more or less the needs of the human heart." Buddhism evolved from a system of ethical principles to something more complex. "Buddhism ceased to be an ethnic system pure and simple; it took in some religious and philosophical elements which were not entirely free from superstition and symbolism. This departure as it were from the traditional path marks the beginning of the so-called Mahayana."[32]

Nishijima edited the first year of *Light of Dharma* but he was sent back to Japan in 1902, and the quality of the journal rapidly declined.[33] It is not clear who took an active part in editing the periodical after this. No other editor was ever specifically named. By volume four it seems that there was not a consistent hand at the helm. There were more editorial mistakes; volume five was entirely incorrectly labeled and the issues were rife with spelling errors. In the later issues, the content was considerably thinner and less interesting. There appear to have been distribution problems as well; the library of the University of California at Berkeley, which either subscribed or was given gratis copies of *Light of Dharma,* clearly was not receiving its issues in a timely fashion. Issues published in 1905 were sometimes two months late.

It could be that others did not have the command of the English language necessary to carry on with the work, or that few others had the enthusiasm or time for the project. As the Hongwanji grew, it clearly would have been more and more difficult to keep up with a laborious and difficult project that included soliciting and reprinting articles, managing the subscriptions, and overseeing finances and the actual production and distribution on a regular basis. *Light of Dharma* began as a bimonthly periodical, producing six volumes a year; beginning with volume three in 1903, it moved to a quarterly publication schedule publishing in April, July, October, and January.

The death knell for *Light of Dharma* sounded in April 1906. The April issue was, according to the editor, ready for distribution when the earthquake hit on the morning of the April 18. The editorial in the January 1907 issue indicates their distress:

> We had all ready for issue the April number when the fire took place, but nothing of it was left but the ashes when the fire was over. We have been doing our best to resume the work of the mission in all its branches since the disaster but it has taken a longer time than we expected to do all this. We urgently hope that our readers will continue their sympathetic support of our work in the time to come as they have in the past and that they will assist us to build a permanent home in the new San Francisco for the teachings of our lord Buddha . . ."[34]

Three more journals were issued in 1907, after which *Light of Dharma* quietly folded. *Light of Dharma* was not the last English-language Buddhist periodical published during this era; nor was it the only one published by groups affiliated with Nishi Hongwanji. In fact, with the exception of the *Buddhist Ray,* every other Buddhist periodical published in the United States during this time period was produced by a Jōdo Shinshū church or a group affiliated with a Jōdo Shinshū church. Hawaii Hongwanji published *Dobo,* the organ of the Young Buddhist Association and the longest continually published Buddhist publication in the United States before World War II.[35] *Dōbō* (1900–1941), *Berkeley Bussei* (1939–1942), *Bhratri* (1932–1935), and *Pacific World* (1925–1928) all focused on the Nisei generation. As American-born native English speakers, the Nisei faced a special set of challenges that, ironically, the modernist tradition reflected in Buddhist periodicals were uniquely situated to address. Because English was their native language, the modernist idiom suited their needs. Having grown up Buddhist in a Christian America, some Nisei developed a sense of inferiority about their Buddhist heritage, so Buddhist periodicals promoting white converts as exemplars of the future universal, nonsectarian Buddhism, gave Nisei men and women role models who helped defend their faith.

Conclusion

A single epigraph framed each issue of *Light of Dharma,* a quotation from Paul Carus's *Gospel of the Buddha.* It reads, in part: "The Dharma of the Tathagata does not require a man to go into homelessness or to resign the world . . . the Dharma of the Tathagata requires every man to free himself from the illusion of self, to cleanse his heart, to give up his thirst for pleasure and lead a life of righteousness." From beginning to end, the editors of *Light of Dharma* sought to convey to its audiences an idealized Buddhist universalism, a utopian hope for Buddhist unity and doctrinal symmetry based on a single, reasonable theology. The religious community envisioned by these texts was simple and organized around the essential truth of the Dharma of the Tathāgata, easily adopted and practiced by ordinary human beings. The reality of religious faith was quite a bit more complicated. The unacknowledged racialization of Buddhism through the erasure of Asian culture and implicit denigration of Asian Buddhist practitioners along with increasing levels of overt discrimination against the Japanese community in the United States made this picture a utopian fantasy. The fact that *Light of Dharma* folded on the eve of the signing of the Gentleman's Agreement is a coincidence, but significant nonetheless. The response of Japanese Buddhist priests was a notable shift, away from the optimistic project of conversion and persuasion toward self-protection and isolation. As the Japanese community grew, racist discrimination against the community flourished. Buddhism came under attack by politicians, community leaders, and ordinary citizens as "Mikado worship," a suspicious devotion to the emperor of

Japan. No amount of good press could surmount the intransigent bigotry of white Americans. Even Japanese Christians were suspect—witness a 1923 campaign to keep a Christian Church from being built in Hollywood on the grounds that the Japanese were "taking over."[36] The editors of *Light of Dharma* struggled valiantly in the face of insurmountable opposition against even the most modest of their aims.

What do these periodicals tell us and what is their value in the historiography of Buddhism in the United States? English-language Buddhist periodicals function as both "text" and "Text." In addition to their value as a chronicle of the transmission of Buddhism to the West, and as a location of primary documents worth remembering, studying, analyzing, and interpreting (text), these journals are also a site of intercultural exchange and interaction. Buddhist modernism was forged in the pages of these journals; what they said, what they left out, what was valued, what was disparaged (Text). Little work has been done on the Buddhist theology that was written in these journals. Existing in a liminal space between actual practice and academic theorizing, the sermons, poems, songs, letters, and discourses on the basics of Buddhist doctrine were a negotiation between tradition and modernity, between East and West. The tension between the Japanese Buddhist devotion to Shinran and the virtual silence in *Light of Dharma* about anything pertaining to Shinran or the *Lotus Sutra* is both heartbreaking and puzzling. If the aim of the editors was to convert white Americans to Buddhism, clearly they did not intend to convert them to any form of Shin Buddhism. The fact that *Light of Dharma* was "devoted to the teachings of the Buddha" and not Shinran or Hōnen indicates that for these Japanese missionaries the priority was to promote a universalistic "neutral" Buddhism unencumbered by too close an association with Japanese culture. The Buddhism presented in *Light of Dharma* reflected a modernist bias favoring the ostensible objectivity of Orientalism over the messy subjectivity of Asian Buddhisms.

These Texts also reflect yet another dynamic of Orientalism: intercultural mimesis and prestige exchange. On the one hand, white Western converts to Buddhism were prized and celebrated because they demonstrated the superiority of Buddhism, or at least its ability to appeal to modern, rational Westerners. White Buddhist converts were a source of pride for Asian Buddhists in the same way as "native" converts were a source of pride for Christian missionaries. White converts demonstrated the compatibility of Buddhism with the Western temperament. On the other hand, white Buddhist converts garnered greater authenticity by traveling to Asia, studying with real monks and living in real monasteries, learning a real Buddhist language, and acquiring a real Buddhist name. Hermann Vetterling adopted the pseudonym Philangi Dasa to assert his status as a genuine interpreter of Buddhism. Who, after all, would listen to a Buddhist named Hermann? Sister Sanghamitta/Marie de Souza Canavarro adopted a similar strategy; Allan Bennett/Ananda Mettya and James McKechnie/Silacara were able to trade on their experiences traveling and living in Buddhist cultures to consolidate their identity as authentic Buddhists. Buddhism in this modernist idiom relied on uneven exchanges of prestige between white and Asian Buddhists.

Buddhist periodicals as Texts also draw our attention to the narrative quality of identity construction within a religious context. White converts and sympathizers such as Bennett quite literally created their Buddhist identity in public, and largely through the medium of text. In the pages of these Buddhist periodicals, white and Asian Buddhists exchanged their thoughts about Buddhism as well as communicated their sense of what it meant to be Buddhist. For example, although the modernist idiom is dominated by the idea of Buddhism as a rational faith, a great deal of the language in Buddhist periodicals is devotional. Adopting Buddhism was an act of faith and functioned as a belief, even when they spoke of Buddhism as a rational religious choice. This seems contradictory, but it reflects the unfinished nature of Buddhist modernism in the early-twentieth century. The newness of Buddhism in a global context prompted converts and sympathizers to defend their faith. The fact that many of these modernists were also involved in Theosophy, Swedenborgianism, and other New Thought movements that were routinely disparaged by religious authorities may explain why they were so insistent on presenting their religious choice as a rational one. Furthermore, Buddhist modernists insisted on the religious nature of their beliefs, but in a way that matched a contemporary sensibility. In order for Buddhism to be taken seriously, Buddhist modernists stressed the logical, even psychological nature of the Dharma as well as its clear moral imperatives. To be a Buddhist, particularly for white converts, was to walk a knife's edge between rationalism and faith. Both the written texts and the act of writing in public provided a means to negotiate this delicate balancing act.

These Texts can act as important tools in our interpretive arsenal, especially because they clearly demonstrate the degree to which Issei Buddhism traded on the tropes of modernism and used them as evangelizing tools. Buddhist periodicals reflected the larger world of connections and interrelationships that formed the foundation of a universal Buddhist modernism.

Notes

1. "Light of Dharma: A Journal," *Light of Dharma* 1/1 (April, 1901).
2. "Light of Dharma: A Journal," *Light of Dharma* 1/1 (April, 1901).

3. In his description of Americans who were interested in Buddhism in the Victorian era, Thomas Tweed makes a critical distinction between those few who converted to Buddhism and those who possessed Buddhist sympathies. See Thomas A. Tweed, "Nightstand Buddhists and Other Creatures: Sympathizers, Adherents, and the Study of Religion," in *American Buddhism: Methods and Findings in Recent Scholarship,* Duncan Ryuken Williams and Christopher S. Queen, eds. (Surrey, U.K.: Curzon Press, 1999), pp. 71–90.

4. Perhaps the most cogent description of Buddhist modernism is Donald Lopez's introduction to *A Modern Buddhists Bible: Essential Readings from East and West* (Boston: Beacon Books, 2002). It is from him that I borrow this evocative phrase.

5. Frank Luther Mott, *History of American Magazines, Vol. III 1865–1885* (Cambridge, Mass.: Harvard University Press, 1957), pp. 5, 11.

6. See Thomas A. Tweed, ed., *Contacts and Exchanges in Print Culture: Encountering Buddhism in U.S. Periodicals, 1844–1903, Vol. 1 Buddhism in the United States, 1840–1925* (London: Ganesha Publishing Ltd, 2004).

7. Thomas A. Tweed, introduction to *Contacts and Exchanges in Print Culture* (London: Ganesha Publishing Ltd, 2004), p. xviii.

8. For most of the twentieth century, sociological studies dominated the study of Japanese American Buddhism. As such, they reiterate the prevailing paradigms of immigrant assimilation. The most well-known is Tetsuden Kashima, *Buddhism in America: The Social Organization of an Ethnic Religious Institution* (Westport, Conn.: Greenwood Press, 1977). Only recently has there been work that either challenged the immigrant assimilation paradigm or presented a transnational analysis or perspective. See Brian Hayashi, *For the Sake of Our Japanese Brethren: Assimilation, Nationalism, and Protestantism among the Japanese of Los Angeles, 1895–1942* (Stanford, Calif.: Stanford University Press, 1995).

9. On Buddhist reform and trans-sectarian movements, see James Ketelaar, *Of Heretics and Martyrs in Meiji Japan: Buddhism and Its Persecution* (Princeton: Princeton University Press, 1990). See also Kiba Akeshi, "Tradition and Reform in Modern Japanese Buddhism," *Zen Buddhism Today: Annual Report of the Kyoto Zen Symposium* 13 (1996): 27–38.

10. Judith Snodgrass, *Presenting Japanese Buddhism to the West: Orientalism, Occidentalism, and the Columbian Exposition* (Chapel Hill: University of North Carolina Press, 2003), p. 155.

11. Snodgrass, *Presenting Japanese Buddhism to the West,* p. 115.

12. Biographical information is drawn from Tomoe Moriya, *Yemyo Imamura: Pioneer American Buddhist* (Honolulu: Buddhist Study Center Press, 2000).

13. Moriya, *Yemyo Imamura,* p. 7.

14. Ibid., p. 5.

15. Ibid., p. 24.

16. Ernest and Dorothy Hunt were typical white Buddhist sympathizers, with a longstanding association with the Japanese American community. After Imamura's death, they had a falling out with the leadership of Nishi Hongwanji and spent the rest of their lives as members of the Soto Zen sect in Honolulu. See Louise Hunter, *Buddhism in Hawai'i: Its Impact on a Yankee Community* (Honolulu: University of Hawai'i Press, 1971).

17. English language sources on Tai Xu are limited. For a brief note on Tai Xu and the International Buddhist Association, see Holmes Welch, *The Buddhist Revival in China* (Cambridge, Mass.: Harvard University Press, 1968), p. 56. See also, Don A. Pittman,

"The Modern Buddhist Reformer T'ai Hsu on Christianity," *Buddhist Christian Studies* 13 (1993): 71–83.

18. The *Navayana* was a mimeographed periodical edited by Ernest Hunt. The American Religions Collection at the University of California, Santa Barbara has retained several issues of the *Navayana*, which are irregularly numbered. Volume 1, no. 12 contains a "Reply to Mrs. Rhys-David," a response to a letter in volume 1, no. 9, of which there is no copy.

19. See Gananath Obeysekere and Richard Gombrich, *Buddhism Transformed: Religious Changes in Sri Lanka* (Princeton: Princeton University Press, 1988) and Stephen Prothero, *The White Buddhist: The Asian Odyssey of Henry Steel Olcott* (Bloomington: Indiana University Press, 1996).

20. See Patricia Lee Masters and Karma Lekshe Tsomo, "Mary Foster: The First Hawaiian Buddhist," in *Innovative Buddhist Women*, Karma Lekshe Tsomo, ed. (Surrey, U.K.: Curzon Press, 2000), pp. 235–48.

21. Lakshman Jayawardene, "Versatile Anagarika Dharmapala—Communicator par Excellence," *Daily News* [Sri Lanka], available at: http://web.archive.org/web/20070210083136/http://origin.dailynews.lk/2002/09/17/fea04.html.

22. Allan Bennett was involved in magic and esoteric practices. He was orphaned, but later adopted in his adolescence by Macgregor Matthews who initiated him into the Order of the Golden Dawn. Thus, Bennett was sometimes referred to as Allan Bennett Macgregor. Several websites discuss Bennett's early life: See, for example, "Mountain Temple of the Golden Dawn: Allan Bennett," available at: http://home.earthlink.net/~xristos/GoldenDawn/biobennett.htm, accessed February 15, 2009.

23. The Buddhist Society of Great Britain and Ireland and the Theosophical Society between them begat the Buddhist of the Theosophical Society, the London Buddhist League, and the Buddhist Society. The British Maha Bodhi Society (1926) also contributed to the proliferation of groups and periodicals; between 1900 and 1941, England had seen the rise (and often the demise) of *Buddhist Review* (1909–1922), *British Buddhist* (1926), *Buddhist Lodge Monthly Bulletin* (1925–26), *Buddhism in England* (1924), and *Middle Way* (1924-present). It is nearly impossible to tell the players without a score card. Happily, one exists: see Christmas Humphreys, *Sixty Years of Buddhism in England* (London: The Buddhist Society, 1968).

24. *Buddhist Review* 1/1 (1909): 142.

25. "Review of Ryusaku Tsonoda's *The Essence of Japanese Buddhism*," *Buddhist Review* 3/1 (1915): 74.

26. *Buddhist Review* 2/3 (1910): 240.

27. Here I distinguish between a dharma name conferred on a student by a teacher and Buddhist pseudonyms that are clearly self-appellations.

28. *Buddhist Ray* 1/11(1888).

29. "Our First Volume Completed," *Light of Dharma* 1/6 (February 1902): 27.

30. "Editorial," *Light of Dharma* 1/5 (December 1901): 28.

31. *Buddhist Review* 3/2 (1910): 205. The appropriation of Buddhist holidays is an intriguing, and as yet uninterrogated aspect of the movement of Buddhism from Asia to Europe and the United States. Buddhist periodicals routinely covered the celebration of "Wesak," as a kind of pan-Buddhist celebration that commemorated the birth, death, and

enlightenment of the Buddha. We know little about how Wesak and Hanamatsuri, for example, were acculturated in a Western context.

32. D. T. Suzuki, "Mahayana Buddhism," *Light of Dharma* 2/3(August 1902): 80.

33. As of February 1902, no editor was listed.

34. "San Francisco's Disaster and Our Mission," *Light of Dharma* 6/1(January 1907): 20

35. *Dōbō* was published from 1900 to 1941. Although Otani University library in Kyoto has Japanese-language holdings from 1900 to 1912, the University of Hawai'i Archives only retains English-language copies from 1939 to 1941.

36. A handbill distributed in Hollywood at the height of the campaign deftly summarizes the sentiment of the community: "Japs! You came to care for lawns; we stood for it. You came to work truck gardens; we stood for it. You sent your children to our public schools; we stood for it. You moved a few families in our midst; we stood for it. You proposed to build a church in our neighborhood but we didn't and we won't stand for it! You impose on us more each day until you have gone your limit. We don't want you with us, so get busy and JAPS MOVE OUT OF HOLLYWOOD!" See William C. Smith, "Anti-Japanese Agitation in Hollywood," Survey on Race Relations Records, Box 23, Document 64, Hoover Institution Archives.

6 "Americanization" and "Tradition" in Issei and Nisei Buddhist Publications

TOMOE MORIYA

The 1990s saw several new studies on the subject of Buddhism in America, mostly categorizing the varieties of traditions according to their members' ethnic origins.[1] Even though every ethnic church/temple shares many cultural features of the ethnic group it is respectively associated with, neither its congregation nor its practitioners would necessarily be homogeneous, in part because of the process of "Americanization." This essay focuses on the varieties of discourses on "Americanization" (especially as articulated in Buddhist publications) and "tradition" (as the repository of ethnic identity and what was attributed as located in the Japanese cultural heritage) that appeared in early-twentieth-century America. Rather than focus on social structures (as most studies on the "Americanization" of Buddhism do), I highlight the doctrinal dimension of the dissemination of the Buddhist teachings in the public forum of the periodical.

Reacting to the Americanization movement, which reached its peak during and after World War I, Japanese immigrants, especially Buddhists, searched for a way to articulate their position in American society.[2] Although the anti-Japanese campaign existed from as early as the first decade of the 1900s, the discourses contemporary with the Russo-Japanese War did not usually use the term "Americanization." Nevertheless, discussing these materials is fruitful for understanding how the pioneer Japanese Buddhists saw their mission in America. In other words, the goal of this chapter is not to judge the degree of the Buddhists' Americanization, but to analyze how they formulated the Buddhist teachings during its transmission to America. When referring to "tradition," on the other hand, I will be examining those discourses both around Buddhist terms—as such Amida Buddha, Shinran, "Other Power,"

Hongwanji (the Jōdo Shinshū mother temple in Kyoto), and Zen terms as disseminated by Daisetz Teitarō Suzuki[3]—and to a lesser extent, terms from Japanese culture as large. I will suggest that "Americanization" and "tradition" are not as antithetical as one might normally think.[4]

Studies on Buddhism in America: A Critical Overview

Here I would like to present an overview of previous studies on Buddhism in America to clarify my stance. When studying the Americanization of ethnic Buddhist churches, scholars usually focus on English-language propagation, church administration by lay board members, or ethnic diversity and the decline in membership of Japanese ancestry due to intermarriage. Naturally, these are important factors indicating the degree of organizational acculturation, but here, I would like to focus on Buddhist ideas rather than institutional developments.

In his sociological study on the Buddhist churches in the Sacramento area affiliated with the Buddhist Churches of America (BCA), Isao Horinouchi describes American Jōdo Shinshū as "Americanized or Protestantized Buddhism."[5] He illustrates, with a great deal of useful material, the institutional acculturation processes of establishing Sunday Schools and the Young Men's Buddhist Association (YMBA)/Young Women's Buddhist Association (YWBA), using the titles "church" and "minister," and installing benches in the temple halls—all of which basically followed the structure of the Protestant Church. However, I would like to contest the term "Protestantized Buddhism" because this definition uncritically assumes that Americanization and Protestantization are equivalent to one another. Collapsing these two processes into the former, merely because they resemble each other superficially, I argue can be more confusing than persuasive to describe a complex cultural process.[6] It is likely that, in part because Horinouchi does not include doctrinal issues within the scope of his study, his hypothetical Protestantization model lends itself easily to this too-simple interpretation of the phenomenon as such and hence does not really fit into the reality of the religious identity of the Japanese American Buddhists, nor the doctrinal reinterpretations that accompanied this process. In this sense, Tetsuden Kashima's 1977 study rightly criticized this approach for neglecting America's pluralistic nature in religious organizations: "the path along the narrow walkway toward only Protestantization is very limiting." David Yoo has approached American Jōdo Shinshū from a doctrinal point of view, pointing out that as a "variant of Japanese Buddhism," Shin Buddhism's "notions within Buddhism akin to 'salvation' and 'grace' as well as an emphasis on the laity lent themselves well to religious life in the United States."[7]

When dealing with ethnic diversity in American Buddhism, concepts such as Charles Prebish's "two Buddhisms" or Rick Fields's "divided Dharma" were introduced to distinguish between "white" and "ethnic" types of Buddhism, as the 1960s had seen an influx of the latter, creating a complex and diverse doctrinal and cultural landscape. Curiously, Fields admits the limitations of this classification with, for example, "largely Japanese American Buddhist Churches of America . . . [which] includes thoroughly acculturated fourth-generation Japanese Americans, as well as at least a scattering of white Americans." The question is whether the "divided" Buddhism model fully accounts for the Shin Buddhist churches affiliated with the BCA or the Honpa Hongwanji Mission of Hawaii or whether it merely states that ethnic Buddhists basically "lack the bent-for-enlightenment zeal of some white Buddhists." In this respect, it is interesting to note that for his part, Fields points out that "it is mainly white Buddhists who are busy doing the defining" in the ongoing discussion, concerning the trend of American Buddhism and "confusing plurality of Buddhism in America."[8]

Jan Nattier, on the other hand, coins the following terms in contrast to the existing "two Buddhism" typology: "import, export, and baggage." The first refers to "elite Buddhism" for the privileged, belonging to Zen or Tibetan groups; the second type, described as "evangelical Buddhism" that actively proselytizes like the Sōka Gakkai; and the last category is called "ethnic Buddhism" that functions as cultural/community centers in order to preserve their cultural identity. Richard Seager suggests another threefold typology of groups within American Buddhism: "convert Buddhists," who consist predominantly of Euro-Americans though including some Asian, African, and Native Americans; "immigrant or ethnic Buddhists," who are mostly Asian immigrants and refugee birthright Buddhists; and "old-line Buddhists," who, for generations, have practiced Buddhism in America such as the Asian Americans, particularly of Chinese and Japanese descent.[9]

These arguments are useful categories to bring to such diversity of Buddhist groups according to each one in terms of its identity and religious and social activities. Yet as long as scholars support the Protestant or dualistic/divided Buddhism model, the very real issue of the doctrinal Americanization of Japanese Buddhism is unlikely to be fruitfully discussed in the scholarship. Recognizing this, Lori Pierce points out the "significance and influence of Asian American communities in the development of American Buddhism" and describes the situation in the Territorial Hawaii as a "hybrid form" of Buddhism. Although it may not be "the largest and most racially diverse," as was the Soka Gakkai International that developed in the postwar period, the Shin Buddhist churches, both on the Hawaiian Islands and the mainland, included small numbers of local Euro-Americans who helped maintain the so-called English departments from its early stages of development, despite racial discrimination on the part of the dominant culture.[10]

What has not been fully discussed up to now is the acculturation of the Buddhist teachings in relation to social engagement. In spite of their century-old history in America, the majority of Shin Buddhist churches seem focused primarily on maintaining only their ethnic character rather than on encouraging their ministers and members to actively engage themselves in social problems, which is not always true of their counterparts in Japan. However, following works like Alfred Bloom's emphasis on social perspectives of Buddhist teachings in an American context, or the Project Dana of the Honpa Hongwanji in Hawaii that has been carried out for over a decade now, I would like to explore, from this angle, a Buddhist philosophy that has tried to deal with what actually has been going on in American society.[11]

There have been some recent studies on American Buddhism that have tried to deal with socially engaged Buddhism. In the United States, this new Buddhist movement, sometimes called "*Navayana*" or "*fourth yana*," consists most prominently of Euro-American converts who have "attempted to explore what it would mean to bring together social, political, economic, and ecological concerns with traditional Buddhist practice," due to a "reform-minded tradition in American religious history" that was influenced by the Judeo-Christian tradition. Yet, it was the Vietnamese Buddhist monk, Thich Nhat Hanh, who first introduced the idea of socially engaged Buddhism to the West during the Vietnam War in response to the great suffering of his people. He called for nonviolent action and attempted to transform the traditional Buddhism of that country into a more activist engagement in social issues.[12] Although the emergence of socially engaged Buddhism occurred in the postwar period, we might understand some of the Japanese Buddhist temples in prewar Hawaii and the U.S. mainland as earlier models of this kind of Buddhism, despite the fact that the term was neither invented nor used as such.

Nonsectarian or Sectarian: Interpretative Discourses of Pioneer Issei Ministers

In his historical study on Victorian Euro-American Buddhists, Thomas Tweed contends that the *Light of Dharma*, an English publication of the Nishi Hongwanji Mission, based in San Francisco, was of high quality and "exerted [great] influence." He also mentions their various connections with Theosophists, prominent contemporary scholars, and "several of the most influential American Buddhist apologists," who contributed to the magazine, not to mention Asian Buddhists such as Anagarika Dharmapala and D. T. Suzuki. Statistics of magazine subscriptions between 1901 and 1907 show us that the ethnicity of subscribers consisted of 97 percent non-Asians and 65 percent urbanites.[13] This clearly suggests a pointed connection between Euro-American sympathizers and Asian Buddhists. Moreover, only six years after the World's Parliament of Religions held in 1893, the first Japanese Shin Buddhist ministers arrived in San Francisco. Considering the racist campaign and the media's agitation against the wave of Japanese immigrants following the Russo-Japanese War, perhaps it represents an exceptionally fortunate time for Buddhism in America prior to the surge of Beatnik Zen.[14]

Kakuryō Nishijima, one of the pioneer Issei ministers in San Francisco, wrote an article that tried to correct, for the sake of the English-speaking readers, "the misunderstandings and misrepresentations of some of our prominent modern scholars, whose knowledge of Buddhistic [*sic*] teachings has been derived entirely from the Pali writings of Southern Buddhism and are strictly in accordance with the teaching of the Hinayana [*sic*] Schools." As Roger-Pol Droit's work reveals, nineteenth-century Buddhist studies in the West largely misinterpreted Buddhism, as it is understood from the viewpoint of current scholarship. The Mahāyāna newcomers from Japan, especially Shin Buddhist ministers, inevitably had to identify themselves as a somewhat different kind of Buddhist given their lifestyles included marriage, an unshaved head, and no special dietary restrictions.[15] Western sympathizers, it seems, were often confused by the similarity between traditional teachings of Shin Buddhism, such as the sole reliance on Amida Buddha and the "Other Power," and Christianity. Such misinterpretations were further abetted by the prevailing notion of Jōdo Shinshū as a religion resembling Christianity, which had been created by previous literature such as *Shinran and His Work* (1910), a book by an Anglican missionary to Japan, Arthur Lloyd, a representation of this branch of Buddhism that Christmas Humphreys, the founder of the Buddhist Society in London and former Senior Prosecuting Counsel, described as a "form of Buddhism which on the face of it discards three-quarters of Buddhism. Compared with the Teaching of the Pali Canon it is but Buddhism and water." He then raises the skeptical question: "Is it Buddhism?"[16]

Concerning the explanation of Nirvāna, Nishijima writes that the misconception about this concept within contemporary Buddhist studies reflects Theravāda Buddhism because it teaches "its aspirants that the only legitimate object of yearning should be for deliverance from existence and its attendant sufferings" and goes on to express that the Mahāyāna doctrine teaches that "there are four classes of Nirvana; two of them are designated as Hinayana-

Nirvana [*sic*] while the other two are known as Mahayana-Nirvana. They are: (1) Honrai-Jishojo-Nirvana; (2) Uyo-Nirvana; (3) Muyo-Nirvana; (4) Mujusho-Nirvana." What is notable about this passage is both the transliteration of Japanese Buddhist terms and his explanation of nonsectarian Buddhist doctrine without mentioning Shinran or Amida, which is not usually the case in Japanese orthodox Shin Buddhist scholarship. Compare this to Tetsuei Mizuki, the second Kantoku of the Nishi Hongwanji Mission, who concludes his lecture on "Buddhism" by mentioning a creed of Rennyo, one of the chief priests of Hongwanji whose name is known exclusively to the members of the denomination: "Rejecting all religious austerities and other action[s], giving up all idea of self-power, we rely upon Amitabha [*sic*] Buddha (source of light) with the whole heart for our salvation in the future life, . . . believing that at the moment of putting our faith in Amitabha Buddha, our salvation is settled."[17]

Even though the majority of the pioneer ministers had received higher education and were graduates of prestigious universities in Japan,[18] such literal translations of Japanese Buddhism may have confused the English-speaking audience and even caused them to question the credibility of Shin Buddhism, as suggested by Humphreys' doubtful notions. Reading the Mizuki's speech, one wonders what the *Light of Dharma* editor means when he declares that the mission intends to "set forth to English speaking people the principles of the [Buddhist] religion, the ethics and the philosophy of Lord Buddha."[19] The reason for this ambiguous stance—that is to present both basic Buddhist principles as found in the teachings of Śākyamuni Buddha ("Lord Buddha") and the teachings of "other power" and faith in Amitabha Buddha—in the propagation by Issei ministers lies in their ways of responding to the various religious needs of both the Issei Japanese and the Euro-American Buddhists who were connected to the Nishi Hongwanji Mission.

It is also instructive to note the January 1904 issue of a Japanese-language monthly journal, the *Beikoku Bukkyō*[20] (*Buddhism in America*), whose mission statements include: "We believe that Śākyamuni Buddha is the incomparable person who discovered the Truth," and "We are in a fortunate environment of being able to free ourselves from a den of a parochial Japanese religious atmosphere and develop our intuitive ability in this new, free country." The editorial also stated that "Buddhism in America should find its way out of the old bounds of Japanese Buddhism and the conservative customs, and with its real compassionate nature, should be built upon a solid foundation." These statements suggest that a sense of universalism was shared by pioneer Issei ministers. Moreover, the years used in the dates on the cover page of every issue of the *Beikoku Bukkyō* were written in the Japanese, Buddhist, and Western forms.[21]

When the war with Russia began, however, the February issue supported Japan's role in the international arena and became less critical of the conservatism in the Japanese religious circle. The editorial of the *Light of Dharma* reports that although it regrets that the war with Russia has begun, "the Japanese residents in the United States should be pleased to learn of the Japanese victories both on sea and land." It also notes that California Japanese raised a war fund of over one million dollars, and another million was raised by "all the Japanese Buddhist denominations."[22] More Japanese writers contributed to following issues, but the devastating earthquake of 1906 caused a publishing delay. The Nishi Hongwanji Mission eventually stopped publication altogether in 1907, which meant that the *Beikoku Bukkyō* became its main periodical. This demise of this English journal, along with the exclusion of Japanese pupils after the earthquake from public schools,[23] may have impeded English-language propagation to Nisei Americans, despite the development of Japanese-speaking Sunday schools and the church-affiliated Japanese language schools. These language schools taught Nisei the Japanese language and culture, gradually shifting the emphasis of instruction to language learning alone, even hiring Euro-American teachers in the process.[24]

In the early 1910s, the committee of businessmen who were running the Panama-Pacific International Exposition tried to avoid the passage of the anti-Japanese bills, even as legislation in California was being debated in favor of their passage. As Roger Daniels suggests, "it was generally felt that the Japanese exhibit would be one of the most important features of the fair, [therefore,] the directors [of the Exposition] were prepared to . . . prevent anti-Japanese legislation." Despite the exposition board of directors' "extensive efforts" to repeatedly visit the state capitol to meet the legislative members under Governor Hiram Johnson, the Alien Land Law of 1913 was ultimately passed, causing more disputes on both sides of the Pacific and both coasts of the U.S. mainland.[25]

It was under these circumstances that the BMNA hosted the World Buddhist Conference in San Francisco, August 2–7, 1915, concurrently with the Panama-Pacific International Exposition that ran from February to December of 1915. Delegates from Japan, the Territory of Hawaii, India, Ceylon, Burma, and Mexico attended the six-day conference. They eventually adopted a five-article resolution wishing "to correct and eliminate the prejudice against Buddhism that . . . Buddhist propagation in America would cause the exclusion of Japanese" and extending, curiously enough, an appeal to end World War I. The fifth article read that they appointed Mokusen Hioki, Sōgen Yamagami (both of them of the Sōtō Zen school), and Kōyū Uchida (BMNA) as representatives to hand this resolution to President Woodrow

Wilson.[26] Despite such seemingly abstract and idealistic themes evinced here, it is clear that the Buddhists, particularly the Japanese ones, saw the anti-Japanese legislation of California as being detrimental to the welfare of their members and decided to take action.

As Kōyū Uchida, the fourth Kantoku of the BMNA (from 1905 to 1923), recalled, ministers struggled between the ideals of *kaikyō,* or propagation to non-Japanese sympathizers/converts, and the reality of the overwhelming proportion of Japanese members. Uchida maintained that they were "not satisfied to settle in America as an 'extension of Japanese Buddhism' or 'religion that followed immigrants,'" even though the reality of the first thirty years remained just that: "[Buddhist] churches for the Japanese residents in America."[27]

Yet the ministers' discussions made clear that as missionaries to the United States, they believed in the universality of the Buddhist teachings, which they thought could be transplanted to America without much concern for cultural differences in dealing with Shin Buddhist terminology, even as nonsectarian teachings were written and preached to meet the religious needs of the Euro-American audience. Because "Buddhism" meant essentially Jōdo Shinshū for them, their efforts to make sense of their propagation among Americans turned out to be merely a one-way transmission of Buddhism from Japan. Their implicit assumption that Buddhism was intrinsically a Japanese religion also led them to voice support for the Japanese government during the Russo-Japanese War. Still, we should regard the 1915 antiwar resolution as a notable expression, and an important precedent to Nishi Hongwanji's Son'yū Ōtani's postwar pacifist declaration of 1921.[28]

"The Duty of Japanese Mahāyāna Buddhists": D. T. Suzuki's Discourses

Unlike the majority of Japanese immigrants, Daisetz Teitarō Suzuki lived mainly among Euro-Americans. For example, he helped Paul Carus translate Chinese and Japanese philosophical literature into English at the Open Court in La Salle, Illinois. Even though he lived relatively isolated from the Japanese community, he arrived in the United States just two years before the first Jōdo Shinshū missionaries landed in San Francisco in 1899. Curiously, when dealing with the early history of Japanese Buddhism in America, we usually find case studies of the Nishi Hongwanji Mission or the BMNA but no mention of the still young Suzuki.[29]

At the invitation of the Nishi Hongwanji Mission, D. T. Suzuki traveled to the West Coast in the fall of 1903. He reported to Carus that "unfortunately, they are all very poor and as I understand, the headquarters in Japan advise them to cut short [*sic*] their expenses as low [*sic*] as possible. There are many things that should be done in connection with their missionary work, but they are all left undone and I heard some complaint[s] among the American Buddhists."[30] His countrymen in San Francisco "did not interest [him] very much." Their Buddhist missionary work among Euro-Americans struck him as a "failure," although their work among the Japanese "may be all right."[31]

Suzuki's articles, on the other hand, reveal that he discussed religious ideas quite often and frankly with non-Japanese sympathizers:

> I confess that I was considerably puzzled whenever I was asked what Buddhism teaches concerning personal immortality. Let me propose to you a counter-question and ask: "What do you mean by personal immortality?" . . . "Do you wish to depict in your imagination a duplicate of our earthly home life up in your future birth?" If so, I cannot understand why you desire such an absurd form of personal immortality, which is not worth striving after by enlightened minds. . . . Christ is bodily dead, Buddha is bodily gone,—both more than a thousand years ago. But spiritually they are still living, will continue to live in the hearts of their disciples, sympathizers, and interpreters."

It appears that his discussions were more successful than that of Shin ministers at conveying at least one aspect of Buddhist teachings to a Euro-American audience. It was not only a matter of their English proficiency, but in their basic premise to address people from a Judeo-Christian tradition.[32]

In 1900, Suzuki wrote an article in entitled, "Religious Duty of My Fellow Japanese Mahāyāna Buddhists in the World," for the San Francisco YMBA's *Kaihō* (Bulletin), which later changed its name to the *Beikoku Bukkyō*. According to Suzuki, Western discourses on Buddhism had been based on linguistic studies of Pali or Sanskrit texts, neglecting the spirituality of East Asian Mahāyāna Buddhism: Japan was the sole country in which the Mahāyāna teachings had still survived. Therefore, he felt that the Japanese Buddhist denominations should cooperate to form a nonsectarian organization that could send highly educated religious people overseas to study so that the Western comprehension could be something more than merely archaistic literal translations or superficial misunderstandings of it as idolatry. Eventually they would "speak or write in the Western languages to propagate the essence of Mahāyāna Buddhism among the Westerners." For this reason, Suzuki regarded Carus's *The Gospel of Buddha* more highly than the English and French literal translations of Bunyū Nanjō and Ryōun Fujishima's *Short History of the Twelve Sects of Japanese Buddhism*, because he believed that "it would do nothing [to help the understanding of] general readers." For him, "in order to propagate a religion among people of another country, one has to think like them, feel like them, and express in their native language."[33]

But, Suzuki was also a dedicated member of the *Shin Bukkyōto Dōshikai* (the New Buddhist Society), founded in Tokyo in 1899, whose nonsectarian membership consisted of intellectual lay Buddhists who "tried to secure the status of a modern religion by engaging themselves positively in social issues."[34] One of its mission statements stipulates a "healthy belief" as the most essential, which Suzuki interpreted as referring to a this-worldly, rational, and intellectually acceptable belief system that accorded with science, which obviously required the rejection of "superstition." Moreover, he interpreted the meaning of a "healthy belief" as "not contradicting scientific knowledge," and "superstition" as "oppos[ing] to the progressive spirit."[35]

He did not, however, wholeheartedly support the idea of mixing science and analytical intellect with religion. He confessed to his friend Kitarō Nishida that "I have been reflecting deeply that Zen is remarkable for being free from logical arguments. . . . I think it is not a Zen way to make all sorts of distinctions or apply various kinds of philosophical ideas."[36] To understand this, it may be helpful to consider the Gifford Lectures and *The Varieties of Religious Experiences* by William James, which Suzuki highly appreciated and recommended to Nishida. He later wrote to Nishida, "contrary to Mr. Carus' discourses on religion, [James's writings] directly touch the human heart, and [James] does not exclude religious experience as delusive superstition but studies it as a psychological fact, which shares the same idea as mine."[37] Nevertheless, he spent most of his time working with just Paul Carus, who he gradually found to hold quite different views on religion from his own. According to the typology of late-Victorian American Buddhists, Carus was the "rationalist type," who, under the influence of Enlightenment rationalism, "focused on rational-discursive means of attaining religious truth and meaning as opposed to revelational or experiential means and emphasized the authority of the individual in religious matters rather than that of creeds, texts, officials, or institutions." Compared with Suzuki's keen interest in Swedenborg while in the United States, as detailed by Tweed and Yoshinaga, perhaps it was ironically the strict rationalism of Carus that drove him indirectly to the study of mysticism.[38]

Criticizing the "excessive formality in Japanese legislature," he commented favorably on American society's respect for freedom and generosity, noting his regret for the racist lynchings in the South at the time.[39] He respected the democratic attitudes of Americans, but did not appreciate their racist double standards. He disapproved of the authoritarian attitudes of the Japanese government as "quite undemocratic in this civilized age,"[40] hoping for a move toward the democratization, while favoring that culture's poetic lifestyle, which "appreciates lovely flowers and admires [the beauty of] the moon" and enjoys "a kind of popular literature, '*hokku*'"(seventeen-syllable poems).[41]

This reveals Suzuki's particular enthusiasm, as a Buddhist from the East, for presenting to Westerners a Buddhism in a "civilized," nonsectarian form—quite different from the one created by Western academia. In one sense, he tried to integrate scientific analysis into modern Buddhist life. For him, religious life needed to be based upon one's religious beliefs, and actual life should be ethically carried out with diligence and founded on modern scientific knowledge, which may explain the reason for his righteous indignation at social injustices. He even criticized the imperial family for "remain[ing] extremely distant and sanctified as in the past, while the nations respond to imperial edicts as if they were something supremely grateful."[42] Witnessing the settlements and philanthropic activities of Christian churches in Chicago, he thought about the direction of the labor movements in Japan and commented on the four great vows of the bodhisattva. He told Nishida, "the reason why Mahāyāna Buddhism placed this vow [i.e., "However innumerable sentient beings there may be, I vow to save them"] at the beginning was to present the ultimate meaning of human life directly, for it will be no use to live this life without being able to save the measureless sentient beings."[43] These interests in social equality eventually led him to express his reinterpretation of "socialism,"[44] which was a kind of prototype of Buddhist socialism articulated from a purely religious perspective, not in economic analysis but in the bodhisattva vow to save the innumerable sentient beings.

Amplifying his comments on social issues, I will now turn to his article on Buddhism in relation to war. The July 1904 issue of *Light of Dharma* begins with Suzuki's article entitled, "A Buddhist View of War," which begins: "Every religion strives to bring about universal peace on earth" while accepting human life is full of grief and despair. He maintains that the reason for our suffering is "our subjectivism," which determines "our destiny on earth and in heaven." This emphasis on "subjectivity" leads him to conclude that "mysticism is the very source from which religion drinks to her heart's content." With this mystical understanding of Buddhism, "war is abominable, and there is no denying it. But it is only a phase of the universal struggle that is going on and will go on, as long as one breath of vitality is left to an animate being." Because the sociopolitical aspect of war is derived from subjectivity, one should evaluate a highly motivated soldier who fights without "ego," who "clears every obstacle in the way . . . In him there is no hatred, no anger." Suzuki even calls this attitude "spiritual," because it "lies [in the] divinity of our being." This expression is not Suzuki's own invention, he claims, but "a recurrent theme in Buddhist discussions on warfare," and can be found in *Sermons of a Buddhist Abbot*, a book Suzuki translated for his master, Shaku Sōen.[45]

In sum, Suzuki was primarily instrumental in transmitting the Buddhist teachings in the context of Mahāyāna Buddhism to Euro-American sympathizers. For him, this was the "duty" of Japanese Buddhists, and his lectures and articles were therefore geared toward a Euro-American audience. The result was also a kind of a one-way transmission. Unlike the Shin Buddhists, his approach was more relevant, with comparative explications of Buddhism based on his understanding of the Judeo-Christian tradition. As he wrote later, Jōdo Shinshū and the Nichirenshū are "the creation of the Japanese religious mind," whereas Zen, in his view, was not essentially restricted to any particular culture and applicable to all circumstances.[46] In other words, he thought that Zen did not have to modify itself further to become Americanized, whereas Shin Buddhism needed to reinterpret its doctrine. Moreover, his version of the Buddhist viewpoint of war downplays its gravity by relegating it to a worldly perception, without expressing sorrow of the war bereaved or the agony of dying soldiers. In a sense, his attitude may be called a "political" indifference to politics. This attitude was actually quite similar to the logic of contemporaneous Buddhists in wartime Japan who praised victory in war and the quest to secure an equal relationship with Western powers in the international arena. In spite of the aggressive presentation of Buddhism at the time of the Russo-Japanese War, however, it is crucial to carefully scrutinize Suzuki's discourses after meeting with his American wife, Beatrice Erskine Lane, which disclosed more compassionate aspect of Buddhism, which revealed his complex ideas.[47]

The Middle Way: Yemyō Imamura's Discourses on Americanization

In the several historical studies on Japanese immigrants and Buddhism in the Territory of Hawaii, Yemyō Imamura has nearly always been prominently featured, which is not surprising given his long tenure as bishop of the Honpa Hongwanji Mission of Hawaii (from 1899 to his sudden death in December of 1932). Yet although most of the later postwar studies were mostly based on the seminal work of Louise Hunter, her 1971 historical study was the only one to examine Imamura's religious thought in any detail.[48]

Hunter successfully uncovered how Japanese Buddhism in Hawaii made an effort to make sense of itself during that critical period. In the midst of the Americanization campaign of the 1910s and 1920s, the English-speaking press in Hawaii sensationally wrote up Buddhism as "non-American" or "anti-American," denouncing both Buddhism and Shintoism as "antithetical to Americanism."[49] For example, some Americanizers stated that "The ideals and political life of the United States depend ultimately and absolutely upon the Christian American home. True Americanization can not bloom in a Buddhist Oriental household." Likewise, "Hawaii was claimed for Christ many years ago and we must refuse to allow our fair islands to be permeated with paganism [i.e., Buddhism] in whatever form it may assume."[50] This nativistic rhetoric exemplified, in a way, the dichotomous perception of Buddhist (often equated with nationalistic/militaristic) Japan and Christian American territory (including Hawaii).

As is well known, the Honpa Hongwanji Mission of Hawaii and other Buddhist denominations such as Jōdoshū or Sōtōshū ran many Japanese language schools through affiliated temples. Imamura was a typical Issei leader and enthusiastic about teaching Japanese to the Hawaii-born children of Japanese ancestry. As Eileen Tamura suggests, the Americanization drive targeted these schools as promoting divided loyalty to America and "hostility focused on Japanese language, and continued after the [First World] war ended." In Noriko Asato's chapter in this volume and elsewhere, she demonstrates that the Federal Survey of Education in 1919 was conducted amid the "religious conflict between Christian and Buddhist clergy" and that this conflict resulted in "[elevating] Christianity as a means and measurement of Americanization, while it demeaned Buddhism as a sign of Japanese origins and ethnic identity." Thus, an Americanizer in 1921 would write: "Inevitably the existence of these schools teaching Japanese and especially the leaning of the Buddhist institutions towards Japan offered a golden opportunity to the exaggerated nationalistic spirit that followed the [First World] war."[51]

Despite criticism against Buddhism and Japanese culture and language, Imamura's thought revolved around ideas such as democracy, Americanism, pacifism, and religious freedom from a Buddhist point of view. Although available sources presently include both English and Japanese publications, because most of the previous studies use only English-language materials, I would like to introduce some of his Japanese writings to clarify his ideas. By examining both English and Japanese discourses, we may uncover how he reinterpreted Buddhism in the process of being transplanted to American soil and to illustrate his Buddhist social ethics.

Largely influenced by the Americanization movement in the surrounding society, the Honpa Hongwanji Mission had started institutional reforms in the 1910s. The language school curriculum was altered under the guidance of Ryūsaku Tsunoda, who was assigned as the new principal of the Hongwanji-affiliated Japanese High School in 1909. Tsunoda reported in a *Hawaii Shokumin Shimbun* article on April 10, 1911, that he chose the new textbooks with the intention of educating Nisei Americans to become "a bridge between Japanese and American cultures." Fukuzawa Yukichi, a Japanese liberal intellectual, had written a series of popular essays on ethics under the title *Fukuō hyakuwa* (A Hundred Stories by an Old Fukuzawa), and this was selected to replace the *Shūshin* textbooks authorized by Japanese government.[52] In 1915, the Honpa Hongwanji's language schools were reformed into "*Gakuen*" or "educational homes" aiming "to render some help in fitting the children for American life." Chie Honda's study points out that these "educational homes" joined the Hawaii Japanese Education Association and adopted textbooks edited by the association in 1917. Furthermore, the Honpa Hongwanji Mission edited several volumes of its original textbooks dealing with Buddhist ethics that taught cultural and family values in accord with American society by taking out the parts about the emperor or Shintō.[53]

Meanwhile, starting in the mid-1910s, Imamura began to consider more universal aspects of Buddhist teachings. He wrote in the preface to Tsunoda's English book on Shin Buddhism (published in 1914): "what we have been teaching in our church and school is so little known, or, rather, to my great regret, has so often been grossly misrepresented to the public, that some of them often speak slightingly of our faith as if it were a form of superstitious idolatry, and our educational work as a system of bigoted nationalism that lays a stumbling block on the way of Americanizing our people."

The theme of universalism was also reflected in his interpretation of the spirit of Shinran as oriented "to induce all nations and all races on the earth, with no regard to their color and rank, to unite in the work of forming one large family, with our Buddha Amida as their universal parent."[54] In the Honolulu YMBA's *Dōbō* magazine of 1916, he described Amida as the "three Ls," namely "Life, Light, and Love." His intention was to articulate Buddhism more comprehensibly to both Issei and Nisei Buddhists, as well as to the Euro-Americans: The "compassion" and "wisdom" contained in these three Ls (interestingly, an English-language construct) were not confined to the Japanese alone but pertained to anyone, regardless of race or ethnicity. With this understanding of Buddhist universalism in mind, he established the English department with help from *haole* Buddhists, especially Ernest Shinkaku Hunt.[55]

Imamura's interventions in contemporary political issues consisted of publishing books on Buddhist democracy with antiwar messages in 1918 and ideas on religious freedom in 1920. These writings, as far as I know, have not been examined in any kind of detail. Hunter describes Imamura's

Democracy According to the Buddhist Viewpoint as "puzzling," whereas Robert Armstrong, a missionary of the United Church of Canada, critically refers to Imamura's idea as the one that "logically and forcefully destroys all social and moral standards."[56] These pick up on passages such as the following:

> If autocracy has no absolute value, neither has democracy. If democracy is right, why should not autocracy be right also? We Buddhists believe that in this world as well as in the ideal world of Amita [*sic*] there are no absolutely determined values or particular things that cannot be reduced to some other terms, and therefore that autocracy does not unconditionally exclude democracy, nor does democracy [unconditionally exclude] autocracy, they are after all two aspects of a thing which is in itself above such opposites. . . . This principle of equalisation [by the nondualism of Buddha-nature] exists in each of us, and as far as this alone is regarded we are all autocrats and at the same time we are all democrats.[57]

To understand Imamura's point of view, one needs to take it in the context of polarizing debates between democracy and autocracy, Christianity and Buddhism. In other words, he was questioning the exclusionary attitudes of those who were propagating "democracy," which ended up treating unfairly the Japanese immigrants who were regarded as "aliens ineligible to citizenship." Imamura's interpretation of Buddhist democracy did not originate from a given political program, but was based on Buddhist teachings. This kind of stance can be derived from the Buddhist doctrine of the Middle Way, that is, not simply situating oneself in a moderate, safe zone but in impartial, strict neutrality.[58]

A fact previous studies hardly mention is that Imamura's antiwar messages were written *during* World War I. In the preface to his book, he quotes a famous line from the *Longer Sukhāvatīvyūha Sūtra*, which reads, "Wherever the Buddha goes, all under Heaven is harmoniously ordered. . . . The land is prosperous, and the people live in peace. There is no need for soldiers or weapons."[59] Concerning the fact that it was published in 1918, this is clearly interpreted as a Buddhist peace appeal. Imamura not only advocated peace based on his religious convictions, but also put it into practice, when it was resolved at the 1919 ministerial meeting to remove the war memorial monument in each temple.[60] The following is a quote from his 1918 book: "[In Buddhism,] Caste distinctions were abolished, all the brethren in the faith stood on equal footing . . . As a sort of corollary to the spirit of universal brotherhood, Buddhism strongly declares against war. Avarice, antagonism, disharmony, self-aggrandisement, and other evils which go to make up the motives of any war are singularly absent in the history of Buddhism."[61]

On the other hand, his 1920 book summarizes "Americanism" as follows: (1) it is unacceptable to exclude other religious creeds in the name of Americanism; (2) it is a flexible ideology and constantly adapting to new circumstances; and (3) it is not a pure, unmixed, and exclusive ideology but inclusive and comprehensive. According to Imamura, this pluralistic Americanism occurs throughout U.S. history, which constantly produced new philosophies such as the pragmatism of William James and John Dewey, thinkers he paid great attention to for their pluralism, empiricism, and repudiation of authoritarian ideas.[62]

Contesting the notion that the Japanese were "autocratic," Imamura suggested derisively that the Daughters of the American Revolution ran parallel with the "Japanese style" of respecting anything old and unchanging, and that "such are not popular even in Japan now." More importantly, he stressed that religion in American history was not limited to Puritanism alone, as numerous other denominations had developed in its history, some of them even resembling Buddhism. His refrain was the argument claiming religious freedom for Buddhists in a country predominantly of Judeo-Christian origin. Because of the tradition of religious pluralism secured by the First Amendment guarantees each American freedom of religion, he asserted that "it is nonsensical to discriminate against someone because of his or her religious affiliation."[63]

Imamura's idea of Americanization was thus not a switch of loyalty from the Japanese emperor to the Stars and Stripes—nor "a hundred percent Americanization" in which a Buddhist might have to throw away his or her religious beliefs—but rather a cosmopolitan outlook, recognizing both American and Japanese cultures equally. What enabled this viewpoint was the effort to respond to the challenges of the Americanization campaign and a perception of Buddhist history in which the universal teachings of Buddhism could flower in each country, adapting to its particular culture.[64] According to Imamura, because these teachings had traveled eastward from India to Japan via China and Korea and finally across the Pacific, Buddhism in America was fortunate to inherit the accomplishments of Buddhists in those countries and would thus add a new vision to it.[65]

In contrast to pioneer missionaries on the mainland and D. T. Suzuki, Imamura more whole-heartedly adopted the logic of Americanization; hence his approach can be called a two-way transmission. Living in a society relatively hostile to Buddhism, it was inevitable for Imamura to contemplate what would be the most essential to his religion and a better way to convey its teachings to Euro-Americans. Perhaps it was up against this hostility that Imamura learned to give greater due to both Japanese and American cultures, consequently developing the idea of Buddhist democracy and extending religious freedom for Buddhists in America.

In War Time: Discourses of Nisei and "White" Buddhists

The Fall 1941 issue of the *Berkeley Bussei* introduced, a new young Nisei minister, Kanmō Imamura,[66] who had just taken over the Berkeley Buddhist Church. As the word "*bussei*" (abbreviation for *bukkyō seinenkai,* or the Young Buddhist Association) suggests, the majority of the staff and contributors of this journal published by the YBA consisted of university students. Written predominantly in English, the journal characteristically feature issues revolving around Buddhism, their thoughts and anxieties about their lives and the future, the YBA Convention, sports and cultural activities, introductions of alumni and newcomers, and other items reflecting the actual activities of the YBA.[67]

Kanmō's first essay in it asserts that Buddhists should have a "cosmopolitan" mind. According to him, Buddhists should stand on the "truth" taught by Buddha, rather than on arguments such as "democracy" or "*Yamato damashii*" (Japanese spirit). The Buddhist truth is free from prejudice and means to bring about the happiness of every human being without appealing to arms, so one should be careful to tell what is really based on the "truth" and avoid being deceived by others. Although his argument reminds us of his father's, his emphasis here is on democracy and equal treatment of each culture based on Buddhism.[68] Ironically, only a few months after this article expressing Buddhism's nonviolent stance was published that the war broke out with Japan. Kanmō told his new bride, Jane, "The Constitution will protect us. This is America," but they were incarcerated just like other California Japanese in 1942 and then were sent to a camp in Gila River, Arizona.[69]

Before the outbreak of the war, Kanmō's hometown of Honolulu hosted the Pan-Pacific YMBA Conference (July 21–26, 1930). Located at the crossroads of the Pacific, Hawaii was already playing a vital role in the international arena by hosting the first and second conferences of the Institute of Pacific Relations in 1925 and 1927, and the Pan-Pacific Women's Conference in 1928. It was under these circumstances that Kōnen Tsunemitsu, a journalist with a Nishi Hongwanji ministership, met with Yemyō Imamura and several Honolulu YMBA staff members to discuss holding an international conference with Buddhists from the Pacific Rim countries in 1928. In the same year, Ernest Hunt, who had already received ordination in the Theravāda order in Burma and now in the Mahāyāna tradition under Imamura, conducted a ceremony of initiation for about sixty Euro-American Buddhists. In April

1928, the progressive Chinese Buddhist monk Tai Xu visited Honolulu on his way to China and talked with Imamura and Hunt about establishing "a Hawaii branch of the newly formed International Buddhist Institute, which was dedicated to breaking down sectarian barriers and working for a united Buddhism everywhere."[70]

Unfortunately, the relationship between the International Buddhist Institute, presided over by Hunt, and the Honpa Hongwanji Mission gradually came to an end after new bishop Gikyō Kuchiba assumed the position in 1935.[71] During the peak of anti-Japanese sentiment, Julius Goldwater, a Jewish American convert who had received ordination through Hunt in Honolulu, aided hundreds of Japanese Americans who had been forced into the War Relocation Authority camps during World War II, supplying them with Buddhist service books and materials for them to continue their religious practices, even at the cost of being viewed as "some kind of clever traitor" by his own affluent German Jewish family and being called a "Jap lover" by non-Japanese Americans.[72] Prior to this, he had already formed relations with Japanese Buddhists; one of his articles appeared in the Spring 1941 issue of the *Berkeley Bussei*, which reads, "Any form of discrimination is against the simple Buddhist's way of living, but discrimination is also part and parcel of relative existence. Thus nationalism has now come into our mode of living, and while this in itself may be very beneficial, I like to think that it will not make for hatred or feelings as against other nationalities." He goes on to discuss the Nisei's willingness to accept Japanese Buddhism as observed at the YBA Convention, while pointing out their intense need for American Buddhism "for understanding purposes, and for living purposes." In an effort to clarify the ambiguous stance of Nisei Buddhists, he defined "American Buddhism" as "the simple teachings to be found in Buddhism rephrased in American terminology to the extent that with every contact there is immediate vitality in association with the living today." But he was also not very rigorously attached to nonsectarian practices. Rather, he considered sectarianism a necessary evil because "we are in various degrees of unfoldment and need various treatments rather than one medicine to cure everything." What we need most now is to "be Buddhists": "then there can exist the real Buddhism and thus as Americans there will be at once American Buddhism."[73]

Perhaps Kanmō's educational background (he studied in Hawaii until his sophomore year of high school, when he moved to Tokyo to enter Keiō University) led him to understand Buddhism as "cosmopolitan," but this understanding seems to reflect something more than just the experience of studying overseas. He adopted the ideas of "democracy" and "constitutional right" to legitimize his rights as a Japanese American, and that of "cosmopolitan" to identify himself as an American Buddhist. As a Nisei Shin Buddhist minister, his approach attempted two-way transmission, which developed into his postwar religious activities with English-speaking Nisei and Euro-Americans.[74] Goldwater, as a Euro-American Buddhist, had to face both some Japanese Buddhists' reactionary attitudes toward Japanese culture and Euro-Americans' racist hostility, which made him turn to a cosmopolitan aspect of Buddhism. He did not reject Bussei's preference for Japanese culture, but he stressed the need to identify oneself as a Buddhist first. Only then, to make teachings more familiar, should terms be rephrased in "American terminology." His approach was also a two-way transmission, and it remained consistent even during the most difficult period.

Conclusion

We have observed several cases of the Americanization process of Japanese Buddhism, particularly Jōdo Shinshū and to a lesser extent, Zen traditions. Issei and Nisei Buddhists wanted, though in different ways, to spread Mahāyāna Buddhism among both Westerners and Japanese, because they believed in the teaching's universality. What made them take different approaches were their understanding of American and Japanese cultural differences and their relationships to Buddhism, as well as their reactions to a surrounding society that was gradually becoming more hostile. The attitudes Issei Buddhist intellectuals held in common were (1) nonsectarianism, (2) relative evaluation of ethnic cultures, (3) internationalism, (4) interests in Buddhist ethics and social justice, and (5) a tendency toward Americanization. Americanization would not have taken place if Buddhist thinkers were not searching for ways to respond to the actual, sociopolitical challenges posed by the surrounding society. I have tried to uncover just a fragment of the diverse processes in the Americanization of Japanese Buddhism and the collaboration of Japanese and Euro-American Buddhists.

Notes

Earlier versions of this essay were presented at the Asian Pacific Americans and Religion Research Initiative Conference in Berkeley, California, in 2002, and the Annual Meeting of the American Academy of Religion in Atlanta, Georgia, in 2003. Unless noted, English translations of Japanese-language materials are by the author. My appreciation goes to Peter Lait for proofreading an earlier draft. Citations from the *Light of Dharma* and the *Berkeley Bussei* were photocopied from the Buddhist Churches of America Archives, the Japanese American National Museum. I would like to thank Brian M. Hayashi, Kenneth K. Tanaka, Muneyoshi Togami, and Toshimaro Ama whose valuable suggestions helped improve the earlier draft. I also wish to acknowledge the assistance of Wayne Yokoyama, and the staff of the JANM, Wakayama Civic Library, Naritasan Buddhist Library, and Ōtani University Library. This chapter was supported in part by Grant-in-Aid for Young Scientists (program B, no. 15720014) and a research grant from Hannan University.

1. Overall lists of academic theses and doctoral dissertations on Buddhism in America were compiled by Duncan Ryûken Williams. See appendixes in Duncan Ryûken Williams and Christopher S. Queen, eds., *American Buddhism: Methods and Findings in Recent Scholarship* (Richmond, Surrey, U.K.: Curzon Press, 1999).

2. John Higham, *Strangers in the Land: Patterns of American Nativism, 1860–1925* (Baltimore: Johns Hopkins University Press, 1984); Eileen H. Tamura, *Americanization, Acculturation, and Ethnic Identity: The Nisei Generation in Hawaii* (Urbana: University of Illinois Press, 1994).

3. I will spell his first name as Daisetz in this chapter.

4. There are two distinct schools within Jōdo Shinshū: Jōdo Shinshū Hongwanji-ha (commonly known as Nishi Hongwanji) and Shinshū Ōtani-ha (Higashi Honganji). I will discuss with only the former, as Michihiro Ama's chapter in this volume deals with the latter in detail. Although the pioneer Shin Buddhist missionaries to America called their institution the Hongwanji Branch Office or simply the Buddhist Mission, I refer to them as the Nishi Hongwanji Mission (prior to 1914) for convenience. That year, the general meeting adopted the name, the "Buddhist Mission of North America" (hereafter BMNA), which remains until the wartime incarceration of the Japanese Americans, when they changed the name to "Buddhist Churches of America" (hereafter BCA) at a meeting in Topaz Camp in 1944. In this way, the three names will be used accordingly. The head of the administration of both the North American and Hawaii Missions was called *Kantoku*, which means director or superintendent, and was later to be elevated to *Sōchō*, or bishop, in 1918.

5. Isao Horinouchi, *Americanized Buddhism: A Sociological Analysis of a Protestantized Japanese Religion* (Ph.D. diss., University of California, Davis, 1973), p. 8.

6. Tomoe Moriya, "Amerika gasshūkoku ni okeru nikkei bukkyō to esunishitī: beikoku bukkyōdan (BCA) o chūshin ni," *Kindai Bukkyō* 9 (2002): 73.

7. Horinouchi, *Americanized Buddhism*, p. 340; Tetsuden Kashima, *Buddhism in America: The Social Organization of an Ethnic Religious Institution* (Westport, Conn.: Greenwood Press, 1977), p. 213; David K. Yoo, *Growing Up Nisei: Race, Generation, and Culture among Japanese Americans of California, 1924–49* (Urbana: University of Illinois Press, 2000), p. 45.

8. Charles S. Prebish, *American Buddhism* (North Scituate, Mass.: Duxbury Press, 1979); Rick Fields, "Divided Dharma: White Buddhists, Ethnic Buddhists, and Racism," in *The Faces of Buddhism in America*, Charles S. Prebish and Kenneth K. Tanaka, eds. (Berkeley: University of California Press, 1998), pp. 196–97, 200–204; Charles S. Prebish, *Luminous Passage: The Practice and Study of Buddhism in America* (Berkeley: University of California Press, 1999), chapters 1–2; Rick Fields, *How the Swans Came to the Lake: A Narrative History of Buddhism in America*, 3rd ed. (Boston: Shambhala Publications, 1992), p. 200.

9. Jan Nattier, "Who is a Buddhist?: Charting the Landscape of Buddhist America," in

Faces of Buddhism in America, pp. 189–90; Richard Hughes Seager, *Buddhism in America* (New York: Columbia University Press, 1999), pp. 9–10.

10. Lori Anne Pierce, *Constructing American Buddhisms: Discourses of Race and Religion in Territorial Ha wai'i* (Ph.D. diss., University of Ha wai'i, 2000), pp. 224–25; David W. Chappell, "Racial Diversity in the Soka Gakkai," in *Engaged Buddhism in the West*, Christopher S. Queen, ed. (Boston: Wisdom Publications, 2000), p. 184.

11. Toshimaro Ama, *Why Are the Japanese Non-Religious? Japanese Spirituality: Being Non-Religious in a Religious Culture*, trans. Michihiro Ama (Lanham, Md.: University Press of America, 2004), pp. 27–38; Alfred Bloom, "Shin Buddhism in America: A Social Perspective," in *Faces of Buddhism in America*, pp. 32–47; Christopher S. Queen, preface to *Engaged Buddhism in the West*, p. x.

12. Christopher S. Queen, introduction to *Engaged Buddhism in the West*, pp. 2, 6; Donald Rothberg, "Responding to the Cries of the World: Socially Engaged Buddhism in North America," in *Faces of Buddhism in America*, pp. 267, 273; Seager, *Buddhism in America*, pp. 202–3. See also Thich Nhat Hanh, *Vietnam: Lotus in a Sea of Fire* (New York: Hill and Wang, 1967), as well as Sallie B. King, "Thich Nhat Hanh and the Unified Buddhist Church: Nondualism in Action," in *Engaged Buddhism: Buddhist Liberation Movements in Asia*, Christopher S. Queen and Sallie B. King, eds. (New York: State University of New York Press, 1996), pp. 321–63.

13. Thomas A. Tweed, *American Encounter with Buddhism, 1844–1912: Victorian Culture and the Limits of Dissent* (Chapel Hill: University of North Carolina Press, 1992), pp. 32, 163. Other periodicals, such as the *Dōbō* (The Brotherhood) and the *Bukkyō no sekai* (The Buddhist World) from Territorial Hawaii, the *Beikoku Bukkyō* (Buddhism in America) and the *Berkeley Bussei* from California, survived for a longer period, enabling us to look into their characteristics over time and the transition of themes in the articles. Limits on space here only allow me to discuss a few particular individuals' articles.

14. Roger Daniels, *Asian America: Chinese and Japanese in the United States since 1850* (Seattle: University of Washington Press, 1988), chapters 4–5.

15. Kakuryo Nishijima, "Hinayana and Mahayana," *Light of Dharma* 1/2 (1901): 4; Roger-Pol Droit, *Le Culte du Néant: Les Philosphes et le Bouddha* (Chapel Hill: University of North Carolina Press, 2003); Richard M. Jaffe, *Neither Monk nor Layman: Clerical Marriage in Modern Japanese Buddhism* (Princeton: Princeton University Press, 2001).

16. Arthur Lloyd, *Shinran and His Work: Studies in Shinshu History* (Tokyo: Kyobunkwan, 1910); Christmas Humphreys, *Buddhism: An Introduction and Guide* (Harmondsworth, England: Pelican Books, 1951, reprint, London: Penguin Books, 1990), pp. 164–65.

17. Nishijima, "Hinayana and Mahayana," p. 5; Shōjitsu Ōhara, "Iwayuru beikoku bukkyō to shinshū kyōgaku," *Ryūkoku Kyōgaku* 3 (1968): 5–17; Tetsuei Mizuki, "Buddhism," *Light of Dharma* 1/1 (1901): 23.

18. Nishijima graduated from Bukkyō/Takanawa Bukkyō University (present-day Ryūkoku University), Mizuki from Tokyo Imperial University. The first *Kantoku* of the Nishi Hongwanji Mission, Shūye Sonoda, and the fourth *Kantoku*, Kōyū Uchida, were both Tokyo Imperial University graduates as well.

19. "Our Second Year Completed," *Light of Dharma* 2/6 (1903): 214.

20. *Beikoku Bukkyō* was published by the San Francisco YMBA and written only in Japanese. Ministers took turns in editing this Japanese monthly as well as the English journal, *Light of Dharma*.

21. "Wagato no shinjo," "Wagato no shugi," "Wagato no hofu," *Beikoku Bukkyō* 5/1 (1904): 2.

22. "Iwayuru bunmei no hanmen," *Beikoku Bukkyō* 5/2 (1904): 2–6; "Our War Fund," "Subscriptions of Buddhist Churches," *Light of Dharma* 4/1 (1904): 175.

23. Roger Daniels, The Politics of Prejudice: The Anti-Japanese Movement in California and the Struggle for Japanese Exclusion (Berkeley: University of California Press, 1962), p. 34.

24. Kashima, *Buddhism in America*, p. 33; Noriko Asato, *Teaching Mikadoism: The Attack on Japanese Language Schools in Hawaii, California, and Washington, 1919–1927* (Honolulu: University of Ha wai'i Press, 2005); Tomoe Moriya, "Kariforunia-shū ni okeru bukkyōkai fuzoku nihongo gakkō no seikaku," in *Amerika nihonjin imin no ekkyō kyōikushi*, Ryō Yoshida, ed. (Tokyo: Nihon tosho sentā, 2005), pp. 115–24.

25. Daniels, *Politics of Prejudice*, pp. 51–64.

26. "Sekai bukkyō taikai kiji," *Beikoku Bukkyō* 16/9 (1915): 2–5; "Bukkyō taikai zatsuji," *Beikoku Bukkyō* 16/9 (1915): 9.

27. Kōyū Uchida, "Hokubei kaikyō sanjūnen no kaiko to shōrai no tenbō," in *Sōkō bukkyōkai kaikyō sanjūnen kinenshi*, Sōkō Bukkyōkai Bunshobu, ed. (San Francisco: Kageyama Tetsujirō), pp. 20–23.

28. Brian A. Victoria, *Zen at War* (New York: Weatherhill, 1997), pp. 60–62.

29. As Wayne Yokoyama points out, contrary to Suzuki's involvement with the Nishi Hongwanji Mission in the United States, it is "a curious fact since Suzuki hardly involved himself with the Nishi Hongwanji while in Japan." Perhaps this somewhat slight relationship could be the reason for overlooking the connection between Suzuki and the early period of the North American mission. Wayne S. Yokoyama, "DT Suzuki's Involvement with the Nishi Hongwanji in the United States," in *The Proceedings of the Eleventh Biennial Conference of the International Association of Shin Buddhist Studies* (Berkeley: Institute of Buddhist Studies, September 12–14, 2003).

30. Suzuki to Paul Carus, San Francisco, September 17, 1903, *Suzuki Daisetz zenshū Vol. 26*, Shōkin Furuta, et al., eds. (Tokyo: Iwanami shoten, 2003), p. 233. English original.

31. Suzuki to Ryōkichi Yamamoto, La Salle, February 10, 1904, p. 246. English original.

32. Daisetsu T. [*sic*] Suzuki, "Individual Immortality," *Light of Dharma* 3/3 (1903): 67–68; Suzuki to Carus, San Francisco, August 30, 1903, p. 232. English original.

33. Daisetz Suzuki, "Waga nihon no daijō bukkyōto ga sekai ni okeru shūkyōteki sekinin," *Kaihō* 1/4 (1900), reprinted in *Suzuki Daisetsu Zenshu (old edition) vol. 31* (Tokyo: Iwanami shoten, 1971), pp. 84–89.

34. Kyūichi Yoshida, *Nihon kindai bukkyōshi kenkyū* (Tokyo: Kawashima shoten, 1992), p. 325. As Yoshida suggests, the history of modern Japanese Buddhism saw two Buddhist movements at the turn of the century with opposite platforms, the *Shin Bukkyō* (New Buddhism) and *Seishin-shugi* (Spirituality).

35. Daisetz Suzuki, "Doku 'shin bukkyō' dai nikan dai ichigō," *Shin Bukkyō* 2/4 (1901): 183.

36. Suzuki to Kitarō Nishida, [La Salle,] November 11, 1897, p. 108.

37. Suzuki to Nishida, La Salle, September 23, 1902, p. 222.

38. Tweed, *American Encounter with Buddhism*, p. 61. For detailed historical studies of Suzuki's interest in Swedenborgianism, see Shinichi Yoshinaga, "Daisetz to suēdenborugu: Sono rekishiteki haikei," *Shūkyō tetsugaku kenkyū* 22 (2005): 33–50; Thomas A. Tweed,

"American Occultism and Japanese Buddhism: Albert J. Edmunds, D. T. Suzuki, and Transnational Religious Flows," paper presented at the 19th World Congress of the International Association for the History of Religions, Tokyo, March 30, 2005.

39. Daisetz Suzuki, "Nemurarenu yogoto-roku: jo," *Shin Bukkyō* 3/3 (1902): 157.

40. Suzuki to Yamamoto, [La Salle,] September 6, 1905, p. 273.

41. Suzuki to Yamamoto, [La Salle,] February 12, 1905, p. 268.

42. Suzuki to Yamamoto, [La Salle,] June 14, 1898, pp. 150–51. In the margin, Suzuki reminded Yamamoto to be careful not to openly criticize the imperial family.

43. Suzuki to Nishida, [La Salle,] January 21, 1901, p. 209.

44. Suzuki to Nishida, December 3, 1902, [La Salle,] pp. 224–25. Despite his sympathy to "socialism," Suzuki never met Japanese socialists in the United States. See also Kiyohide Kirita, "D. T. Suzuki on Society and the State," in *Rude Awakenings: Zen, the Kyoto School, and the Question of Nationalism*, James W. Heisig and John C. Maraldo, eds. (Honolulu: University of Hawaii Press, 1994), pp. 52–74. For a historical context of socialism in relation to Buddhism in Meiji Japan, see Yoshida, *Nihon kindai bukkyōshi kenkyū*.

45. Daisetz Teitaro Suzuki, "A Buddhist View on War," *Light of Dharma* 4/2 (1904): 179–82; Victoria, *Zen at War*, pp. 26–27.

46. Daisetz T. Suzuki, *Zen and Japanese Culture* (Princeton: Princeton University Press, 1959).

47. Tomoe Moriya, "Suzuki Daisetsu ni okeru Beatrice Lane no igi," in *Tsuisō Suzuki Daisetsu: Botsugo yonjū nen kinen kikōshū*, Tsutomu Kaneko, ed. (Kamakura: Matsugaoka Bunko, 2006), pp. 349–51.

48. Louise H. Hunter, *Buddhism in Hawaii: Its Impact on a Yankee Community* (Honolulu: University of Ha wai'i Press, 1971); Horinouchi, *Americanized Buddhism*, pp. 40–109; Kashima, *Buddhism in America*, pp. 56–57; Tamura, *Americanization*, pp. 204–205.

49. Daniel Erwin Weinberg, *The Movement to 'Americanize' the Japanese Community in Hawaii: An Analysis of One Hundred Percent Americanization Activity in the Territory of Hawaii as Experienced in the Caucasian Press, 1919–1923* (M.A. thesis: University of Ha wai'i, 1967), p. 72.

50. Vaughan MacCaughey, "Some Outstanding Educational Problems of Hawaii," *School and Society* 213 (1919): 102; Henry P. Judd, "The Repaganization of Hawaii," *Friend* 89 (1920): 188.

51. Tamura, *Americanization*, p. 147; Noriko Asato, "Mandating Americanization: Japanese Language Schools and the Federal Survey of Education in Ha wai'i, 1916–1920," *History of Education Quarterly* 43/1 (2003): 37; Doremus Scudder, "Hawaii's Experience with the Japanese," *Annals of the American Academy of Political and Social Science* 93 (1921): 113.

52. Yemyō Imamura, ed., *Hawaii kaikyōshi* (Hawaii: Honpa Hongwanji kaikyō kyōmusho bunshobu), pp. 213–26. After resigning as principal in Hawaii, Tsunoda moved to New York and taught Japanese cultural history at Columbia University. Donald Keene, "Remembrances of Tsunoda Sensei," in *Ryusaku Tsunoda Sensei, 1877–1964,* The Ryusaku Tsunoda Memorial Book Fund, ed. (Tokyo: The Ryusaku Tsunoda Memorial Book Fund, n.d.), pp. 25–36. For detailed accounts of Tsunoda in Hawaii, see Takashi Utsumi, "Tsunoda Ryūsaku no Hawaii jidai: 1909nen no tofu zengo o megutte," *Waseda Daigakushi Kiyō* 30 (1998): 121–74; Takashi Utsumi, "Tsunoda Ryūsaku no Hawaii jidai sairon: 1909–17nen no taizai kikan o chūshin ni shite," *Waseda Daigakushi Kiyō* 31 (1999): 91–124.

53. Yemyō Imamura, *A Short History of the Hongwanji Buddhist Mission in Hawaii* (Honolulu: The Publishing Bureau of Hongwangi [*sic*] Buddhist Mission, 1931), pp. 20–21; Chie Honda, "Dainiji sekai taisenzen no Hawaii ni okeru Jōdo Shinshū Honpa Honganji no Nihongo gakkō: Honolulu o kyoten to shita fukyō katsudō to no kanren de," in *Amerika no nikkeijin: Toshi, shakai, seikatsu,* Toshio Yanagita, ed. (Tokyo: Dōbunkan, 1995), pp. 187–90.

54. Yemyō Imamura, introduction to *The Essence of Japanese Buddhism*, Riusaku Tsunoda. (Honolulu: The Advertiser Press, 1914), pp. 5–7.

55. Yemyō Imamura, "Shimin keihatsu undō ni tsuite," *Dobo* (1916), reprinted in *Chōshōin ibunshū*, Hawaii Honolulu Hongwanji, ed. (Honolulu: Hawaii Honolulu Hongwanji, 1937), p. 74; Hunter, *Buddhism in Hawaii*, pp. 151–71.

56. Hunter, *Buddhism in Hawaii*, p. 105; Robert Cornell Armstrong, *Buddhism and Buddhists in Japan* (London: Society for Promoting Christian Knowledge, 1927), p. 70.

57. Yemyō Imamura, *Democracy According to the Buddhist Viewpoint* (Honolulu: The Publishing Bureau of Hongwanji Mission, 1918), pp. 21, 26–27.

58. Although written postwar, Imamura's expression could perhaps be illuminated by the words of Thich Nhat Hanh. In his essay on nonviolence, he recalls that during the Buddhist struggle for peace in Vietnam, they "had to overcome both communist and anticommunist fanaticism and maintain the strictest neutrality. . . . Both warring parties claimed to speak for what the people really wanted, but . . . The Buddhists only wanted to create a vehicle for the people to be heard—and the people only peace, not a 'victory' by either side." Thich Nhat Hanh, *Love in Action: Writings on Nonviolent Social Change* (Berkeley, Calif.: Parallax Press, 1993), pp. 39–40. Also, one should keep in mind the concurrent political history of imperial Japan while the relatively successful development of the democratic and labor movements were taking place.

59. Luis O. Gómez, trans., The Land of Bliss: The Paradise of the Buddha of Measureless Light: Sanskrit and Chinese Versions of the Sukhāvatīvyūha Sūtras (Honolulu: University of Ha wai'i Press, 1996), p. 215.

60. "1919 nendo kaikyōshi-kai ketsugi yōkō," July 26–30, 1919, Collections, Department of Religious Studies, University of Tokyo.

61. Imamura, Democracy According to the Buddhist Viewpoint, pp. 8–9.

62. Yemyō Imamura, *Beikoku no seishin to shūkyō no jiyū* (Honolulu: Honpa Hongwanji Hawaii kaikyō kyōmusho bunshobu, 1920), p. 13. Although Imamura simply listed William James and John Dewey as pragmatistic philosophers, they had, of course, important differences. D. T. Suzuki's interest in pragmatism was based on James's discourses on religious experience, whereas Imamura related it to democracy and religious pluralism. Like most Issei leaders on the islands, Imamura was a member of the Hawaii Japanese Education Association. Imamura's commitment to Nisei education most likely led him to Dewey, who published *Democracy and Education* in 1916.

63. Imamura, Beikoku no seishin to shūkyō no jiyū, pp. 24–26, 30, 56.

64. Imamura cited in his book on Americanism an excerpt from the *Shorter Sukhāvatīvyūha Sūtra,* which portrays the beauty of the Pure Land where each color of various lotuses blooms and shines in the way they naturally should. I appreciate Bishop Chikai Yosemori of the Honpa Hongwanji Mission of Hawaii for informing me of the importance of this sūtra. For an English translation, see Gómez, *Land of Bliss*, p. 146.

65. Yemyō Imamura, "Bukkyō no sekai ni okeru shimei," *Dōbō* (1917), reprinted in *Chōshōin ibunshū*).

66. Born in Honolulu in 1904 as the son of Yemyō Imamura, Kanmō was first assigned to Waipahu as a minister before transferring to Berkeley in August 1941.

67. The postwar issues have a variety of contributors, including Gary Snyder, Taitetsu Unno, Allan Watts, Hajime Nakamura, among others.

68. Kanmo Imamura, "Bukkyōto wa sekaijin (cosmopolitan) nari," *Berkeley Bussei* (Fall 1941).

69. Jane Michiko Imamura, *Kaikyō: Memoirs of a Buddhist Priest's Wife in America* (Honolulu: Buddhist Study Center Press, 1998), pp. 11–15. For Buddhism during the Japanese American incarceration, see Duncan Ryûken Williams, "Camp Dharma: Japanese-American Buddhist Identity and the Internment Experience of World War II," in *Westward Dharma: Buddhism Beyond Asia,* Charles S. Prebish and Martin Baumann, eds. (Berkeley: University of California Press, 2002), pp. 191–200.

70. Hunter, *Buddhism in Hawaii*, pp. 154, 164–67, 170–71; Kōnen Tsunemitsu, *Nihon bukkyō tobeishi* (Tokyo: Bukkyō shuppankyoku, 1964), p. 65.

71. Ernest H. Hunt, interview by Mrs. Culver, n.d., file "Buddhist," Ha wai'i War Records Depository, Special Collections, Hamilton Library, University of Ha wai'i.

72. Elaine Woo, "Rev. Julius Goldwater; Convert to Buddhism Aided WWII Internees," *Los Angeles Times* (June 23, 2001): A7. See also Tetsuden Kashima's interview with Goldwater. Kashima, *Buddhism in America,* pp. 98–103.

73. Julius A. Goldwater, "Our Future," *Berkeley Bussei* (Spring 1941).

74. After returning to California in 1945, Kanmō Imamura took care of the Senshin Buddhist Hostel for ex-internees in Los Angeles with Goldwater and Arthur Takemoto, then went back to Berkeley, where he founded the Buddhist Study Center (present-day Institute of Buddhist Studies).

PART 4

Patriotism and War

If a central concern of Issei Buddhism was to help first-generation immigrants and their children in the Americas negotiate the difficulties of labor, language, and a culture hostile to them, the period after Pearl Harbor was one of the most trying of circumstances. Although much has been written on the incarceration experience of roughly 120,000 Japanese Americans during World War II, very little has touched on the interior life of the internees nor on the role of religion in times of war and crisis. The two chapters in this section highlight the role of faith among internees as well as those in Hawaii (which was under martial law), but through very different source materials. Keiko Wells brings to light the "song culture" among Japanese Americans in Hawaii, especially those composed during the war to grieve those Nisei who had been killed in combat after they had volunteered (or were later drafted) for service in the military, both in the European theater (as part of the famous 100th Battalion/442nd Regimental Combat Team) or the Pacific theater (as part of the Military Intelligence Service). Akihiro Yamakura, on the other hand, draws on a previously unpublished wartime internment diary of the Bishop of Tenrikyo (a so-called new religious movement that was classified during the war as "Shintō"—though having both Buddhist and Shintō elements as part of this "new religion") to paint a picture of a Issei minister with pro-Japanese sensibilities.

Keiko Wells's study of Buddhist song cultures in Hawaii begins with its composition and singing in the context of labor songs on the plantations and songs of nostalgia for migrants, but extends to a detailed examination of Buddhist songwriters who, both prior to the war and during it, sang extensively through Buddhist motifs.

Wells, a specialist in American folksongs and culture and someone who has previously written on black spirituals and other kinds of religious music, reveals how Buddhist song transmission and song making in the 1930s to 1950s, participated in a local Hawaiian religious and cultural framework. She suggests that this song culture was a mixture of Japanese folksongs, Buddhist sutra chanting, and Western music traditions (especially as seen in Ernest Hunt's 1924 *Vade Mecum*, a compilation of, among other items, Buddhist "hymns" accompanied by Western music).

One of the key songwriters that Wells takes up is Haru Matsuda of Kona. Some time after her son's blood-stained uniform gets returned by the army after his death on the battlefields of Italy, this Issei Buddhist mother composed the following song lyrics to deal with the death:

A WAR SONG

Thousands of miles away from the homeland,
the bright red sunset in Italy looms so far away,
My beloved child is buried under stone.
It is too sad to simply say that he was a brave soldier,
who dashed toward the enemy before anyone else.
Though he killed so many foes, now he lies asleep there.
Oh, how fierce the fighting must have been.
    His fellow soldier suddenly fell beside him. Carl ran over.
    He could not let his friend just lie on the ground,
    though there were the strict military prohibitions against proceeding without orders.
Carl encouraged him, held him in his bosom,
    and put a bandage on him; all on the battlefield.
It was that moment when Carl was shot, and fell.
Oh, my beloved Carl, you became a part of Italy's soil.
    Six years have already passed; finally you have come back to us loving parents
    who have waited and waited for your return
    to your homeland, Hawaii.
You have come back guided by the compassionate hands of America.
You have come back silently. You have come back silently.
Namu Amida Butsu, Namu Amida Butsu.

Although sung to the tune of a Japanese war song (*Gunka*), it is clear that the "homeland" here is Hawaii and that Buddhism had helped the family come to terms with their acceptance of his death and their feeling that they were part of America through his sacrifice to the U.S. Army. No longer using his Japanese name, Gorō, "Carl" and other Nisei Buddhist soldiers who proved their loyalty to the United States come to represent the idea that Americanism is not a matter of race and religion. This notion that one can be a Buddhist and a loyal American came to be recognized even by the U.S. Army (albeit somewhat after the war) as Buddhist soldiers received dharma wheels on their tombstones, "B" on their dog tags, and Buddhist chaplains in the corps.

Bishop Hashimoto of Tenrikyo represents a somewhat different, and equally understudied, perspective on the wartime Japanese American experience. Targeted by the U.S. government as "subversive" because of his role as a religious leader in the community, Hashimoto experienced a number of high-security internment camps operated by the Department of Justice. Akihiro Yamakura's chapter highlights the role that religion played in his arrest, the denial of parole, and the extension of his imprisonment. Indeed, whether in the Department of Justice camps or the War Relocation Authority camps (where the majority of the 120,000 were incarcerated), both Buddhists and Shintoists found themselves at a disadvantage compared with Christians at every stage in the wartime experience. Attempts by Buddhist leaders to demonstrate loyalty to America (for example by denouncing the Japanese military, promoting U.S. war bonds, or encouraging blood donations to the Red Cross) ran up against wartime hysteria. What would today be called "hate crimes" were also directed against Buddhists, such as an incident in which local white boys took their shotguns to the Fresno Buddhist Temple and used the front entrance of the building for target practice. Their potshots were particularly aimed at the ancient Buddhist symbol called the *manji,* which represented an aerial view of a *stūpa* and which adorns many Buddhist temples around the world. An ancient Indian symbol, the *manji* coincidentally—and unfortunately—resembles a German Nazi swastika (though reversed, and predating the swastika by thousands of years). But the weeks and months in the wake of Pearl Harbor were no time for the Issei to try to educate their non-Buddhist neighbors about the difference between a *manji* and a swastika. Trying to convince their neighbors of their loyalty to the United States would only prove fruitless for Buddhists at a time when many Americans, including the U.S. government, viewed their faith as inherently suspicious and foreign. To America they were still Japanese, and so the enemy.

Government agents saw those who had converted to Christianity as more "Americanized" and less of a threat during the initial sweep after Pearl Harbor. Once in camp, Catholics and Protestants received higher levels of cooperation from camp authorities to set up their "barrack churches"; Christians had an advantage when it came to leave clearance as white Christians vouched for their loyalty; and whereas Buddhists returned to their hometowns after the war to find dozens of Buddhist temples vandalized, almost all Japanese Christian churches were protected by white coreligionists. What Yamakura suggests is that those deemed Shintoists were under even more suspicion by the government than the Buddhists were. Particularly with Bishop Hashimoto, because he had served previously in Tenrikyo missions in Asia (as part of the Japanese empire) and had supported the Japanese militarist expansion in Asia, he was seen as a particularly "dangerous" enemy alien. Prior to the war, his and other Tenrikyo sermons were increasingly filled with calls to support Japan from a sense that their ancestral homeland was being unfairly singled out as an aggressor in that European and American empire expansion was normal, but Japanese expansion—that of a nonwhite race—was not. Racism, Yamakura suggests, was as much a factor in Issei wanting to find pride in being Japanese (including its military success on the Asian mainland) as Japanese military ideology and propaganda.

The history of the internment experience has almost always left out the viewpoint of those like Hashimoto, who was pro-Japanese. Tens of thousands of Japanese Americans had conflicted senses of identity, loyalty, and questions about what kind of "democracy" and "land of the free" would incarcerate people solely on the basis of race. By examining Hashimoto's diaries, Yamakura brings to light a major faction within the Japanese American community who, though not disloyal to the United States, had strong ties to and affection for Japan. Yamakura's study thus provides a valuable corrective to the dominant narrative of the incarceration experience, which relies altogether too much on English-language Nisei (and mostly Christian) sources to tell the story.

Where Wells's essay uses songs to show how religion permeates and sustains daily life, Yamakura uses Hashimoto's first-hand accounts of his incarceration in camp to illuminate the complex loyalties demanded by religion and state that are further shaped and transformed by individual experiences—in this case, Hashimoto's experience of marginalization in the United States. Together, the essays by Wells and Yamakura show how the use of unexpected sources can tell a much more complex and nuanced history of American Buddhism and the Japanese American experience than have been told to this point.

7 The United States–Japanese War and Tenrikyo Ministers in America

AKIHIRO YAMAKURA

In the period leading up to the U.S.-Japanese war (World War II), the U.S. government had been increasingly suspicious of Japanese religions practiced in Hawaii and the mainland. A 1941 report compiled by the Office of Naval Intelligence, the intelligence unit of the U.S. Navy, depicted Japanese in the United States as "inherently a religious race" who "depend upon the authority, the ritual, and the doctrines of Shintōism or Buddhism, or both religions, to act as moral factors to guide their personal conduct and to aid their spiritual well being, both in life and hereafter." The report further explained that the priests of both religions were held "in high regard" and "looked upon" as "leaders in the communities"; the "anti-American and possibly subversive elements" it discovered in the Japanese communities were traced "almost invariably" to these priests. Their existence and influence within the ordinary Japanese immigrant community was a source of alarm: "Because of these priests, the nationalistic, Emperor-worshiping doctrines of Shintoism were kept alive among those Japanese whose tendencies were toward pro-Japanism and the fancied mission of the Yamato people. In the same way, certain priests and believers in Buddhism allowed the original meaning of their creed to become adulterated by the desire for Japanese expansion and the philosophy of Japanese supremacy over the other people of the earth."[1]

Tenrikyo[2] was one of the Japanese religions regarded as particularly suspect by the U.S. government before and during World War II. In a "History of Provost Marshal's Office," prepared by G-2, the Intelligence Office of the U.S. Army, Tenrikyo was mentioned along with six other Shintō sects of Izumo Taisha, Kotchira [Kompira] Jinsha, Daijingū [Hawaii Daijingū], Inari Jinsha, Katō Jinsha, and Maui Jinsha, and one Buddhist sect of Nichiren as dangerous religions. Membership in those sects, the document argues, "should be considered an adverse point" in any evaluation of subversive or disloyal activity.[3] Many Tenrikyo ministers in mainland United States and in the territory of Hawaii were arrested and interned during the war. Historian Bob Kumamoto argues that the Federal Bureau of Investigation (FBI) classified Shintō priests in the United States "potentially dangerous" for believing "that their bodies belong to their god and sovereign, the Emperor of Japan." Citing newspapers in San Francisco, he claims that "[t]he Konko and Tenrikyo Churches in San Francisco were of particular interest," because the priests of these faiths "were reportedly receiving secret military instructions from Japan."[4]

During the wartime incarceration of the Japanese Americans, it seems that Tenrikyo was particularly conspicuous, as much so as other major Japanese religions (Buddhism, Japanese Protestantism, and Catholicism) despite the miniscule proportion of the incarcerated population who subscribed to this faith. The War Relocation Authority (WRA), a civilian organization created in 1942 to oversee the detention of Japanese Americans, categorized the inmates according to their religions: Buddhist, Protestant, Catholic, "Tenri-kyo and similar sects" (meaning "sects of popular Shintō"), and Seichō no Iye, even though Tenrikyo followers comprised only 0.4 percent of the total inmate population in the WRA custody.[5]

The bishop of the Tenrikyo North American mission during the war received extraordinarily harsh treatment from the U.S. government. He was left at large for the first two months after the attack on Pearl Harbor, then was interned in five different internment facilities in California, North Dakota, New Mexico, Texas, and New Jersey. He remained incarcerated until April 1947, a year and eight months after the surrender of Japan, longer than most other Japanese internees.

Typically Tenrikyo ministers, including its North American bishop, carefully avoided politics, especially anti-American or antiadministration activities, both before the war and during the internment. Why, then, were these Tenrikyo ministers arrested and the bishop kept in internment so long after the war? What about their faith and behavior provoked such intense suspicions on the part of the U.S. government? How did the bishop respond to the incarceration and perceive how he and his compatriots were treated? These are the themes of this chapter.

It should be noted that what caused the arrest and internment of Tenrikyo ministers also applies to almost every Japanese religious sect and denomination that was doing missionary work in the United States before World War II. Although Tenrikyo especially aroused the U.S. government's suspicions—for example, Tenrikyo's collaboration with the Japanese government's policy of sending its emigrants to Manchuria, a puppet state of the Japanese empire, in the 1930s and the early 1940s—Tenrikyo ministers in the United States shared much with other religious ministers. Therefore, examining the wartime treatment of Tenrikyo ministers can shed light on how other Japanese religious ministers adopted to the American environment foreign to them: how they were treated by a host society that was more or less unfriendly, even hostile on occasions; how the U.S. government dealt with those Japanese who were trying to spread "dangerous" faiths; and how the ministers tried to survive the hardships of the U.S.-Japanese war.

Modern Japan, State Shintō, and the Spread of the Tenrikyo Faith

The constitution of the empire of Japan (proclaimed on February 11, 1889), the emperor system, and State Shintō were principally responsible for a powerful, centralized, Japanese state placing the nation under tight control.[6] Although the constitution granted a certain "freedom," it did so with certain limits. Although Article 28 stipulated religious freedom, freedom shall be enjoyed "within the limits not prejudicial to peace and order, and not antagonistic to their duties as subjects." Whereas shrines of State Shintō were government institutions, and whereas the emperor was sacred and inviolable, religious workers of Buddhism, Christianity, and other Shintō sects had severe restrictions on the exercise of this "freedom."

The Imperial Rescript on Education (*Kyōiku chokugo,* 1890) supplemented the Meiji Constitution with the prescription to indoctrinate the nation in total devotion to the emperor and the state, demanding absolute loyalty and willing sacrifice.[7] As Helen Hardacre argues, the rescript "was far more consequential as a result of its use than because of its content." Some four million copies of the work were printed; those copies were distributed to all public schools, and all schoolchildren were required to memorize it from the second grade. Under the instruction of the Ministry of Education, monthly ceremonies of reciting the rescript and worshiping the imperial photo soon developed everywhere in Japan. Shintō priests actively participated in and promoted these ceremonies.[8]

Under these circumstances, State Shintō, even though it functioned as a religion in practice, was legally reduced to a set of rites and customs and was therefore not treated as a religion. The rescript gave it ideological underpinnings. The state transcended the various declared religions whereas priests of Shintō and Buddhism were left to compete "freely" with each other to serve the state's objectives. This is what religious scholar Yoshio Yasumaru calls "separation of church and state, Japanese style."[9]

This ideological apparatus reached its perfection in national education during the war with the introduction of *kokumin gakkō* (national people's schools) dedicated to indoctrinating children into loyal subjects of the emperor. According to Yoko Irie, the National People's School Order of 1941 aimed at educating subjects of the empire: for lower graders, it instilled admiration for the emperor and the emperor system, dedication to the emperor and the state, and patriotism without any rational explanation; for upper graders, it aimed to create loyal subjects who were conscious of Japan's leadership role in the Great East Asia Co-Prosperity Sphere. Irie cites numerous enthusiastic responses to the indoctrination on the part of children and teachers. These children, who were imprinted with ultranationalism, she argues, while tasting the pleasures of burying themselves in a sense of national unity and conformity, were less equipped to judge things of their own accord.[10]

How did Tenrikyo fit into the restrictive "freedom" of religion and the government's policy demanding conformity? Ever since Tenrikyo began spreading its faith in the mid-nineteenth century, it was under constant persecution from the government. According to *The Teachings and History of Tenrikyo,* compiled by Tenrikyo Overseas Mission Department, "Tenrikyo, neither Shintō nor Buddhism, was regarded as being a malicious god and a heretical religion." The local authorities and nearby shrines investigated Tenrikyo activities persistently, and the police often took the foundress and her chief disciples into custody. The foundress was treated especially harshly; "she was taken to police stations or jails eighteen times in all including the last detention of fifteen days in February at the age of 89."[11]

In 1895, the Ministry of Home Affairs issued a secret directive to all the police stations in all prefectures to suppress Tenrikyo. The Tokyo Metropolitan Police Department issued a directive to the same effect, which was published in newspapers.[12] The government subsequently exerted strong pressure on Tenrikyo to change its doctrine and rituals, threatening to disband Tenrikyo by force unless it complied.[13] In order to avoid the annihilation of their faith, Tenrikyo gave in. It reformed its rituals to conform to State Shintō; it compiled the Meiji version of the *Doctrine of Tenrikyo* in 1903, which emphasizes the sacredness of the divinity of the emperor and the followers' duty to the state as subjects of the emperor. Tenrikyo was forced to compile *The Doctrine* in conformity to State Shintō, and the product was quite divergent from the original doctrines of the faith.[14]

State control of religious life and the pressures to conform to State Shintō, however, was somewhat offset by the state's protection provided to religious organizations considered orthodox. In the Great Promulgation Campaign from 1870 to 1884, the state attempted "to author a religious doctrine and undertook to promulgate it systematically by enlisting as National Evangelists members of every religious organization except those refusing to be so co-opted," and leaders of many popular religious movements were drawn into this project. They thus "traded their independence and autonomy for the prestige of a connection with the state."[15] As historian Shigeyoshi Murakami argues, "persecution coupled with protection was the consistent policy on religions under the Imperial Constitution."[16] After more than three decades of persecution, starting in the mid-1870s, Tenrikyo was finally recognized as a legal religious organization in 1908. *The Teachings and History of Tenrikyo* describes the period between the legalization of the faith and the end of World War II as "the period of conforming to the laws."[17]

In 1926, Tenrikyo Church Headquarters announced that its prime objective in mission efforts would be overseas. The following year it established the Overseas Mission Department and mission headquarters in Manchuria, Tianjin (T'ientsin), and Shanghai.[18] Tenrikyo's overseas mission started in Korea, then went on to China. These mission activities started in the 1890s through various parts of Asia, such as Korea, the Northeast region of Asia ("Manchuria"), and Taiwan. It was the earliest among Shintō sects to do so, and as early as established Buddhist sects. Among Shintō sects, Tenrikyo carried out the largest scale of mission activities in terms of the length of the mission, the area covered, and the number of churches and fellowships built.[19] The Tenrikyo mission in Manchuria is unique, taking the form of a mass migration, sending its followers to build "Tenri Village" there.[20]

The Japanese government sent 270,000 agricultural emigrants to Manchuria to help effectively occupy the colony and to support the war effort in China between 1932 and 1945. In 1934, Masaharu Hashimoto, who later became the North American bishop, was appointed head minister of the first Tenrikyo church in Tenri Village in Manchukuo. In the same year, Tenrikyo sent its first emigrant group of 43 families consisting of 205 people. In 1935, a second emigrant group of 20 families consisting of 112 people were sent. Hashimoto, who was in charge of the initial development of Tenri Village, reminisced in 1941, when he was in office as North American bishop: "I'm filled with joy to observe a unique pioneer town 'Tenri Village' sustaining a sound and steady development and contributing, however in a small way, to the Imperial policy toward Manchukuo."[21]

In 1942, Tenrikyo collaborated with the government's project of sending a million families, totaling five million emigrants. Between 1943 and 1945, it sent on its own 402 households; it planned to send another 200 households, but the war ended before the program was completed.[22] By the Japanese defeat, there were 211 Tenrikyo churches in Korea, 124 in Manchuria, and 46 in the rest of China.[23] Thus, the Tenrikyo mission in Asia followed the flag of the Japanese Empire.

Most of the Japanese who migrated to Japan-occupied areas in Asia must have enjoyed the prestige of a nation that had become a "first-rate" world power in the early-twentieth century, alongside the United States and Great Britain. Tenrikyo ministers and followers were no exceptions. Masaharu Hashimoto once escorted students of the Russian Language Studies of Tenri Foreign Language School (now Tenri University) on a field trip to Manchuria and Far East Russia in 1928. When visiting Harbin, soon to be the economic hub of Northern Manchuria under Japanese occupation, Hashimoto felt safe in the foreign land because of the strong presence of the empire. "Japanese overseas," Hashimoto wrote in his memoir, "never have their worth or prestige recognized as an individual apart from their mother land. Oddly enough, it is the state behind the individuals that counts. To be a Japanese enables us to enjoy the dignity and pride as a citizen of a first-rate power. . . . To the extent that Japan has a strong presence in Harbin, we Japanese can walk with our head held high and feel secure and relaxed."[24]

Tenrikyō and the Surge of Patriotism in the 1930s

In the United States, by contrast, it was becoming increasingly difficult for the Japanese to walk with their head held high, especially starting in the early 1930s. Whereas many Japanese admired and respected the West, especially the United States, many Americans were increasingly suspicious of and hostile toward Japan and the Japanese. Many Japanese in the United States became increasingly defensive and apologetic about Japanese overseas policies, although the stances toward them were diverse, and sometimes even divided in the Japanese communities. Although many of them admired the American way of life, they simultaneously felt the need to support the expansive policy of the Japanese empire as a source of their ethnic pride and identity.

Since at least the early Meiji era, the Japanese held quite different attitudes to the West, especially the United States and Great Britain, than to Asia, especially China and Korea. The Japanese generally admired Western civilization, and some Japanese attempted to emulate life styles of the British and Americans. Yutaka Yoshida, historian of modern Japan, emphasizes the significant amount of Americanization preceding the U.S.-Japanese war. "In pre-war Japan, the living standard of the Japanese peaked around 1935–1936, until which the American life style had been the model for the Japanese in general and the aspiration of the white collar in particular, at least in the urban area."[25] This Americanization, along with the admiration for American consumer goods and material life, significantly deterred the full development of anti-American sentiments in the 1930s.

Tenrikyo followers did not escape these influences. Hashimoto reminisced in his autobiography that when he was appointed bishop of Tenrikyo Mission Headquarters in America in 1939, "Tenrikyo Headquarters then had abundant talent for the post, and it was the assignment every one wished; it meant going abroad to America, an advanced country."[26]

Tenrikyo mission efforts in North America took a fundamentally different form than its mission work in Asia. Tenrikyo overseas missions on the Asian continent and in the South Pacific generally followed the flag of the empire, whereas Tenrikyo ministers to the United States, Hawaii, and Canada followed the path of emigrant laborers. Some Tenrikyo followers migrated to North America themselves as immigrant laborers and only later started missionary work. Even though Tenrikyo won a number of converts among the native people in Asia,[27] the converts in North America were almost exclusively other Japanese immigrants. North American missionaries, including the bishop, did not have to speak English, and therefore acquired little command of the language; they almost always ate Japanese food and remained almost exclusively within Japanese communities on the West Coast and in Hawaii.[28] Before World War II, these communities lived a largely segregated existence.

But this phenomenon was by no means wholly accounted for by Tenrikyo ministers and followers. Japanese in the United States were excluded from the mainstream society, denied naturalization, forbidden to possess or lease land for more than two years, and segregated into ethnic enclaves along the West Coast. The segregation and exclusion of the Japanese was a part of larger racist patterns of the U.S. society, where racial segregation was not only a widely practiced social custom but was also constitutionally sanctioned by official policies of the federal and state governments (beginning with the Supreme Court decision in *Plessy v. Ferguson*[29] in 1896 and ending with the decision in *Brown v. Board of Education*[30] in 1954).

The report of the Tolan Committee, which investigated the "evacuation" of the Japanese and made an affirmative recommendation in 1942, noted the high concentration of the Japanese and gave a cause: "As a result of restrictions, legal or otherwise, the Japanese have remained concentrated near the points of immigration where they were originally brought to provide a cheap agricultural labor supply."[31] In a report on the implementation of the "evacuation" policy, the Western Defense Command used this concentration as the rationale for the exclusion measure. "Because of the tie of race," the report argued, "the intense feeling of filial piety and the strong bonds of common tradition, culture and customs, this population presented a tightly-knit racial group." "Whether by design or accident," it went on, "virtually always their communities were adjacent to very vital shore installations, war plants, etc."[32]

The Western Defense Command thus suggested disloyalty on the part of the Japanese on the West Coast.

This conspiracy theory was based on a half-truth at best. As I have already mentioned, the Japanese on the West Coast and in Hawaii, including Tenrikyo followers, admired the American way of life and recognized the importance of maintaining friendly relations with the host society; some of them, especially the second-generation population, eagerly tried to assimilate into American culture. At the same time, strong emotional ties with the mother country (as manifest in moral and monetary support for it) were a natural strategy for maintaining pride and integrity among Japanese Americans confronting the humiliations of discrimination, exclusion, and segregation. For the Issei population, most of whose activities were strictly contained within their ethnic communities, their social status in this "tightly-knit" society was determined by the comparable social status they would have enjoyed in their mother country.

By the late 1930s and the early 1940s, the Japanese government's persecution of Tenrikyo and the consequent stigma attached were long forgotten. The decent social status Tenrikyo enjoyed at home at that time can be illustrated with a few examples. Hashimoto's memoir, diary, and autobiography make occasional references to rather comfortable relations with Japanese government agencies, and even report occasional favors granted to Tenrikyo ministers. The field trip to eastern Russia and Manchuria, for example, would not have been possible without government approval.

Furthermore, Hashimoto, as North American bishop, was granted what looks like a special favor by the Japanese army. He visited Japan for both official and personal business in July 1941. When because of the deteriorating bilateral relations, Hashimoto had difficulty finding a return passage in September, he sailed to Shanghai and tried to find a ship to the United States but to no avail. In the meantime, he received news that passage to the United States would probably be available at Yokohama, so he negotiated with the Japanese army in China for transport on a military plane. The first negotiation was unsuccessful, but finally, with the help of a certain Tenrikyo follower, he secured a flight back to Japan in a military plane provided by the Imperial Army.[33] Even though the initial negotiation did not succeed, the very fact that he went to the army to negotiate for flight service during the war with China reflects the status and prestige of Tenrikyo in the Japanese empire at this time.

If the social prestige they enjoyed in the ethnic communities and the prestige of their mother country in the international society were sources of pride to buttress themselves against the social humiliation of discrimination and racial segregation in the host society, it was only natural for the Japanese religious ministers to want to contribute to the cause of the empire. Japanese Christians, Buddhists, Shintōists, and Tenrikyo followers, almost without exceptions, enthusiastically contributed to the early war efforts of the empire, especially after Japan began to fight China in 1938. According to the Japanese Association of America, the leading Issei economic and political organization in the prewar days, Japanese Christians donated care packages, created soldier-relief funds, and even sent donations to cover part of the expense for "comfort" houses. The Hokubei Bukkyō Dan (North American Buddhist Mission) even sent its ministers to cheer up "Imperial soldiers" fighting in the "China Incident" during 1937 and 1938. Konkōkyō sent a fourteen-member "comfort" mission headed by North American Bishop Yoshiaki Fukuda to China to encourage Japanese soldiers; they visited Japanese army troops deployed in Korea, Russia, the Russian-Manchurian border land, and Northern China with 5,600 care packages, about 700 pounds of candy, and "patriotic" donations.[34]

If not in the amount of donations, Tenrikyo did no less in terms of its enthusiasm. After the "China Incident," the mission headquarters in Los Angeles occasionally held prayer services specifically to enhance the prestige of the empire, praying for the health of the soldiers going to the front.[35] Sermon lectures and notices to followers were increasingly filled with calls for dedication not only to the Tenrikyo faith but also to the cause of the Japanese state in the middle of a "national emergency."[36]

The devotion of Tenrikyo followers in America was not limited to expressions of patriotism and a spirit of cooperation with the war efforts of the mother country. They also made great efforts to make monetary contributions, like many other religious organizations from Japan. In July 1937, shortly after Japan opened fire with China, Tenrikyo Young Men's Association responded to a campaign to donate war planes started by the *Osaka Asahi Shimbun*.[37] A total of $1,060.65 were sent from 41 churches, 9 Tenrikyo followers' associations, and 159 individual followers in America.[38] The *Osaka Asahi Shimbun* reported Tenrikyo's "donation for 'wings of the mother land,'" and the "ardent patriotic sincerity also found among Tenrikyo followers overseas."[39] Kunio Higashida, who lived close to the mission headquarters at that time, often saw Bishop Hashimoto "enthusiastically commanding a number of followers in producing care packages for the front."[40]

Because a patriotic surge also developed among Americans, the pro-Japanese behaviors and activities of the Japanese in America were increasingly putting them in jeopardy. The two world wars triggered a sense of American patriotism, triggered fears of foreign elements, and an intense movement of Americanization, including attempts to force assimilation, as historian Philip

Gleason argues.[41] He argues that this trend of Americanization and forced assimilation was given added impetus by World War II.[42]

World War II made many Americans, especially government leaders and politicians, feel that national unity was absolutely essential. President Franklin D. Roosevelt put precedent on victory over anything else. His administration attempted to elicit large war efforts from the Americans and "utilized techniques earlier developed by national advertising and by the media," for instance war bonds "to sell the war." It also used the movie industry and the Office of War Information to command the nation's support of the war. In these campaigns for selling the war, truths were sometimes sacrificed for the sake of the war propaganda.[43] Contribution to the state and its war efforts were now the obligation of the nation.

Discussing wartime civil liberties, historian Richard Polenberg argued that wartime restrictions upon individual liberties took various forms depending upon "the nature of war, the kind of opposition that existed, the type of internal threat perceived, the relative strength of various immigrant groups, the composition of the Supreme Court, and the outlook of the Roosevelt Administration."[44] For the Japanese in the United States, most of these factors worked against them.[45] The result was widespread war hysteria and intense anti-Japanese feelings among many Americans.[46]

War and Tenrikyo Ministers

Before Hashimoto visited Japan in July 1941, he applied for return visas for his wife and daughter, thinking that their visas would come during his stay in Japan. But only his daughter's, not his wife's arrived. Unable to take his wife with him, he left his daughter behind, and returned to Los Angeles alone in November 1941, intending to summon both of them when he obtained his wife's visa. Before he could do so, however, the war broke out.[47]

Japanese at home, including many Tenrikyo followers, exulted over the attack by the Japanese navy on Pearl Harbor. Hashimoto's wife, Kei, worried in her diary about her husband's safety and expressed her grief of living apart from him. At the same time, however, she was overjoyed with the opening of the war with the United States, writing:

> The imperial rescript [of declaring a war] describes America's arrogant behaviors of having insulted our country to this day, our patience and restraint for the sake of establishing a Great Co-Prosperity Sphere, and the emperor's desperate determination that we had no choice but to go to war for the sake of our nation's prestige and survival. When I read our majesty's heart-rending determination, I braced myself. I could not stop my tears from running down.

> At the same time I cried cheers for our majesty's declaration of war and replied to our majesty in my mind that I would exert myself to the utmost in fulfilling my duty day and night with "the spirit of gaining nothing but a victory" for the sake of our majesty and our country.[48]

This might sound to contemporary ears like a remarkable statement for a housewife whose husband had returned to a belligerent country as an enemy alien, but it indicates how much the Japanese emperor system in conjunction with State Shintō had affected ordinary Japanese minds, including those of Tenrikyo followers. It is now our common knowledge that many Japanese were excited about the empire's declaration of war against *kichiku Bei-Ei* (diabolical America and Britain).

This exultation was shared by some Japanese in the United States, but many of them immediately had sober reflections on the grave situation they now faced. Tenrikyo followers in America became immediately aware of the implications of the attack. Bishop Hashimoto had had the "harrowing experience" of burning all kinds of important documents such as correspondence between the church headquarters in Tenri, Japan, and the mission headquarters in Los Angeles; letters from the Tenrikyo *Shinbashira* (the spiritual leader of Tenrikyo), his parents, and friends; and the mission journal. He recorded his thoughts in his diary: "The moment I thought I was standing on the enemy land, a cold chill ran through the spine. There was no place to run away to. I have no choice but to wait for the subsequent development leaving everything to fate." Susumu Yoshida, secretary of the mission headquarters and Hashimoto's assistant, reminisced: "The surprise I felt at the opening of the Japanese–United States war was beyond description. I did my utmost to give minimum trouble to anyone else around us as a person in charge of an organization, but you can't use any cheap trick in the war between the states. I couldn't do anything else but to let nature take its course."[49]

President Roosevelt made the public proclamation, in which he declared as "enemy aliens" such persons as "all natives, citizens, denizens, or subjects of the hostile nation or government, being of the age of fourteen years and upward, who shall be within the United States and not actually naturalized." "Alien enemies deemed dangerous to the public peace or safety of the United States by the Attorney General or Secretary of War," he continued, "are subject to summary apprehension."[50]

Several hours after the attack on Pearl Harbor, the arrest of Japanese "dangerous aliens" began. Many were abruptly taken from their homes and detained without any charge; most were arrested for no apparent reason other than being leaders of the Japanese community, being members of organizations that were considered pro-Japanese, having strong emotional ties with their mother country, or, in the case of fishermen, being capable of sending signals to the enemy by shortwave radio. Those arrested were sent to Justice Department detention stations and camps, which were temporary detention facilities for those arrested, where they were given alien hearings.[51] The purpose of the hearings was to record evidence and make recommendations to the attorney general about whether they would recommend release, parole, or internment for the arrested.[52] Almost 7,000 Japanese on the mainland and 875 in Hawaii were eventually sent to the Justice Department's internment camps on the mainland.[53]

A large group of Tenrikyo ministers were arrested as a part of this roundup, totaling fifty people (thirty-six on the mainland and fourteen in Hawaii). Bishop Hashimoto was arrested by three plainclothes FBI agents at the mission headquarters in Los Angeles on February 19, 1942, which happens to fall on the day when President Roosevelt issued Executive Order 9066, which authorized the removal of the entire Japanese American population from the West Coast. Detained in the Los Angeles County Jail and Tujunga Federal Prison for a few days, he was sent to Fort Lincoln, Bismarck, North Dakota. He was subsequently given a hearing to determine how he would be treated during the war.[54]

The hearing board, consisting of a judge, a prosecutor, and an FBI agent, began, according to Hashimoto's recollection, by acknowledging that he was in charge of sixty-four Tenrikyo churches in North America and that he was a man of considerable education and wisdom. The board asked him, for example, questions such as: when, how long, and in what capacity he had served in the military in Japan; why he had returned to Japan with his family (wife and daughter) immediately before the war; whether he had predicted the coming of the war at the time; how he assessed the Great East Asia Co-Prosperity Sphere Japan was advocating; how he thought Japan should deal with occupied territories such as the Philippines; whether he regarded the emperor as God; whether he would obey the emperor's orders; whether he would lead the Tenrikyo followers and take up arms to expel an invasion army from Japan if they landed on the mainland United States; and whether he thought the attack on Pearl Harbor was right or wrong.[55]

According to his personal file kept by the FBI, the Alien Enemy Hearing Board on June 5, 1942, found him "a dangerous enemy alien" and recommended that "he be interned for the duration [of the war]." The following evaluation of him may have been what determined his fate: "The Board cannot take the statement of the detainee as to his loyalty to the United States at their face value in view of his position of importance in the Japanese Colony and in view of his broad ideas. The O.N.I. reports that they have evidence that detainee made statements very detrimental to the United States, but the Board did not ask the detainee to verify such statements because they were quite sure that the detainee would deny them, in view of his other testimony."[56]

John Edgar Hoover, director of the FBI, clarified the content of the Office of Naval Intelligence report referred to here: Hashimoto, Hoover wrote, "has been organizing in the Los Angeles area to assist an invading force."[57] Another FBI document reveals the existence of an informant, probably Japanese American, behind this judgment. The FBI investigation leading to his arrest, the document explained, was "predicated upon a report from [agent's name deleted] whose identity is known to the Bureau," which said: "Reliable confidential Jap informant of this office states" that Hashimoto "is president of the Tenrikyo, a Jap religious sect, and is in this country for the purpose of spreading Jap. Propaganda among both Nisei and Isei [*sic*] Japs. . . . Subject has stated that he is endeavoring to organize both Nisei and Isei [*sic*] Japs for their future duties to the Jap government in the event of Jap invasion of the U.S."[58]

Hashimoto and other Tenrikyo ministers were thus arrested and interned in a variety of places, such as Fort Missoula, Montana; Fort Lincoln, Bismarck, North Dakota; Santa Fe, New Mexico; and Lordsburg, New Mexico. Ministers picked out for prolonged internment ended up in Crystal City Internment Camp, Texas, a family internment camp established by the federal government to allow internees and their families to remain together.[59] Many of the Tenrikyo minister internees were of advanced age, and the internment was so trying that one of them was paralyzed and three ministers died. One head minister of a church had a stroke in 1942 while at Santa Fe Internment Camp, which left his body paralyzed.[60] The same year, a prominent member of a church in California died of nephritis at Fort Lincoln Internment Camp.[61] In 1943, two head ministers of churches in California and one head minister of a church in Hawaii passed away at Santa Fe Internment Camp.[62]

The families of the interned ministers were also affected. For example, the family of Manabu Yama, head minister of a church in Hawaii was deprived of subsistence when Yama was arrested: They were subsequently "voluntarily evacuated" to a WRA center at Jerome, Arkansas, in order to join Yama.[63] Learning that he could be with his family in a WRA camp if his parole was granted, Yama submitted his petition for parole or release on November 15, 1943. The commanding general, Hawaiian Department, U.S. Army, recommended his parole, but the Alien Enemy Control Unit, Department of Justice, did not concur. In view of the fact that Yama had not requested repatriation, the Prisoner of War Division, Department of War, resubmitted his case to the Alien Enemy Control Unit for reconsideration.[64] It concluded, however, that his case and three others they were considering concurrently "do not present proper records for parole," because Yama and another internee "are Shintō priests, and the other two are very recent arrivals whose Japanese background and education has not had the opportunity to be counteracted by long residence in this country or in Hawaii."[65] Yama's family was kept waiting for a year in Arkansas, finally reuniting as internees at Crystal City Internment Camp in March 1944.

Of these hardship cases of internment, Hashimoto's is unique. Soon after Hashimoto received the order of internment in Fort Lincoln, North Dakota, on July 5, 1942, his fellow Tenrikyo followers already incarcerated in Poston Relocation Center, Arizona, began an effort to win his release, collecting over 280 signatures on a petition. He was given a second hearing in Santa Fe Internment Camp, New Mexico, on December 7, 1945, exactly four years after the attack on Pearl Harbor. Four months later, on April 8, 1946, he received a deportation order. Tenrikyo followers again carried a campaign for his release, writing up a petition that emphasized why he had returned to the United States on the final ship before the war, leaving his wife and daughter behind in Japan.[66]

The petition for his release remained unanswered for almost half a year. He then decided to apply for employment at Seabrook Farms in Bridgeton, New Jersey, a food-processing and cannery company that was both contributing to the wartime policy of food production and making a lucrative business as one of the largest and most successful food-processing companies in the nation. According to historian Mitziko Sawada, the company was trying to tap into a large variety of labor sources, including female college and high-school students; immigrant workers from the Caribbean and Mexico; black migrant workers from Florida; white migrant workers from West Virginia, Kentucky, Tennessee, and Arkansas; and even German prisoners of war.[67]

The company, with the cooperation of the WRA, which wanted to release as many "loyal" Japanese Americans in their custody as possible, recruited approximately 2,500 Issei and Nisei from the WRA centers. Immediately after World War II ended, Seabrook Farms employed 178 Japanese Peruvians who had been deported by the Peruvian government to the United States and were also interned at the Justice Department internment camps.[68]

Sawada's pioneer work on the Japanese American workers in Seabrook Farms does not mention two more groups of workers of Japanese ancestry in Seabrook Farms. One group is about 300 "renunciants"; they were a part of 5,589 Japanese Americans who, under threat of mistreatment by the WRA, renounced citizenship and consequently were designated by the WRA as "native Japanese aliens."[69] The other is a small number of Japanese "enemy aliens" who remained interned in the Justice Department internment camps even after the end of the war. Hashimoto belonged to the last group, which he called with a bit of sarcasm "the hard core of the dangerous enemy aliens."[70]

When his application for employment at Seabrook Farms was accepted, he was overjoyed. He was quite disappointed, however, and felt deceived the moment he saw "the miserable, filthy, and poorly furnished barracks" surrounded by barbed wire, where he was supposed to live during his employment. The living conditions in this residence, Hashimoto wrote, "was worse than any other internment camp since the days of Bismarck [Fort Lincoln], and quite intolerable indeed." The working conditions, especially, the 13-hour-long night shift, were so trying on him that his heart disease reappeared. Waiting in the extremely long food line in the company cafeteria at every meal was also hard; so was commuting from his barrack to the factory by bus, which took thirty to forty minutes each way. The pecuniary reward for this hard labor was surprisingly meager. He worked for 39.6 hours in the first week at 67.5 cents per hour; his first paycheck was $26.73, from which $14.39 was deducted as Social Security, state tax, income tax, union dues, meal tickets, etc. His net income for the first week, therefore, was $12.34. In his second week, he worked much longer, 66.1 hours. For this labor he was paid $44.62 with the deduction of $23.35; his net pay was $21.27. "This was the result of my spine-shattering labor," Hashimoto wrote, "I was barely surviving as if I were living on my own flesh and blood."[71]

Hashimoto endured all this hardship for seven months, because he had to avoid disgrace of deportation, not as an individual but as North American bishop of Tenrikyo mission. He complied with the U.S. government policy of food production, thereby producing "good rationale for his eventual release."[72] However, his perseverance approached its limit during his months of strenuous, miserable, and humiliating labor at Seabrook Farms.

On February 27, 1947, Hashimoto received the news that his wife Kei passed away on February 14. For the next month and a half, he struggled with a mixture of despair, deep grief, regret, and retrospection of his wife, while enduring the hardships of his employment. His over seventy-years-old mother and his thirteen-year-old only daughter were now alone in a war-devastated country. His own church in Nagasaki was completely demolished by the atomic bomb. Many churches subordinate to his in Korea, Manchuria, and China were shuttered as followers fled back to Japan "with nothing but their clothes on." His two brothers were devastated by the war. His wife's death was the last straw. Hashimoto reported to the Immigration and Naturalization Service office in Philadelphia in person and withdrew his suit for the stay of his deportation order on April 21, 1947, had himself released next day, and returned to Japan for good.[73]

In the autobiography he published after the war, he described the U.S. policy vis-à-vis the Japanese in the United States during the war as "cruel, ruthless, and inhumane." Referring to the misery, grief, anxiety, and extreme hardship the Japanese suffered at the hands of the U.S. government, Hashimoto argued, "there is nothing more preposterous for America at its extreme end of anti-democracy to advocate 'democratizing Japan' after having done tyranny of that magnitude."[74]

Conclusion

The fates of the Japanese in the United States in general, that of Tenrikyo ministers in particular, and that of Bishop Hashimoto most specifically, were the result of the Americanization movement and the accompanying xenophobia in the United States as well as intense Japanese nationalism triggered by the aggressive and militaristic policy of the Japanese Empire. The main causes leading to Tenrikyo ministers being incarcerated and its bishop held for a very long time, even after the defeat of Japan are (1) the aggressive, nationalistic, and militaristic policy of the Japanese empire, which in turn triggered intense nationalism and patriotism in prewar Japan; (2) the nearly inevitable accommodation and compromise of almost all the religious organizations during the period, including Tenrikyo, to the imperialistic expansive policies of the state, and the occasional identification of Tenrikyo leaders and followers with their government's overseas expansion and aggression; (3) the fact that Tenrikyo ministers in the United States confined the sphere of their daily lives and their missionary activities to Japanese ethnic community; (4) statements and behaviors of Tenrikyo followers in the United States cooperating with the war policy of their home government; and, finally, (5) development of intense patriotism, Americanization movement, and xenophobia, which created political and social circumstances quite adverse to the Japanese population in the United States.

Tenrikyo endeavored to survive in extremely adverse circumstances in Meiji Japan and managed to conform to the national policy of the empire—perhaps so enthusiastically that the conformity obscured, at least on the surface of it, its identity as a unique religion, which in itself is neither Shintō nor Buddhist. Leading up to the U.S.-Japanese war, it even came to enjoy some prestige in the State Shintō system. This status of Tenrikyo at home, combined with enthusiastic expressions of patriotism and dedication to the imperial policy by Tenrikyo followers in the United States, clearly alarmed the federal government.

The *Ofudesaki*,[75] one of the Tenrikyo scriptures, reveals the divine words of God the Parent revealing itself as the Creator of all human beings: "I am the original God who created human beings of this world."[76] However, contemporary Tenrikyo followers, including those in America, came quite close to accepting the emperor as God, at least in words, if not in heart and mind. Some followers in America must have expressed the emperor's "divinity" rather casually, and those expressions caught the attention of the American intelligence agencies. An FBI document I obtained through the Freedom of Information and Privacy Act reveals how the FBI observed Hashimoto and Tenrikyo in America. Referring to Tenrikyo as one branch of "the Shinto Cult," it argued: "This sect teaches that a Japanese is born only to give his body and life in the service of his Emperor. He is taught that his first loyalty is to his religion, one of the chief individuals or deities of which is simultaneously the head of the Japanese Government."[77]

In hindsight, it was careless and unwise for Japanese nationals living in America to express loyalty to the emperor and to refer to his "divinity" in the late 1930s and the early 1940s. Yet it certainly was not unconstitutional in light of freedom of speech (Amendment 1, U.S. Constitution),[78] particularly when expressed among fellow Tenrikyo followers. Moreover, it definitely should not have been a rationale for the particularly harsh treatments accorded to Tenrikyo ministers: the sudden removal from their residence, separation from their mission and families, lengthy incarceration, and the stigma of "dangerous enemy aliens." Bishop Hashimoto, in particular, suffered extreme agony and dishonor as one of the "select few internees" who remained interned long after the end of the war. To cap it all, he had to accept deportation, an extreme stigma he had struggled to avoid at all cost. The interned Tenrikyo ministers and their families certainly did not deserve such treatment. The U.S. government interned those who were not "dangerous to the security of the United States" at an unnecessary cost and left Hashimoto, who had accepted his assignment to the United States with a sense of honor and appreciation, with deeply disturbed and suspicious feelings about American "democracy."

Notes

1. H. S. Burr, U.S. Navy Reserve, District Intelligence Officer, U.S. Navy, "Naval Intelligence Manual for Investigating Japanese Cases in Hawaii," RG 389: Record of the Office of the Provost Marshal General, 1941-, Japanese Internment and Relocation: Hawaii Experiences, University of Hawaii, Hamilton Library, Special Collection, Box 3, A-40, pp. 50–51.

2. Tenrikyo Church Headquarters officially spell the religion without a macron as "Tenrikyo" instead of "Tenrikyō," a practice I will follow here.

3. Office of the Chief of Military History, United States Army, "History of Provost

Marshal's Office: United States Army Forces Middle Pacific and Predecessor Commands during World War II—7 December 1941–2 September 1945," vol. 24, pt. 5, appendix "A": Japanese, p. 815, Japanese Internment and Relocation: Hawaii Experiences, University of Hawaii, Hamilton Library, Special Collection, Box 2, CH-5.

4. Bob Kumamoto, "The Search for Spies: American Counterintelligence and the Japanese American Community, 1931–1942," *Amerasia Journal* 6/2 (Fall 1979): 65.

5. War Relocation Authority, *War Relocation Authority, Vol. 3, The Evacuated People: A Quantitative Description* (Washington, D.C.: GPO, 1946; reprint New York: AMS Press, 1975), p. 79.

6. Meiji Japan had struggled to create a unified, centralized, powerful nation. In 1871, it abolished *han* (feudal domains) and established a centralized *ken* (prefectural) system, thereby creating a politically unified nation. It also invented a concept called *kokugo* (the language of the nation) by suppressing numerous local dialects. Lee Yeounsuk, *"Kokugo" to iu shisō: Kindai Nihon no gengo ninshiki* (Tokyo: Iwanami shoten, 1996), pp. v–vi. The constitution, as legal historian Kazuhiro Takii argues, was a response to the world phenomenon of rising nationalism in the nineteenth century on the part of the Meiji government, which was desperately attempting to win approval and respect of the Western nations. Kazuhiro Takii, *Bunmeishi no naka no Meiji kenpō: Kono kuni no katachi to seiyō taiken* (Tokyo: Kōdansha, 2003), pp. 10–11, 144–45. The new government further attempted to create a unified philosophical value among the nation by inventing a state religion based on State Shintō.

7. Kang Sang-jung, *Nashonarizumu* (Tokyo: Iwanami shoten, 2001), pp. 54–73.

8. Helen Hardacre, *Shintō and the State, 1868–1988* (Princeton, N.J.; Princeton University Press, 1989), pp. 122–23.

9. Yoshio Yasumaru, *Kamigami no Meiji ishin: Shinbutsu bunri to haibutsu kishaku* (Tokyo: Iwanami shoten, 1979), pp. 208–9.

10. Yoko Irie, *Nihon ga "kami no kuni" datta jidai: Kokumin gakkō no kyōkasho o yomu* (Tokyo: Iwanami shoten, 2001), pp. 8–10, 201–2, 220.

11. Tenrikyo Overseas Mission Department, ed., *The Teachings and History of Tenrikyo* (Tenri, Japan: Tenrikyo Overseas Mission Department, 1986), pp. 110–11.

12. Ibid., p. 115; Nobutaka Inoue et al., eds., *Shinshūkyō jiten* (Tokyo: Kōbundō, 1990), p. 493.

13. *The Teachings and History of Tenrikyo*, p. 115.

14. Makoto Hiraki, "Meijiki ni okeru Tenrikyo no Chōsen-Kankoku dendōshi," *Chōsen gakuhō* 119/120 (July 1986): 14.

History suggests that Tenrikyo's choice to conform to the authorities was inevitable. Between 1921 and 1944, the authorities persecuted thirty-eight religious organizations; they prosecuted three of them twice and completely destroyed one of them, Ōmotokyō, by arresting and putting in custody members of the cadre and tearing down the main sanctuary. Among the persecuted were four dissident organizations splintering off from Tenrikyo. One of them, Honmichi, was persecuted twice. As a part of the second persecution, in 1944, its founder Aijirō Ōnishi was sentenced to life. *Shinshūkyō jiten*, pp. 495–506.

15. Hardacre, *Shintō and the State*, pp. 7–8, 22.

16. Shigeyoshi Murakami, *Kokka Shintō* (Tokyo: Iwanami shoten, 1970), pp. 204–5.

17. *The Teachings and History of Tenrikyo*, p. 120.

18. Ibid., p. 123.

19. Inoue et al., *Shinshūkyō jiten*, p. 611.

20. For the details of Tenrikyo's involvement in the enterprise of Manchuria migration, see Masaharu Hashimoto, *Tenrikyo seinenkai Manshū imin jigyō o kataru* (Tenri, Japan: Private Publication, 1941).

21. Ibid., p. 1.

22. Wataru Ōya, *Kyōha shintō to kindai nippon: Tenrikyo no shiteki kōsatsu* (Osaka: Tōhō shuppan, 1992), pp. 124–25.

23. Tenri University Oyasato Institute, *Tenrikyo gaisetsu* (Tenri, Japan: Tenri University Press, 1981), p. 107.

24. Masaharu Hashimoto, "So-Man kikō," in *Kikō: Satsukibare Vol. 1,* Masaharu Hashimoto and Akio Sano, eds. (Tenri, Japan: Private Publication, 1958), pp. 77–78.

25. Yutaka Yoshida, "Sengo 'Nihonjin' no rekishi ninshiki/sensō kan no hensen," in *Rekishi ninshiki ronsō,* Tetsuya Takahashi, ed. (Tokyo: Sakuhinsha, 2002), p. 33.

26. Hashimoto, *Tako: Jijoden Vol. 2* (Tenri, Japan: Haru Hashimoto, 1955) (hereafter cited as Hashimoto's *Autobiography*), p. 104.

27. Inoue et al., *Shinshūkyō jiten*, pp. 611–14.

28. Toyohiko Tsuji, "Introduction," in *Tenrikyo beikoku fukyō jūnenshi,* Susumu Yoshida, ed. (Los Angeles: Tenrikyo Mission Headquarters in America, 1938), pp. 52–55. Tsuji was the first bishop of North America, serving from 1934 to 1939. He was succeeded by Hashimoto.

29. 163 U.S. 537 (1896).

30. 347 U.S. 483 (1954).

31. U.S. Congress, *House Report No. 1911: Report of the Select Committee Investigating National Defense Migration, House of Representatives,* 77th Cong. 2d Sess., p. 12.

32. John L. DeWitt, *Final Report: Japanese Evacuation from the West Coast, 1942* (Washington, D.C.: GPO, 1943), p. 9.

33. Hashimoto, *Autobiography,* pp. 114–16.

34. Zaibei Nihonjinkai, ed., *Zaibei Nihonjinshi* (San Francisco: Zaibei Nihonjinkai, 1940, reprint, Tokyo: PMC shuppan, 1984), pp. 364, 418–19, 425, 453.

35. *Amerika,* no. 70, May 1, 1938, p. 2. *Amerika* was a monthly organ of the Tenrikyo Mission Headquarters in America; it was started in January 1937, combining the mission headquarters' monthly reports and *Rokuji News,* an enlightenment magazine for Nisei followers.

36. *Amerika,* no. 22, October 1, 1938, pp. 1, 2, 4.

37. The *Osaka Asahi Shimbun* (July 20, 1937): 1; (July 30, 1937): 15.

38. *Amerika,* no. 9, September 1, 1937, p. 1. The statistics were compiled by this author based on ibid., pp. 2–3; and *Amerika,* no. 10, October 1, 1937, pp. 3–4.

39. The *Osaka Asahi Shimbun* (August 4, 1937): 11.

40. Interview with Kunio Higashida, Los Angeles, August 14, 1994.

41. Philip Gleason, "American Identity and Americanization," in *Harvard Encyclopedia of American Ethnic Groups,* Stephen Thernstrom et al., eds. (Cambridge, Mass.: Harvard University Press, 1980), p. 40.

42. Philip Gleason, *Speaking of Diversity: Language and Ethnicity in Twentieth-Century America* (Baltimore, Md.: The Johns Hopkins University Press, 1992), pp. 163–64.

43. John Morton Blum, *V Was for Victory: Politics and American Culture during World War II* (New York: Harcourt Brace Jovanovich, 1976), pp. 15–52; Richard Polenberg, *War and Society: The United States, 1941–1945* (New York: J. B. Lippincott, 1942), pp. 51–53.

44. Polenberg, *War and Society,* pp. 37–38.

45. Discussing each of these factors is not in the scope of this chapter. For the racist characteristics of the war, especially a diabolical image of the Japanese as a despised enemy, see John W. Dower, *War without Mercy: Race and Power in the Pacific War* (New York: Pantheon, 1986); for the role of the Supreme Court in the Japanese removal and incarceration, see Peter Irons, *Justice at War: The Story of the Japanese American Internment Cases* (New York: Oxford University Press, 1983); for the composition of the Supreme Court that worked against the incarcerated Japanese Americans, see Melvin I. Urofsky, *Division and Discord: The Supreme Court under Stone and Vinson, 1941–1953* (Columbia: University of South Carolina Press, 1997); and especially Paul L. Murphy, *The Constitution in Crisis Times, 1918–1969* (New York: Harper & Row, 1972), p. 246.

46. In 1981, the Commission on Wartime Relocation and Internment of Civilians acknowledged "race prejudice, war hysteria and a failure of political leadership" as "the broad historical causes which shaped the decision" to exclude and incarcerate over 120,000 Japanese and Japanese Americans. Commission on Wartime Relocation and Internment of Civilians, ed., *Personal Justice Denied: Report of the Commission on Wartime Relocation and Internment of Civilians* (Washington, D.C.: GPO, 1982), pp. 1, 18.

47. Hashimoto, *Autobiography,* p. 118.

48. Haru Hashimoto, ed., *Haha: Hashimoto Kei shinobugusa Vol. 2* (Tenri, Japan: Haru Hashimoto, 1953), pp. 72–73. This is an edited collection of Kei Hashimoto's diary she had kept between April 21, 1921, the day of her wedding, and February 2, 1947, twelve days before her death; outgoing and incoming letters; and drafts of her sermon lectures. Its copyright page indicates Haru Hashimoto, daughter of Masaharu and Kei, as editor, but Haru herself says the real editor must have been her father Masaharu, because she was a high school student at that time. This is a valuable supplement to Masaharu's memoir, diary, and autobiography.

An equally tragic case of separation, although in a different way, of a husband and his wife during the U.S.-Japanese war is vividly described in Louis Fiset's *Imprisoned Apart,* a copy of which the author kindly gave me. It not only is a moving human story but also provides a very interesting case of a husband interned in an Immigration and Naturalization Service (INS) detention camp and his wife incarcerated in a War Relocation Authority camp during wartime. Louis Fiset, *Imprisoned Apart: The World War II Correspondence of an Issei Couple* (Seattle: University of Washington Press, 1997).

49. Susumu Yoshida, "Special Contribution," *Ichiretsu* 236 (May 1974). *Ichiretsu* is the postwar organ of the Tenrikyo mission headquarters in America in Los Angeles. Yoshida, born in Saga Prefecture in 1909, was sent to Los Angeles as secretary working under Bishop Hashimoto. He was arrested and interned in several camps of the Department of Justice. Meanwhile, his wife and daughters were forcibly removed to Poston Relocation Center, Arizona. After the war, he took over the Hashimoto's post as North American bishop and then was appointed bishop of the mission headquarters in Hawaii. He became a naturalized American citizen after he retired. He passed away in Los Angeles in 1993.

50. Proclamation, No. 2525, by the President, December 7, 1941, cited in House Select Committee Investigating National Defense Migration, *Report of the Select Committee*

Investigating National Defense Migration, Fourth Interim Report, 77th Cong., 2d sess., 1942, H. Rept. 2124, p. 294.

51. The most detailed and most precise account of the process and procedures of removal and incarceration of the Japanese nationals in the United States and Japanese Americans during the U.S.-Japanese war is perhaps Tetsuden Kashima, *Judgment without Trial: Japanese American Imprisonment during World War II* (Seattle: University of Washington Press, 2003). For the process of the arrest, enemy alien hearings, and internment, consult its chapter 3, especially figure 3 on p. 44.

52. Fiset, *Imprisoned Apart,* p. 46.

53. As for the actual number of Japanese internees held by the Department of Justice during World War II, as Tetsuden Kashima explains, different sources give varying numbers. What "appears to be the most accurate" number is the one given by W. F. Kelly, assistant commissioner for the Alien Enemy Control Program of the department. Kashima arrives at 6,978 for the number of Japanese interned in continental United States and 875 in Hawaii, based on Kelly's report and other references. For the details, consult Kashima, pp. 123–25, especially Table 6.1 on p. 125.

For the details of the Hawaiian Japanese internment case, see Akihiro Yamakura, "Pāruhābā kōgeki to Nikkei 'tekisei' gaikoku-jin," *Shigaku* 67/2 (March 1998): 25–56; for the mainland Japanese case, see Yamakura, "Nichi-Bei sensō boppatsu to Beikokuseifu no hondo zaijū Nihonjin taisaku," *Seijikeizai shigaku* 350 (August 1995): 35–55.

54. Seven hundred eighty-nine Japanese leaders in California (including Hashimoto) were arrested during the first few months after Pearl Harbor. They were sent to the two internment facilities in the interior, Fort Missoula, Montana, and Fort Lincoln, North Dakota. The movement began on the night of February 22, 1942. Hashimoto arrived at Fort Lincoln on February 26. Lemuel B. Schofield, "Memorandum for the Attorney General," February 23, 1942, DOJ 146-13-7-2-9, 2/21/42–2/23/42, National Archives and Records Administration (NARA), Suitland, Md.; and Hashimoto's diary, Hashimoto, *Nankin rokunen* (*Six Years of Internment*), vol. 1 (Tenri, Japan: Hashimoto Haru, 1954) (hereafter cited as *Six Years of Internment*), p. 16. The latter is a detailed diary he kept during his internment. He privately published it in two volumes in mimeographed form in 1954 and 1955.

55. Hashimoto, *Autobiography,* pp. 130–31.

56. Federal Bureau of Investigation, "Masaharu Hasimoto, with alias: Masaji Hashimoto," July 28, 1942, Documents from FBI records, obtained through Freedom of Information and Privacy Act, FOIPA No. 318963/190-, January 11, 1990 [hereafter cited as Hashimoto Personal File].

57. John Edgar Hoover, director, FBI, "Memorandum for Mr. Edward J. Ennis, Director, Alien Control Unit," February 25, 1942, Hashimoto Personal File. This memorandum, as it came into my hand, had a substantial part blackened. I filed a complaint to the FBI following the advice of Japanese American researcher Mrs. Aiko Herzig-Yoshinaga and obtained a version that removed a major part of the blackening.

58. Federal Bureau of Investigation, "Masaharu Hasimoto, with alias: Masaji Hashimoto," February 26, 1942, Hashimoto Personal File.

According to an FBI agent in charge of the Los Angeles office, the Japanese American Citizens League, a patriotic civic organization of American citizens of Japanese ancestry, reported to the FBI that "every Japanese alien returning to his country within the past two years [immediately before Pearl Harbor] has sworn to assist and uphold the present Japanese Government." R. B. Hood, special agent in charge, Los Angeles, Memorandum, "Re: Japanese Activities, Los Angeles," January 20, 1942, Document received from Kenneth Ringle Jr., by the Commission on Wartime Relocation and Internment of Civilians, a copy of which is in the possession of Japanese American researcher Aiko Herzig-Yoshinaga.

59. Hashimoto, *Autobiography,* pp. 128, 148, 183; *Six Years of Internment, Vol. 1,* pp. 1–12.

60. Hashimoto, *Autobiography,* p. 129; *Six Years of Internment,* vol. 1, pp. 25, 44.

61. Hashimoto, *Six Years of Internment,* vol. 1, pp. 40–41.

62. The Tenrikyo Mission Headquarters in America, ed., *50 Years of the Path: A History of the Tenrikyo Mission Headquarters in America, 1934–1984* (Los Angeles: The Tenrikyo Mission Headquarters in America, 1984), pp. 20–21.

63. Interview with Ronald Yama, Honolulu, Hawaii, August 2, 1992.

64. Manabu Yama to Col. I. B. Summer, Director, Prisoner of War Division, Department of War, November 15, 1943; Yama to Summer, January 3, 1943; and A. M. Tollefson, assistant director, Prisoner of War Division, to Yama, January 11, 1944, RG 389-461-2644, F: Yama, Manabu, NARA, Washington, D.C.

65. The view of the Alien Enemy Control Unit, cited in Horatio R. Rogers, Provost Marshal General's Office, U.S. Army, to the INS, March 13, 1944, RG 338-89-123, Box 96, F: Yama, Manabu, ISN-HJ-230-(CI), NARA, Washington, D.C.

66. Hashimoto, *Autobiography,* pp. 134, 159.

67. Mitziko Sawada, "After the Camps: Seabrook Farms, New Jersey, and the Resettlement of Japanese Americans, 1944–47," *Amerasia Journal* 13/2 (1986–87): 120–21. The Seabrook Farms phase, the final phase of the whole project of Japanese removal, incarceration, and resettlement, is very important, yet remain largely unstudied to this day.

68. Ibid., pp. 121, 127.

69. On October 10, 1946, 296 Americans of Japanese ancestry who renounced American citizenship arrived at Seabrook Farms from Crystal City Internment Camp. Like other Japanese "enemy" aliens who worked at Seabrook Farms, their status was "relaxed internees." Although they were granted a certain "freedom," such as visiting a nearby town for amusement, they still remained internees under the custody of the INS. W. F. Kelly, assistant commissioner, Alien Control, to Ugo Carusi, commissioner, INS, "Relaxing internment of Japanese renunciates for employment at Seabrook Farms," October 1, 1946; Kelly to Carusi, "Employment internees—Seabrook Farms," October 4, 1646; Kelly to Thomas M. Cooley, II, director, Alien Enemy Control Unit, INS, October 10, 1946, RG 85, Box 2439, File: 56125/182, NARA, Washington, D.C.

For the details of the renunciation movement and the subsequent litigation to recover their citizenship, see Donald E. Collins, *Native American Aliens: Disloyalty and the Renunciation of Citizenship by Japanese Americans during World War II* (Westport, Conn.: Greenwood Press, 1985). The number of the Japanese American renunciants is given as 5,589 on p. 3.

70. His perception seems well-informed. In January 1947, a few months after Hashimoto arrived at Seabrook Farms, a Miss Mori of a Japanese newspaper in New York inquired concerning a circuit court of appeals decision, which would result in the removal of Japanese internees under alien enemy proceedings. According to the reply by W. F. Kelly,

an INS officer, there were fifty-seven Japanese aliens who could be subject to the removal procedure, of whom twenty-eight were the alien enemies, and the rest were their family members. Of the fifty-seven, twenty-five were at Seabrook Farms and the rest in Crystal City, Texas, which was a family internment camp. Hashimoto was among these Japanese at Seabrook Farms. Thus, Hashimoto was indeed among the very few select Japanese "enemy" aliens whom the U.S. government deemed extremely dangerous to the United States and endeavored to remove from the country. Kelly, "Memorandum for File," January 7, 1947; Kelly to Miss C. Mori, Hokui Shinpo, New York, January 7, 1947, RG 85, Box 2438, File 56125/175-B [file 2], NARA, Washington, D.C.

71. Hashimoto, *Autobiography,* pp. 234, 238, 241–43.

It is true that as many as approximately 2,500 Issei and Nisei in the WRA centers applied for labor at the Seabrook Farms, and many of them appreciated the employment opportunities out of the WRA centers. However, according to Nathaniel Snyder, an officer in charge of "relocating" Japanese Americans from the WRA centers to the East Coast area, the "popularity of Seabrook Farms for relocation . . . in a measure reflects the evils of the evacuation experience and the abnormalities of center life." Nathaniel A. Snyder, Relocation Officer in Charge, the War Relocation Authority, "Final Report of the Philadelphia, Pa., District Office, East Coast Area, War Relocation Authority," February 4, 1946, p. 198, RG 210, Entry 4 (C) Box 5, NARA, Washington, D.C.

Hashimoto's description of his life in Seabrook Farms reveals the utilization and exploitation of the labor of imprisoned people by the federal government and a thriving private enterprise.

72. Hashimoto, *Autobiography,* pp. 221–2.

73. Ibid., pp. 267–68; *Six Years of Internment,* vol. 2, p. 310.

74. Hashimoto, *Autobiography,* p. 200. Hashimoto referred to the GHQ's efforts to "democratize" Japan after the war. According to John Dower, "General Douglas MacArthur and his command ruled their new domain as neocolonial overlords, beyond challenge or criticism." The GHQ imposed "authoritarian, top-down exhortations to dramatically alter the status quo" and to transform Japan into a "democracy." The contradictions of what Dower describes as a "democratic revolution from above" were clear: "while the victors preached democracy, they ruled by fiat; while they espoused equality, they themselves constituted an inviolate privileged caste." The interaction between the American occupiers and the Japanese "was infused with intimations of white supremacism." Dower, *Embracing Defeat: Japan in the Wake of World War II* (New York: W. W. Norton, 1999), pp. 27, 203, 211.

75. What the foundress taught the followers she wrote down for fear that they might forget it. This written instruction, which began to be published in 1927, consists of 1,711 verses in the *waka* (Japanese poetry) form compiled in one volume having seventeen parts. *The Teachings and History of Tenrikyo,* pp. 23–24, 123.

76. The *Ofudesaki,* part III, verse 15, cited in *The Teachings and History of Tenrikyo,* p. 32.

77. Federal Bureau of Investigation, Untitled Document, September 19, 1942, Hashimoto Personal File.

78. A good discussion on constitutionally protected speech during World War II is Richard W. Steel, *Free Speech in the Good War* (New York: St. Martin's Press, 1999).

8 The Role of Buddhist Song Culture in International Acculturation

KEIKO WELLS

Kona, Hawaii, during the 1930s to 1950s was one of the most vibrant regions for Buddhists gathering to sing religious music and to exchange original compositions. Singing had always been a part of Buddhist practice; in the late-nineteenth and early-twentieth centuries, when the Issei were still in Japan, laypersons enthusiastically sang songs whose vocabulary and image structures resembled the popular songs of the time. The Issei had brought this singing culture from Japan along with their religion to Hawaii. Interestingly, however, singing was not a part of religious activity among Shin Buddhists on the U.S. mainland until the temples started using *gathas* (Buddhist hymns) composed by ministers in order to create Sunday services modeled after those of Christians. What factors, then, led people in Kona to be so devoted to singing and composing songs?

Daisetz T. Suzuki, in the seventh chapter of his *Mysticism: Christian and Buddhist,* writes that both Christian and Buddhist mystics experience unconditional spiritual contentment regardless of "a network of great contradictions running through our human life."[1] A person who faces these contradictions in life and abandons them in a fierce struggle with a will to power, experiences the abovementioned unconditional contentment resulting from a deep feeling of interconnected oneness with the Divine Spirit. Sometimes this awareness produces wonderful mystic literature. Mystic literature is often strangely beautiful and powerful, yet hard to explicate line by line.

In the seventh chapter of his book, Suzuki introduces Chiyono Sasaki's song lyric, "*Konomama* (as-it-is-ness of life, good or bad)," as an example of Shin (Jōdo Shinshū) Buddhist mystic literature. Suzuki comments on this song by Sasaki, who was a Nisei Buddhist from Kona: "'*Kono-mama,*' we may think, sounds too easy and there is nothing spiritual or transcendental in it. If we bring this out in the world of particulars, everything here will be left to the struggle for existence and the survival of the fittest."[2]

Suzuki sees spirituality and a transcendent quality in Sasaki's lyric, but does not clearly explain how and under what circumstance her spirituality exploded into verse.[3] The goal of this article is to interpret the Buddhist folksongs in Kona in order to understand the contexts of lyrical spirituality and its transmission over generations in the Hawaiian community.

Three factors enabled a vigorous tradition of Buddhist singing in Kona. First, the Japanese population in Kona was quite dense and relatively independent. According to the 1930 Census, 4,845 of Kona's 9,405 residents were Japanese; about half of the remaining population was Hawaiian, and Caucasians numbered only 120. Most of the Japanese were Shin Buddhists. Unlike in Honolulu, on the Big Island, conflict between Buddhists and Japanese Christians was uncommon. In this environment, Buddhists could comfortably keep the singing tradition they had brought from Japan.

The second factor was a leader in religion and creative activities, Shūun Matsuura, who became the resident minister at Kona Hongwanji in 1936. He was a sensitive young Buddhist whose literary talent was conveyed to the temple members, whom he encouraged to express their religious feelings with words. During the transitional period when the younger generation was emerging from the 1930s to the 1950s, Matsuura consistently guided both the Issei and Nisei to express themselves in song, and he wrote vividly about his experiences with them in his *Hōetsu monogatari* (Stories of Religious Ecstasy).

The third factor in the development of the Kona Buddhist singing culture was the tragic experience of Japanese Hawaiians during the 1940s. In 1941, the Japanese American community was suddenly threatened in the aftermath of Japan's attack on Pearl Harbor. Volunteering for the U.S. Army was one method to demonstrate loyalty to the United States and in 1943 2,686 Japanese American volunteers from Hawaiian Islands went off to fight in the European theater of combat. The 100th Infantry Battalion and later the 442nd Regimental Combat Team, whose ranks were composed entirely of Japanese Americans, the majority of whom were Buddhist, were sent to the most severe European frontlines. This experience of loss inspired Japanese Americans in Hawaii to compose new songs. The Issei parents of the deceased composed Buddhist-inspired ballads and elegies and shared these songs with each other as they struggled to overcome their grief.

These Japanese American Buddhists are particularly well-suited to illustrate the transnational dimensions of the acculturation process of Buddhist spirituality in Hawaii. This essay discusses two Issei lyricists whose spiritual tendency marks the beginning of a devotional tradition in Hawaii. I highlight this song tradition within the context of the World War II experience. The analysis of Sasaki's songs, in particular, reveals which aspects of the Issei song tradition were passed down to this Nisei lyricist. I conclude by exploring how spirituality is transferred through languages in a song by a Nisei lyricist from an English-speaking generation.

Ume Hirano: A Woman Who Gazed into Hell (Poems from 1910s to 1950s)

Not much is known about Ume Hirano, beyond her role as probably the most influential lay religious leader and singer in Kona from the early 1910s to the 1950s.[4] Hirano was married in Japan and had children while she was still in her teens. Her launch into spiritual life began when she had serious doubts about the meaning of life. She was afraid of falling into hell after death because of not knowing the true meaning of "*tariki hongan*" (salvation by other power). After earnest but fruitless searches, she abandoned her family as well as her material riches. Her search ended when she encountered a Buddhist ascetic who told her that she would not be saved unless she let herself "fall" if she must.[5] She understood his words and was awakened to absolute faith in Amida Buddha. Following this episode, she returned to her family.

There is no record of the date of her arrival in Hawaii, but when she came she already knew religious folk songs that were popular among Shin Buddhists in Hiroshima. The songs were didactic and were published in three volumes in 1903 under the title of *Tsūzoku Bukkyō shōkashū* (Buddhist Song Book for the People).[6] This anthology contains two songs known among Kona Buddhists as Hirano's compositions, but she probably learned them by ear at religious gatherings rather than from the anthology.[7] According to Matsuura's *Hōetsu monogatari,* Hirano frequented the informal religious meetings that were held in the houses of laypersons, with or without the presence of a minister, when she was in Hiroshima. The religious songs were circulated among attendants at these meetings mostly by memory; people did not know the names of either the composers or the lyricists. The songs became an important part of their lives as if they were traditional hymns or folksongs.

The lyrics of the two particular songs that Hirano brought to Hawaii convey Shin Buddhist teachings without using difficult religious expressions such as those we find in the *Tannishō* or the *Kyōgyōshinshō.* The images and metaphors in these songs are based on both Buddhist scriptures and folk religious beliefs. The Buddhist teachings are often mixed with Confucian moral lessons and Japanese folk religious values. In Hirano's songs, two religious concepts became integral parts of the spiritual tradition in Kona: the concept connoted by the word, "*Oya*(-sama)," which literally means "a parent" or "parents," and the sensibility that one feels "hell" beneath one's feet in everyday life.

In contrast to the Confucian concept of the "parent," which represents a morally ideal adult, the Japanese Buddhist concept of the "parent" emphasizes the loving side of a parent. The *oya* (a parent or parents) would save the child who is in danger at the risk of the *oya*'s own life; the *oya* awaits the child in any condition with infinite love. The deceased and idealized parent is characterized as a suffering child's wise and compassionate guide to the other world of bliss, a figure that naturally reminds us of the Buddha. In Japanese folk beliefs, the Buddha and ancestors (both termed "*hotoke*") are equally adored. Whereas the Shin Buddhist doctrinal teachings are antithetical to ancestor worship, the notion of the "*oya*" could enter the tradition by identifying Amida Buddha as "*Oya*" ("*Oya-sama*" with the honorary suffix). Through this identification, the Buddha and one's biological parents merged. The overlapping could accelerate in Hawaii because the parents of the immigrants remained far away back in Japan. John Embree points this out in his *Acculturation among the Japanese of Kona, Hawaii* (research conducted in 1937–1938) stating that, for people in Kona, Japan had a mystic power. Embree writes:

> For people of Kona, Japan, the native land, has a mystic power, a mana. Those who are born there possess a spirit, a character which is lacking among those born abroad. Furthermore, those born in Japan who have lately revisited the land of the god have renewed and strengthened their mana. The word of such persons carries and added weight in the affairs of Kona. This sacredness extends to the language. A person who speaks the mother tongue well has much greater prestige than one who does not.[8]

Japan was "the land of god" for the Issei and the land where their *oya*(s) lived. One interesting point is that Amida is usually "he" in English books, but in many Japanese songs, *Oya* appears in the image of a loving mother. Take, for example, one of the songs that Hirano taught to people in Kona, *Gohōgi sōzoku no uta* (A Song about the Inheritance of the Buddha's Teachings). It begins with the self-sacrificing and transcendental love of *Oya,* or Amida as mother:

> In parental love, which pervades the three thousand worlds of the universe,
> nothing is more treasured than a child.
> The pain and toil of having a child began when the child existed in the womb.

As the song continues, the Amida-mother figure further overlaps with the female singer herself. The singer, in the fifth and sixth stanzas, advises the listener to educate one's beloved child with the teaching of *kami* (Japanese folk gods) and *hotoke* (Buddha and deceased ancestors).

> All wisdom is rooted in *Oya*'s teachings.
> Do not think school teaches all. Do not think school education does it all.
> If one truly loves a child, one nurses it, *Nennen korori, Nenkorori,*
> In one's bosom while worshipping *kami* and *hotoke.*[9]

Here we can see Japanese Buddhists in the early 1900s worshipping folk gods (*kami*), Buddha, and deceased ancestors all at once, though in Kona, through the intricate concept of *Oya*(*-sama*)/Amida, who is at times a mother and at times a father.

Hirano is told to have guided some people in Kona to salvation through the phrase, "Fall, make yourself fall."[10] Despite her orientation toward salvation, the songs have more images of hell than of Nirvana. The songs tell us that women, who were believed to be born polluted according to a Buddhist apocryphal sutra, the *Ketsubonkyō,* live in hell from the beginning. The phrase, "fall, make yourself fall," means that one must realize that the life before salvation is nothing but hell; one can be saved only when one realizes that one is in hell.

> WOMEN ARE THE OFFICIAL GUESTS
>
> Knocking on hell's door, [Amida comes in] through the blazing flame,
> Holding [me] up saying, "Come, woman," and leads [me] to this world.
> I hear that I will be saved as I am,
> And that my salvation is confirmed in Amida's thirty-fifth vow.
> I understand, then, that women are the official guests [to Pure Land]. . . .
> The whole blood of Amida was mixed with sweat and oil from the body.
> The three are caked in Amida's endless suffering labor. . . .
> Men cannot go through this gate. This is the official gate for women. . . .
> I am ashamed of myself. Honorable *Oya* is most wonderful and beyond
> human understanding.
> I am impressed and am ready to resume reciting the *Nenbutsu,*
> Namu Amida Butsu, Namu Amida Butsu.

Although according to the *Ketsubonkyō* women are polluted by the nature of their menstrual blood and doomed never to be saved, Amida Buddha made a vow (the thirty-fifth vow) to save them if they took refuge in Amida. Hirano believed that she was polluted and wicked, and she feared what would happen to her after death. Then she realized that her fear and anxiety were the very hell that she should be most afraid of and that she could be saved if only she trusted Amida. The preceding song expresses Hirano's awakening process

The song opens with the suffering of the speaker burning in hell. The image of tremendous pain is placed side by side with Amida's self-torture, which the Buddha tolerates in order to accomplish the thirty-fifth vow to save women. The song abruptly concludes with a tremendous admiration for Amida when the speaker truly understands that Amida would never fail to save her.

Why did Hirano sing more about hell than about the joy of understanding the truth? One reason is that she believed a woman is doomed to fall into hell, so hell was obviously closer to her feelings than Nirvana. The other reason is that her religion was very much influenced by folklore. Ever since the Heian period, Japanese folk tradition suggested disciplining children with illustrations or stories of hell, so Hirano must have been familiar with various images of hell when she left Japan.

Moreover, I suspect that singing about hell could, ironically, ease her homesickness for Japan. Unlike the breathtaking images of hell in Japanese art and literature, images of Nirvana are usually indistinct and often very hard to grasp. Take, for example, a folksong sung by a professional female entertainer from the twelfth century, which says:

> [I know] Buddha always exists, but
> It is different when Buddha appears.
> On the quiet dawn, with no sound being heard,
> I see Buddha faintly in the mist of my dream.
> (*Ryōjinhishō*)

Nirvana is usually described with metaphors of nonexistent flowers, dreams, or other abstract images. Scriptures use images of light from nowhere (not from fire or the sun) to express the sensation of religious awakening and ecstasy, but folksongs seldom include images of heavenly light. Instead, people repeatedly sing folksongs of, as seen in Hirano's songs, darkness in hell and light from destructive fire. Numerous folktales tell us about the terrible experiences of sinners in hell instead of a momentary experience of awakening. It is no wonder that a common young woman such as Hirano was more familiar with the images of hell than with those of Nirvana.

Within this spiritual model centered on hell, it was Hirano's conviction that one must "fall"; that is, one must completely give up one's ego and be willing to give up one's "self-effort" to save oneself from hell. Hirano's teaching, "fall, make yourself fall," became a strong undercurrent of many songs sung and composed in Kona. The following verse from an unknown poet is one example:

> One cannot safely go beyond life, if one relies on oneself.
> Torture, torture yourself, and let yourself go.

Then, you will fall.
Fall, fall!

One must fall before being embraced by Amida, but one cannot be saved if one falls with any expectation of being saved. One must, Hirano taught, just fall.

Haru Matsuda: "My Heart Is a Barbarous Horse" (Poems from the 1940s to 1960s)

Haru Matsuda was a very quiet woman, according to Clara Uechi, Matsuda's second daughter. Though Matsuda often suffered from headaches, Uechi remembers that she never complained of anything. This lyricist left a handwritten notebook that contains song lyrics, including two songs by Hirano, and her own *tankas* (short verses consisting of thirty-one syllables). Haru's husband, Den'nojō Matsuda, handwrote these poems because Haru could only write *hiragana* and *katakana* (phonic characters). Matsuda composed at least 177 verses; most of which seem to date from 1943–44.

Haru Matsuda was born in 1892 in Yamaguchi. She came to Hawaii as a picture bride when she was nineteen. She had eight children with Den'nojō, who was seven years older than her. In 1943 Gorō, the fifth son of the Matsudas, left Honolulu with 2,685 other Japanese American youth for the U.S. mainland as part of the U.S. Army. They were all volunteers who wished to show their loyalty to the United States during World War II. Matsuda missed and worried about her son who was sent to Europe as part of the 442nd Regimental Combat Team. As a Shinshū follower, she suffered from the fact that she had a strong worldly desire: the desire to have him back. She could not simply feel at ease and let Amida take care of everything. She wrote:

I am here, but my heart is with my beloved son.
I go back and forth every day.
I always see him in front of me, he who has departed.
I see him more often than the other sons who live with me.

He does not leave my field of vision.
Close your eyelids, and sleep.
I yearn for a supernatural power.
I want to know how he is doing.
How silly I am, desiring to know the future.
I don't even know what awaits me.
My heart is a barbarous horse.
It rushes about everywhere all the time.

I wish to be embraced by Namu Amida Butsu and not complain,
But, see, this is already a complaint.
I am older. I am weaker, physically and spiritually.
Yet, my worldly desires won't get any weaker.

Who would blame oneself as Matsuda did for wishing her son to return safely from war? Her spirituality is similar to that of Hirano, because both of them struggled mightily with their egos vis-à-vis Amida Buddha's power.

Before Matsuda resolved her emotional and religious dilemmas, she received notice of Gorō's death in Italy. Several months later, the army sent his blood-stained uniform to the Matsudas. Clara clearly remembers the shocking incident: "months later, his blood-stained uniform came back. I don't know why they did that. But I remember my mother opening the package, and I was there, too. The whole living room was filled up with the smell of old blood from the stained uniform. He was shot. I don't understand why it was sent home to us. Months later his ashes came back. And after that we had a memorial service."[11]

Matsuda did not write verses following his death. But six years later, she composed a song lyric that changed words to a popular war song from Japan. The original song that she drew on was *Sen'yū* (A Fellow Soldier) written by Hisen Mashimo (1878–1926) in 1905. This is a ballad that tells the story of a soldier who helps a wounded companion in the midst of combat and witnesses a fellow soldier die in his arms. The lyrics are pathetic and not nationalistic unlike most war songs. *Sen'yū* was especially popular in western Japan and was sung in elementary schools, which means that Matsuda probably knew the song from school in Yamaguchi. In the 1930s, however, people stopped singing it because the Japanese military banned it. The military disliked the song because it expressed the cruelty of war and the sadness of losing a friend to it. Matsuda and many Isseis in Hawaii had left Japan before the ban so they kept singing the song that they learned at elementary schools before coming to Hawaii, even through World War II.

In 1950, Matsuda altered the words to compose her own version of *Sen'yū:* a ballad featuring her son titled *Gunka* (a military song). Matsuda's *Gunka* tells us what happened to him: Carl (she no longer calls her son by his Japanese name, Gorō) sees a fellow soldier fall in the battlefield; he tries to help him, but he himself gets shot to death.

A WAR SONG

Thousands of miles away from the homeland,
the bright red sunset in Italy looms so far away,
My beloved child is buried under stone.

It is too sad to simply say that he was a brave soldier,
who dashed toward the enemy before anyone else.
Though he killed so many foes, now he lies asleep there.
Oh, how fierce the fighting must have been.
His fellow soldier suddenly fell beside him. Carl ran over.
He could not let his friend just lie on the ground,
though there were the strict military prohibitions against proceeding without orders.
Carl encouraged him, held him in his bosom,
and put a bandage on him; all on the battlefield.
It was that moment when Carl was shot, and fell.
Oh, my beloved Carl, you became a part of Italy's soil.
Six years have already passed; finally you have come back to us loving parents
who have waited and waited for your return
to your homeland, Hawaii.
You have come back guided by the compassionate hands of America.
You have come back silently. You have come back silently.
Namu Amida Butsu, Namu Amida Butsu.

The fact that Matsuda calls her son by his English name emphasizes that she understands him as an American: She says Carl was brought back to his parents by "the compassionate hands of America," a gesture that makes America parallel with the compassionate Amida Buddha. Amida received Carl after death in the same way America honored him as a hero, and his parents are thankful to both Amida and America. They feel Carl close to them now because Amida also has received them as they became free from their worldly desire at the time of Carl's death. Carl and his parents are unified in Amida's embrace. In 1950, Den'nojyō wrote a letter to Matsuura saying that Gorō's death had made each member of the family realize absolute Truth.[12] Haru finally was released from her torturous suffering when she wrote the story of Carl's honorable death in this war song.

Transcendental Expressions in Songs

Matsuda was not the only one who overcame the sadness of losing her son with the help of religion and song making. Other song lyrics in her notebook refer to the deaths of Japanese Americans in World War II as well; for instance one of the lyrics, titled *Hōmi no Uta* (A Song of Delicious Teachings of Buddha), written by Haraga (his given name unknown). Matsuda wrote the song down in her notebook on March 9, 1951:

HŌMI NO UTA

Written by a layperson, Mr. Haraga in Honolulu. Mr. Kawano in Honolulu sent it to me and let me write it down. How sweetly he sings here. March 9, 1951.

1. I am a shameless sinful person. I outlived my parents and my child.
The last words of my child were,
"Father, please be in good health until you become one hundred years old."
2. "I am going before you, father. A cherry blossom, falling at the age of twenty-three.
I put my hands together reciting Namu Amida Butsu,
Looking toward the West and saying good-bye."
3. I repeated my son's words, and they hurt me.
I then realized that life is uncertain, transient and empty.
I thought I would go forward, but it was far too dark.
4. I learned that I must listen, so I frequented the temple.
I listened and listened [to sermons] wishing for a pious pure mind.
But it was all in vain.

9. You are suffering because you cannot hear [the truth],
But *Oya* endangers life to save you.
Say "*Oya*" just once to call. Where are you going, leaving *Oya* behind?
10. You are in the middle of light. Here is *Oya* who will never let you fall.
You won't fall, but you are already fallen.
You are fallen, so you won't fall.

13. I happily can listen now, though the road to joy was long and painful.
I intended to listen, but I was wrong.
No intention was necessary.

Joy, all joy! Namu Amida Butsu. Namu Amida Butsu.

This song starts with the death of the speaker's son. The speaker is so hurt that he needs help to find meaning in his life, so he goes to a temple. He visits the temple often and tries to discover the fundamental truth of being by listening to sermons. He hopes that Amida has received his son, but in spite of his religious practice, his anxiety cannot be eased (stanzas 1–4). In stanza 9, the poet speaks of his wish to save his son at the risk of his own life. The speaker here overlaps with Amida Buddha who offers hands of help to everyone with unconditional love. The poet transcends the barrier between himself and Amida. In the following stanza, the voice of a parent (the father-poet/Amida) asserts itself and lets the truth be known to the listener (the son of the poet/the poet himself): One does not have to be afraid of falling because one is already fallen, and that *Oya* (parent/Amida) embraces in the light of bliss. Stanza 10 expresses the same idea as Hirano's: Let yourself fall and you never fall. Here, the poet, the son of the poet, and Amida overlap with each other. The mysterious union of the three invites the reader to join in. No wonder Matsuda comments: "How sweetly he sings." Now that the poet knows the fundamental truth of life and death, in stanza 13, he is full of joy. "Joy, all joy!" he says, and the *nenbutsu* follows. *Nenbutsu* in this context expresses the ecstatic feeling of being united with Amida by letting go of one's ego- or "self-power."

The tragic experiences from World War II were not only personal, but involved the entire Japanese American community in Hawaii. *Iwakuni Ondo: Nisei Butai* (Iwakuni Ondo: Nisei Troops) is a heroic ballad about the 442nd Regimental Combat Team and the 100th Infantry Battalion. The lyrics to this song were printed on five hundred sheets and distributed on the occasion of a memorial service for the deceased soldiers held at the Hongwanji Honolulu Betsuin in 1977. The lyricist is Muon Ozaki, an Issei who was also a reporter at the *Hawaii Times*. Hongwanji, however, did not print the name of the Issei poet on the handout along with the lyrics.[13] Today, hardly anybody knows that Ozaki composed the song. It has been passed on as an anonymous folksong. It now is an important piece of cultural heritage for the Japanese American community in Hawaii.

IWAKUNI ONDO: NISEI TROOPS

(The 442nd Regimental Combat Team/The 100th Infantry Battalion)

In 1941, it was early morning of December 7,
  the fiercest storm came with black clouds.
Our paradise! Broken dreams! Pearl Harbor, burning!
We have cultivated the land, shedding sweat and tears, but now
  our secure foundation is no longer firm.
Peaceful life is washed away in wild waves.
The dark Kuroshio Current rolls in from the Pacific Ocean.

It is said that one has to fight for justice in spite of parents' concern.
They are young volunteers, who devoted their lives to show gratitude to the
  country.
How brave, how admirable! The Nisei troops under the Star Spangled
  Banner!
In Camp McCoy and Camp Shelby, miles and miles away from Hawaii,
  they go through tough military training.
Then, they cross the Atlantic.
Under the scorching sun in Africa Nisei youths march.
Fierce gods, stay away from this fire!

At the battlefield of snow-covered Cassino, and in the endless mud of Anzio,
the 100th Infantry Battalion fights for honor just as fanatically as can be.
A youth writes to his mother in Hawaii, far, far away;
"Mother, please excuse me not writing you so long. I am well in Italy.
I am in Cassino. There is snow everywhere. Deep, deep snow, Mother.
Rome is near."

Before I learned this song from James Kunichika in Honolulu, I had already visited Oahu and the Big Island a few times in search of songs about the 442nd Regimental Combat Team. I had heard about this song from Professor Stephen H. Sumida, who told me that nobody outside the community had access to the song for twenty-some years. During my research I acquired very little information, but in February 2001, I was told that a certain elderly lady knew the song that I was looking for. As she was a member of Hilo Hongwanji, a minister telephoned her for me to ask if she would let me interview her. She declined, but said she had taught the song to a Chinese American man and gave the minister his phone number. When the minister telephoned him, he said he was not allowed to teach the song to anybody from outside the community and refused to see me. He said that I could record the song if he sang it at a Bon Odori festival, but that he would not tell me when and where he might sing it. (O-bon dance festivals are held in each local community divisions throughout the summer months. The singer is invited to sing at different festivals.) The minister would not give me his name and phone number. I was happy to be certain of the existence of the song, but at the same time I was awfully discouraged by how improbable it was that I would ever record the song; living and teaching in Japan, I could obviously not stay in Hilo all summer long videotaping every O-bon festival in the area.

What impresses me is that this song is thought to be very sacred in spite of the fact that there are few people who understand the Japanese lyrics. Even without knowing whether or not the song from Hilo is the same as the one from Honolulu, one thing is certain: Japanese American experiences of World War II left a deep scar on the Japanese American community, and these songs are understood as very important and holy.[14] People in Hawaii had to bear distress unreasonably forced on them; they made a heroic ballad to give meaning to the deaths of their loved ones; they accepted the fact of death and somewhat overcame the grief, while keeping the song secret from outsiders who did not share the same suffering. The painful spiritual drama of the community remains concealed in this semianonymous dance song.

Chiyono Sasaki: In Nirvana "Being as I Am"

Chiyono Sasaki, a Nisei from Kona, Hawaii, inherited the spirituality of Issei Buddhists through folksongs. However, she expressed it with a less distinctly Japanese cultural background and more abstract expressions than Issei singers.

Her biography represents the harsh and confusing lives of Japanese American women during the early settlement days in Hawaii. Sasaki was born in Ka'u, Hawaii, in 1897. She did not have the opportunity to receive an American elementary school education and studied at the Hongwanji Japanese school for only three years. Except for a few easy Chinese characters, she wrote mostly in phonograms (*hiragana* and *katakana*). She did not write in English at all. She married at the age of fourteen or fifteen, but her marriage was not peaceful. Her husband drank heavily and was violent. On one occasion, he tried to shoot her, and on another, he cut her with a knife, leaving a large scar on her neck. As she increasingly felt her life to be in danger, she left him and barely escaped with her daughter.

After the unhappy marriage, she remarried Mr. Sasaki from Japan, who was ten years older than her. She had ten children with him: first came eight boys and then two girls. While working on the leased family coffee farm and taking care of the big family, her troubled mind was not at ease.[15] Tatsuo Munetō, who knew Sasaki well when he was a Kona Hongwanji minister from 1980 to 1986, wrote about what she was like when she was spiritually awakened:

> Deeply troubled by her confusion, she could not resist calling on the Rev. Shūun Matsuura [minister at Kona Hongwanji, 1936–42] in Kealakekua. She was in desperate straits. One afternoon when Chiyono returned home to Keopu from the temple, her husband, Kumatarō, who had just returned from laboring in the coffee fields, scolded her, shouting, "You're always going to the temple! What for?" Chiyono replied, "To listen." "After listening, what did you learn?" yelled her husband. "Nothing," she answered. Kumatarō then said, "What a fool you are!" Hearing those words, something flashed across Chiyono's inner being: "Oh, today, I finally am able to truly listen. Yes, I am able to accept and embrace my foolish self."[16]

Sasaki sent four sons to the war. When the fourth son went, she was so shocked that she almost fainted. In her letter to Matsuura in 1948, she wrote:

> After you left us [for the internment camp in Texas in 1942], our life was not hard materially but spiritually it was most terrible. Four of our sons were drafted. When I was told even our fifth son was going to the war, I realized how deeply

egocentric I was. Suddenly I noticed that the unconditional compassion of *Oya* had been with me and was certainly present. I cried and cried so hard.[17]

She was a devoted Buddhist until her death in 1993 at the age of ninety-five. There still are many people on the Big Island who heard her saying, "Go to the temple and listen."

Sasaki's little notebook (7 × 11 cm, seventy-four pages) contains nine song lyrics and two *tankas*. One song is signed "Sasaki Chiyono," and the authorship for two songs are given to "Hirano joshi" (respectable Ms. Hirano). Sasaki composed at least two of the remaining six songs. Taking two date scribbles into consideration, she likely wrote down the words in her notebook during the period from 1945 to 1948. She also made a tape recording of her songs on September 26, 1983. The first two recorded songs are her own compositions and the next two are the ones she learned from Hirano, who along with Matsuura, was Sasaki's mentor. In an interview with Munetō in 1986, Munetō mentions how much she respected Hirano.

Sasaki inherited Hirano's spirituality and sang about the importance of falling as can be seen in the following song:

> I was told to fall, and I did. Then I found myself on top of a lotus flower.
> I cried for joy. I am truly grateful. I am grateful.
> The voice of *Oya*, "Fall, make yourself fall," came first.
>   I did fall, and then I heard the voice of *Oya* again in joy.
>   I am truly grateful. I am grateful.

Hirano fell into hell where one's egotism burns up in a furious fire. Matsuda fell into the void after she lost her son. Sasaki, on the other hand, fell into the depth of depression when she realized what she considered her own ultimate foolishness. For Sasaki, "to fall" meant "to be truly humble." All three women "fell" by seeing the depths of their egotism, but Sasaki was the best in expressing the ultimate joy of awakening. Her mystic poems have the power to communicate her spiritual experience even to non-Buddhist readers. Here is the poem Daisetz Suzuki referred to in his book, *Mysticism:*

> I am so happy about being as I am, that I naturally bow my head.
> Being good or bad, I am what I am.
> Being false or true, I am what I am.
> Having or not having, I am what I am.
> Rain or shine, I am what I am.
> Crying or laughing, I am what I am.
>
> Being dissatisfied with what I am, how greedy I can be!
> Being as I am does not change; it cannot be changed.

Only *Oya-sama* affirms me, calling, "Come as you are."
Because of not knowing that I am as I am,
I wander around lost and confused.

Because the compassion of *Oya-sama* is all embracing,
 I am now contained within it.
Oya-sama is pleased, and I am happy, too.
Living together with *Oya-sama* daily,
 every time I listen to *Oya-sama* working for my sake,
I feel both ashamed and grateful.
Namu Amida Butsu, Namu Amida Butsu.[18]

Despite of the heavy subject of the poet having "wander[ed] around lost and confused," the tone of the song is light and full of joy. The words are simple; the juxtapositions are also straightforward. The message is only that she can be as she is. The main imagery, herself being one with *Oya-sama,* is not decoratively visionary. The very plainness of this song signifies the simplicity of the truth she communicates to the listener in the poem. This style also expresses the mystic union, or absolute oneness, of everything.

Conclusion

Until the 1970s, even though a number of the Issei were still alive, values from the Meiji period (1868–1912) had survived and were respected in Hawaii, whereas in Japan the same values were mostly rejected because the Pacific War ended in Japan's defeat. Buddhists in Hawaii had trained themselves to be reflective, looked deeply into the darkness of human nature, and expressed their spirituality in songs. When the deaths of many young Japanese American troops deeply hurt the feelings of individuals and the community, the emotionally wounded people made ballads and gave heroic meanings to the lives of the deceased. Nisei poets such as Chiyono Sasaki composed new songs, which were written with simpler vocabularies without decorative images, while maintaining the reflective quality of Issei's religious folk songs even though they expressed joy and gratitude with much less religious dogma or folk beliefs.

Unlike in Kona, in Honolulu, there were serious conflicts between Buddhists and Christians. In order to establish mutual understanding and universalize the teaching of Buddha, Yemyō Imamura, the first bishop of the Honpa Hongwanji Mission of Hawaii, set up an English department in the Hongwanji Mission in 1924 and invited an English Buddhist, Ernest Hunt, to be its director. Hunt compiled a nonsectarian Buddhist service book in English, entitled the *Vade Mecum* clearly modeled after Christian service books. The text does not include sutras (scriptures) for chanting, but it does contain procedures for holding religious ceremonies and hymns for singing. In 1924, hardly any Japanese would have imagined a Buddhist ceremony without sutra chanting. The *Vade Mecum* offers 138 English hymns with Western music. These "hymns" were later called "*gathas*" to avoid a Christian connotation. As years went by, some parts of the ceremonial models and many songs were avoided because of their Christian flavor, but the basic direction taken to adapt Buddhism into a form that does not appear overly foreign for non-Japanese-speaking people continued unabated. In the end, the songs from the *Vade Mecum* constitute another song tradition in Hawaii.

One of the new *gathas,* composed under the tradition of Buddhist hymns in *Vade Mecum,* clearly shows the reflective characteristics that I pointed out in the songs of Hirano, Matsuda, and Sasaki. The lyricist for this *gatha* is Mieko Takamiya, a Nisei from Honolulu who worked for the newspaper, the *Garden Island.* Takamiya's *With These Hands,* which later won a prize at Hongwanji's Gatha Contest in 1965, was written in English:

> With these hands just a part of me, I work and play and feel.
> These hands are busy as can be, yet sometimes they are still,
> In gassho, trustingly to say, I'm one with Amida.
> These hands oft raised in hate and rage, are awful sights indeed.
> Yet these hand held out encourage, and comfort those in need.
> These hands humbly joined together, say "Thank you, Amida."[19]

Here the poet looks at her own hands and checks herself. She goes through the anguish of looking at the ugliness of her ego, but in the end reaches the ecstasy of knowing Amida's compassion. The most important image is the joining of hands: a humble picture of mystic union with Amida.

It has been about half a century since Hirano landed on Hawaii. The reflective spirituality that she and other Issei Buddhists brought from Japan has merged with the sensibility of new generations. The new songs with traditional spirituality are sung with melodies of European music and people choose to sing different songs as time passes. Most religious folk songs are no exceptions, but even new songs often express traditionally surviving spirituality, sensibility, and ways of handling troubled life. Issei Shin Buddhists in Hawaii implanted the reflective and transcendental elements of their Buddhism into their newly adopted cultural soil. Nisei Buddhists kept this tradition alive while transforming the forms of the songs to reflect their position as Americans of Japanese descent.

Notes

I owe special thanks to Rev. Tatsuo Munetō, who generously allowed me use the handwritten notebooks of Sasaki and Matsuda, an interview tape of Sasaki, and a copy of Matsuura's *Hōetsu monogatari,* which is now rare. Without his advice and constant encouragement, this research would not have been completed. I am also grateful to Ms. Clara Uechi and Ms. Margaret Kihara, Mr. James Kunichika, who kindly accepted my requests for interviews in 2002 and 2003. Ms. Kihara allowed me to take Sasaki's song tape to Japan to study. I thank Ms. Kimi Hisatsune, who read my manuscript carefully and gave me suggestions. My gratitude also goes to (in alphabetical order) Rev. Midori Kondo, Ms. Fujie Ichishita, Dr. Hisami Konishi, Rev. Shinkai Murakami, Rev. Toshio Murakami, Ms. Masako Nishikawa, Ms. Lillian H. Noda, Mr. Ralston Nagata, Rev. Francis Okano, Rev. Thomas R. Okano, Prof. Yukuji Okita, Ms. Motoe Tada, Bishop Chiaki Yosemori, who offered me indispensable information and generous help.

English translations of Japanese texts and song lyrics are mine unless noted.

1. Daisetz Teitaro Suzuki, *Mysticism: Christian and Buddhist* (Mineola, N.Y.: Dover, revised edition, 2002), p. 143.

2. Suzuki, *Mysticism,* p. 148.

3. The spiritual trait that I am discussing in this article can be identified with that of the *myōkōnin.* (For an English explanation of *myōkōnin,* see: Suzuki, "The Myokonin" in his *A Miscellany on the Shin Teaching of Buddhism* [Kyoto: Shinshū Ōtani-ha shūmusho, 1949], pp. 71–91. The reason that I do not mention the word "*myōkōnin*" here is that I am not attempting to explain the Japanese American (Hawaiian) Buddhist spirituality as a counterpart of Japanese *myōkōnin.*

4. One finds Hirano's songs both in Matsuda's religious song notebook and Sasaki's notebook. Some poems by Dan'noura (see note 7) evidently imitate Hirano's songs. Matsuura Shūun in his *Hōetsu monogatari* (Stories of Religious Ecstasy) refers to Hirano as the most influential religious person in Kona.

5. Hirano's life story is introduced by Matsuura, *Hōetsu monogatari* (Kyoto: Hyakkaen, 1955), pp. 39–48. Matsuura uses a pseudonym for her.

6. Further information about these songs, *Bukkyo Shōka,* can be found in Keiko Wells, "Shin Buddhist Song Lyrics Sung in the United States: Their History and Expressed Buddhist Images (1), 1898–1939," *Tokyo daigaku Amerika taiheiyō kenkyū* 2 (2002): 75–99.

7. Mitsuyo Dan'noura, another Issei lyricist, writes of her fond memory of meetings and singing songs in Hiroshima in *Ririkoi no sato* (The Village of Ririkoi), p. 48.

8. John F. Embree, *Memoirs of the American Anthropological Association: Acculturation among the Japanese of Kona, Hawaii* supplement to *American Anthropologist* 43/4 (1941): 131.

9. Quoted from Matsuda's notebook. Translations of poems are mine otherwise noted.

10. Tatsuo Muneto, *Dharma Treasures: Spiritual Insights from Hawaii's Shin Buddhist Pioneers* (Honolulu: Buddhist Study Center Press, 1997), p. 21.

11. From an interview with Ms. Clara Uechi in Captain Cook, February 21, 2002.

12. Matsuura, *Hōetsu monogatari,* p. 242.

13. Yukari Nakahara, "Utawareta taiheiyō sensō," *Imin kenkyū nenpō* 8 (March 2002): 65.

14. Bishop Chikai Yosemori told me there also is a Nisei Butai Bon Odori song in Maui.

15. I received personal information about Chiyono Sasaki from her youngest daughter, Ms. Margaret Sasaki Kihara. Interviews in Kailua Kona: February 22, 2002 and March 8, 2003.

16. Muneto, *Dharma Treasures,* p. 21.

17 Matsuura, *Hōetsu monogatari,* p. 233. Fortunately Sasaki's fifth son did not go to the war.

18. Translated by Muneto in *Dharma Treasures,* pp. 22–23.

19. Mieko Takamiya, "With These Hands," in *Praises of the Buddha* (Honolulu: Honpa Hongwanji Mission of Hawaii, Centennial Commemoration Publication), pp. 174–75.

Contributors

MICHIHIRO AMA is a lecturer at the University of California, Irvine. He has published several articles on Shin Buddhism. His forthcoming book, *Immigrants to the Pure Land: Modernization, Acculturation, and Globalization of Shin Buddhism in the Formation of Two Nations States, 1898–1941*, will be published by the University of Hawai'i Press in 2011.

NORIKO ASATO is an associate professor of library and information science at the University of Hawai'i, Manao. She has published a number of journal articles on Japanese language schools. She is also the author of *Teaching Mikadoism: The Attack on Japanese Language Schools in Hawaii, California, and Washington, 1919–1927.*

MASAKO IINO is the president of and a professor in the English department at Tsuda College in Tokyo. She is the author of a number of publications in Japanese including *A History of Japanese Canadians* (awarded the Prime Minister's Award for Publication) and *Another History of US-Japan Relations.* She is coauthor of *Ethnic America* (with Norio Akashi) and coeditor of a number of volumes. She has served as the president of the Japanese Association for Canadian Studies and been on the board of the Japanese Association for American Studies. In 1997, she received the Governor General's Award for Canadian Studies.

TOMOE MORIYA is a professor at Hannan University in Osaka, Japan. Her recent publications include *Yemyo Imamura: Pioneer American Buddhist* and *America Bukkyō no tanjō: 20 seiki shotō ni okeru Nikkei shūkyō no bunka hen'yō.* She has published numerous articles on both Japanese and Japanese American Buddhism in English and Japanese.

LORI PIERCE is an associate professor of American studies at DePaul University in Chicago. She teaches courses on race and American culture, ethnic studies, and Asian American history, including the history of Buddhism in the United States. She is the recipient of a 2009 NEH Summer Fellowship on American immigration and is a 2009–2010 Teaching Fellow at the Newberry Library in Chicago.

CRISTINA ROCHA teaches at the School of Humanities and Languages, University of Western Sydney, Australia. She is the editor of the *Journal of Global Buddhism*. Her writings include *Zen in Brazil: The Quest for Cosmopolitan Modernity;* "The Brazilian Imaginaire of Zen," in R. Pereira and H. Matsuoka (eds.), *Japanese Religions in and Beyond the Japanese Diaspora;* "All the Roads Come from Zen: Busshinji as a Reference to Buddhism in Brazil," *Japanese Journal of Religious Studies;* and the forthcoming *Buddhism in Australia: Traditions in Change* (with Michelle Barker).

KEIKO WELLS is a professor of American literature and American studies at Ritsumeikan University (Kyoto, Japan). She is the author of *Black Spirituals: How It Has Survived Through the Centuries* and *The American Character in Folksong Lyrics: The Hens That Lay Soft-Boiled Eggs,* and the translator of *The Book of Werewolves* written by Sabine Baring-Gould. She has also published numerous articles on black spirituals and Shin Buddhist song lyrics as well as other folksongs and folktales.

DUNCAN RYÛKEN WILLIAMS is the Shinjo Ito Distinguished Chair in Japanese Buddhism and chair of the Center for Japanese Studies at the University of California, Berkeley. He works primarily on Japanese Buddhist history, Buddhism and environmentalism, and American Buddhism. He is the author of *The Other Side of Zen: A Social History of Soto Zen Buddhism in Tokugawa Japan,* translator of four Japanese books, and editor of three volumes including *American Buddhism* and *Buddhism and Ecology.* He is currently completing a manuscript entitled *Camp Dharma: Japanese-American Buddhism and the World War Two Incarceration Experience.*

AKIHIRO YAMAKURA is a professor of American history at Tenri University, Japan. He is the chief editor of two books and the author of over two dozen articles on Japanese American history, law, and religion, including a series of articles on Tenrikyo in the Americas. He is also the editor-in-chief of the *Journal of Americas Studies,* a Japanese journal on transnational perspectives on studies of the Americas.

Index

The Asian American Experience

The Hood River Issei: An Oral History of Japanese Settlers in Oregon's Hood River Valley *Linda Tamura*

Americanization, Acculturation, and Ethnic Identity: The Nisei Generation in Hawaii *Eileen H. Tamura*

Sui Sin Far/Edith Maude Eaton: A Literary Biography *Annette White-Parks*

Mrs. Spring Fragrance and Other Writings *Sui Sin Far; edited by Amy Ling and Annette White-Parks*

The Golden Mountain: The Autobiography of a Korean Immigrant, 1895–1960 *Easurk Emsen Charr; edited and with an introduction by Wayne Patterson*

Race and Politics: Asian Americans, Latinos, and Whites in a Los Angeles Suburb *Leland T. Saito*

Achieving the Impossible Dream: How Japanese Americans Obtained Redress *Mitchell T. Maki, Harry H. L. Kitano, and S. Megan Berthold*

If They Don't Bring Their Women Here: Chinese Female Immigration before Exclusion *George Anthony Peffer*

Growing Up Nisei: Race, Generation, and Culture among Japanese Americans of California, 1924–49 *David K. Yoo*

Chinese American Literature since the 1850s *Xiao-huang Yin*

Pacific Pioneers: Japanese Journeys to America and Hawaii, 1850–80 *John E. Van Sant*

Holding Up More Than Half the Sky: Chinese Women Garment Workers in New York City, 1948–92 *Xiaolan Bao*

Onoto Watanna: The Story of Winnifred Eaton *Diana Birchall*

Edith and Winnifred Eaton: Chinatown Missions and Japanese Romances *Dominika Ferens*

Being Chinese, Becoming Chinese American *Shehong Chen*

"A Half Caste" and Other Writings *Onoto Watanna; edited by Linda Trinh Moser and Elizabeth Rooney*

Chinese Immigrants, African Americans, and Racial Anxiety in the United States, 1848–82 *Najia Aarim-Heriot*

Not Just Victims: Conversations with Cambodian Community Leaders in the United States *Edited and with an Introduction by Sucheng Chan; interviews conducted by Audrey U. Kim*

The Japanese in Latin America *Daniel M. Masterson with Sayaka Funada-Classen*

Survivors: Cambodian Refugees in the United States *Sucheng Chan*

From Concentration Camp to Campus: Japanese American Students and World War II *Allan W. Austin*

Japanese American Midwives: Culture, Community, and Health Politics *Susan L. Smith*

In Defense of Asian American Studies: The Politics of Teaching and Program Building *Sucheng Chan*

Lost and Found: Reclaiming the Japanese American Incarceration *Karen L. Ishizuka*

Religion and Spirituality in Korean America *Edited by David Yoo and Ruth H. Chung*

Moving Images: Photography and the Japanese American Incarceration
Jasmine Alinder

Camp Harmony: Seattle's Japanese Americans and the Puyallup Assembly Center
Louis Fiset

Chinese American Transnational Politics *Him Mark Lai, edited and with an introduction by Madeline Y. Hsu*

Issei Buddhism in the Americas *Edited by Duncan Ryûken Williams and Tomoe Moriya*

The University of Illinois Press
is a founding member of the
Association of American University Presses.

Composed in 10.5/13 Adobe Minion Pro
by Jim Proefrock
at the University of Illinois Press
Manufactured by Thomson-Shore, Inc.

University of Illinois Press
1325 South Oak Street
Champaign, IL 61820-6903
www.press.uillinois.edu